CONCENTRATE Q&A
EU LAW

CONCENTRATE
Q&A
EU LAW

Nigel Foster

LLM Degree Programme Leader at Robert Kennedy College,
Zürich, Switzerland; Visiting Professor of European Law,
Europa Institut, Saarland University, Saarbrücken, Germany

SECOND EDITION

OXFORD
UNIVERSITY PRESS

Great Clarendon Street, Oxford, OX2 6DP,
United Kingdom

Oxford University Press is a department of the University of Oxford.
It furthers the University's objective of excellence in research, scholarship,
and education by publishing worldwide. Oxford is a registered trade mark of
Oxford University Press in the UK and in certain other countries

First edition 2016

Impression: 1

Published in the United States of America by Oxford University Press
198 Madison Avenue, New York, NY 10016, United States of America

British Library Cataloguing in Publication Data
Data available

Library of Congress Control Number: 2018945168

ISBN 978–0–19–881785–7

Printed in Great Britain by
Ashford Colour Press Ltd, Gosport, Hampshire

Contents

Guide to the book

Every book in the Concentrate Q&A series contains the following features:

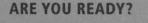

ARE YOU READY?

Are you ready to face the exam? This box at the start of each chapter identifies the key topics and cases that you need to have learned, revised, and understood before tackling the questions in each chapter.

DIAGRAM ANSWER PLANS

Not sure where to begin? Clear diagram answer plans at the start of each question help you see how to structure your answer at a glance, and take you through each point step-by-step.

KEY DEBATES

Demonstrating your knowledge of the crucial debates is a sure-fire way to impress examiners. These at-a-glance boxes help remind you of the key debates relevant to each topic, which you should discuss in your answers to get the highest marks.

SUGGESTED ANSWER

What makes a great answer great? Our authors show you the thought process behind their own answers, and how you can do the same in your exam. Key sentences are highlighted and advice is given on how to structure your answer well and develop your arguments.

QUESTION

Each question represents a typical essay or problem question so that you know exactly what to expect in your exam.

LOOKING FOR EXTRA MARKS?

Don't settle for a good answer—make it great! This feature gives you extra points to include in the exam if you want to gain more marks and make your answer stand out.

CAUTION!

Don't fall into any traps! This feature points out common mistakes that students make, and which you need to avoid when answering each question.

TAKING THINGS FURTHER

Really push yourself and impress your examiner by going beyond what is expected. Focused further reading suggestions allow you to develop in-depth knowledge of the subject for when you are looking for the highest marks.

Guide to the Online Resources

Every book in the Concentrate Q&A series is supported by additional online materials to aid your study and revision: www.oup.com/uk/qanda/

- ● Extra essay and problem questions.
- ● Bonus questions to help you practise and refine your technique. Questions are annotated, highlighting key terms and legal issues to help you plan your own answers. An indication of what your answers should cover is also provided.

- ● Online versions of the diagram answer plans.
- ● Video guidance on how to put an answer plan together.
- ● Flashcard glossaries of key terms.
- ● Audio advice on revision and exam technique from Nigel Foster.

Table of cases

Cases are listed numerically in chronological order within each year. CoJ cases are listed ahead of General Court cases. General Court cases are prefixed T-.European Courts

Commission Decisions

Belgian Courts

French Courts

German Courts

Table of Primary Legislation

International Legislation

Other Jurisdictions

Belgium

France

Germany

Italy

UK

Table of EU secondary legislation

Abbreviations

AG	Advocate General	EL Rev	European Law Review
CAP	Common Agricultural Policy	EMU	Economic and Monetary Union
CFI	Court of First Instance of the European Communities	EP	European Parliament
		ERTA	European Road Transport Agreement
CMLR	Common Market Law Reports	EU	European Union
CML Rev	Common Market Law Review	GATT	General Agreement on Tariffs and Trade
CoJ	Court of Justice of the European Union		
CT	Constitutional Treaty	IGC	Intergovernmental Conference
EC	European Community/ies	NATO	North Atlantic Treaty Organization
ECA	European Communities Act 1972	OEEC	Organisation for European Economic Cooperation
ECB	European Central Bank		
ECHR	European Convention on Human Rights	plc	Public Limited Company
ECJ	European Court of Justice	QMV	Qualified Majority Voting
ECR	European Court Reports	SDA	Sex Discrimination Act
ECSC	European Coal and Steel Community	SEA	Single European Act
EEC	European Economic Community	TEU	Treaty on European Union
EFTA	European Free Trade Area	ToA	Treaty of Amsterdam
ELJ	European Law Journal	WHO	World Health Organization

Exam Skills for Success in EU Law

1

The challenges of EU law

This book provides a number of example questions on European Union (EU) law, fairly typical of those met on degree-level courses on EU law. The chapters open with a brief review of the general matters you need to be aware for the topics under investigation, followed by one or more key debates. Each chapter, apart from this one, consists of a number of questions containing points you need to take into account when answering and each suggested answer commences with a diagram or flow chart outlining the main aspects or elements to be considered.

Achieving success in EU law assessments

The suggested answers are designed to demonstrate how the particular questions should be answered to get a good mark, i.e. an upper-second or better. Note, however, that the writing and marking of law questions (EU law included) is not a simple arithmetic process whereby, once you have written a sufficient number of points, you automatically qualify for a particular grade. Whilst that is one of the elements taken into account, it is also a qualitative assessment of what has been written: in other words, how you have written what you have written. This in turn refers to the style and structure of your answer, the clarity and precision with which you express yourself and the accuracy of your statements and application of law to fact. If you are able to demonstrate wider reading in your arguments, some of which may feature in the 'Key debates' and 'Taking things further' features, this will help you achieve a better mark. So there are more factors taken into account than just writing a list of the points that arise and a simple answer to each. The presence of this extra quality will enhance your mark, so its absence will not allow you to obtain the higher marks. Some Universities will designate percentages they consider appropriate to each part to assist you in deciding how much you write for each part, whereas others will leave that to your discretion, which itself forms part of assessment of your knowledge, skills, and abilities in constructing excellent answers to questions. Note that the answers in this book are not model answers which can be learnt by heart and applied to answer any question on a particular topic, although I have often seen this attempted. It doesn't work because for the most part the person attempting the question simply fails to answer the question set. There is no harm, however, in being able to adapt parts of these answers to particular questions providing you are still answering the question. The answers have been designed with the idea in mind that they are exam-type answers rather than answers for assessed course work, which would require far more detail. To assist in coursework, a short chapter has been added to the end of the book containing tips and advice on how to structure and answer coursework.

Please note though, this book is not a replacement for work, either for attendance at lectures, preparation for tutorials or seminars, or revision for the examination. If used carefully, it will help you prepare answers but will not help you learn the material in the first place. It does not present EU law in a systematic way but instead selects particular issues within questions on which to concentrate.

Using cases in EU law

The choice of example cases provided within some if not most of the answers is rather limited, especially in comparison with textbooks and cases and materials books and in particular when compared to common law subjects. This is deliberate because, for the most part, one case will be sufficient authority for the points of law you wish to convey and this is also a realistic approach bearing in mind that, in an examination, you will simply not have time to reproduce the numbers of cases in the books and by necessity must concentrate your attention on a smaller number of clearly relevant cases. In EU law, for the most part we are not seeking to distinguish, compare, or analogise cases. Unlike the common law subjects, there is far less concern with the facts of the case in that you can only apply a legal principle to a new case if the facts are sufficiently similar. In EU law, the facts are sometimes completely irrelevant, as in, for example, the leading case of *Costa v ENEL*. The facts concern the collection and payment of an outstanding electricity bill by the newly nationalised electricity company. The principle of law established in that case is that of the supremacy of EU law over national law. EU law cases can be one further level of abstraction away from a consideration in detail of the facts, for example, those in the **Article 267 TFEU** preliminary reference procedure where the facts are dealt with by the national courts and questions of EU law are the focus of attention and reason for the reference. Hence, then, it is far more often that the legal principle is the important factor. In some of the substantive law subjects, such as the free movement of goods or persons, the facts can play a more important role and in answering problem questions, you need to identify what the facts are because you still have to apply the law to the facts.

An example from the Free Movement of Persons chapter

We can look at whether part-time work is sufficient to satisfy the definition of the term 'worker'. This in turn is important because if you are a worker for the purposes of EU law, this gives not only the right to reside in the host state but the right to many more rights and benefits.

This is the example involving certain factual issues surrounding Wolfie, who was busking in the street and playing in a band but only for a limited time. The questions are whether these facts support the conclusion that he is a worker for the purposes of EU law.

Is he a worker as a busker? Fundamentally, to be a worker, the definition from *Hoekstra* **(75/63)** is that the person must be employed. The *Levin* **case (53/81)** also requires there to be a genuine economic activity. A busker does not seem to satisfy the criteria of a worker laid down in the case of *Lawrie Blum* **(66/85)**. His busking is not at the direction or remuneration of an employer and he receives donations only; therefore, on these facts, he is not a worker. Does the 80-hours' membership of the band and playing gigs qualify him as a worker? Although the case of *Raulin v Netherlands Ministry of Education and Science* **(C-357/89)** would seem to support this suggestion, again the criteria of *Lawrie Blum* seem not to be satisfied as he is not employed under a contract and the band split.

The facts were important but only for that individual case.

For the most part I have sought to use as example cases the leading and more popular cases in EU law. Don't worry, however, if these do not coincide with the cases you have read, learnt, or been referred to in your course on EU law. As long as they cover the same legal issue or point, they are perfectly acceptable alternatives in an examination. It is the legal point at issue and not necessarily the particular case authority although there are certain leading and classic cases which should be cited, such as *Van Gend en Loos* in relation to direct effects.

The structure and approach to problem questions

As an internal and external examiner for more than 20 Universities now in EU law, I have seen a number of variations on a simple way to remember how to approach problem questions, including IRAC (Identify the issues, Relevant law, Apply the law, and Conclusions), FLAC (Facts, Law, Application, and Conclusions), and ILAC (Issues, Law, Application, and Conclusions). Whichever one you encounter in your own University, they are all aimed at the same thing, which is to provide an easy to remember acronym which in turn sets out the matrix or blueprint for your answer. You will come across IRAC throughout the series of Q&A books. The facts or factual issues are the ones you must identify and are usually in the form of a scenario or series of events clearly within one of the areas of law covered by the chapters. The law, obviously relevant law, can come in a variety of forms, more so in EU law: Treaty law, secondary EU Law, principles of EU Law, national law (often in conflict), or case law (both EU and national case law). The application is, of course, the working part of your answer where you apply the laws you have identified to your facts and which allow you to reach your conclusions, the final part of your answer.

EU terminology

A brief mention will be made here in respect of the terms EU and European Community (EC). Although these have been unified now, following the entry into force of the **Lisbon Treaty**, as the European Union, both will be found in older textbooks and in previous case law. The term European Union was brought in by the **Treaty on European Union (TEU) (also known and referred to as the Maastricht Treaty)** and describes the extension by the Member States into additional policies and areas of cooperation. Following the entry into force of the 2007 **Lisbon Treaty** in 2009, it is correct to refer only to the European Union.

Case citation in EU law

It is assumed that you are familiar with the statutory provisions of Union law and the case law of the CoJ so that references to a case by one name or by a short title will be enough for you to identify the case. Therefore, in order to avoid cluttering up the text, the references to cases will be to the name of the case and the case docket number as given to it by the Court of Justice of the European Union (CJEU but most commonly abbreviated CoJ) (beginning with C) or the General Court (previously the Court of First Instance) (beginning with T). For example, *Van Gend* **(26/62)**. This number identifies a case uniquely, although it is not often used to identify cases for the purposes of examinations. However, by adopting this method it does allow you to look the case up in either the alphabetical or case number numerical case lists in textbooks for further details. Please note though that some textbooks only list the cases by name only and sometimes, because case names are often complicated and can be known by different names, finding them can be very difficult. Oxford University Press textbooks on EU law all, as far as I know, have name and number lists. This book, not being a textbook, makes an exception because you will be working directly from the text of this book, i.e. you will be reading each question and answer as a complete whole, hence you will be unlikely to enter the book via the case references, and so it was considered appropriate only to include one set of case tables. Given that some cases are often known by more than one name or the case names can commence with different words and letters, it seems safer to offer the numeric list, especially as these identify the case uniquely and are also contained in the text.

The citation for cases has been revised by the adoption of the European Case-Law Identifier (ECLI) system, which will apply to national cases also concerned with EU law, which will carry the ECLI prefix. The system was adopted to make electronic tagging of cases and thus access both uniform and easier and works as follows as far as EU Court of Justice cases are concerned: The case name and number in the Court Register are retained but to these are added additional elements as demonstrated by the example provided by the Court of Justice.

The ECLI of the judgment of the Court of Justice of 12 July 2005 in Case C-403/03 Schempp is the following: 'EU:C:2005:446'.

It is broken down as follows:

● 'EU' indicates that it is a decision delivered by an EU Court or Tribunal (for decisions of national courts, the code corresponding to the relevant Member State appears in the place of 'EU');

● 'C' indicates that this decision was delivered by the Court of Justice. Decisions delivered by the General Court are indicated by the letter 'T' and those of the Civil Service Tribunal by 'F';

● '2005' indicates that the decision was delivered during 2005;

● '446' indicates that it is the 446th ECLI attributed in respect of that year.

The new system is being backdated to all cases from 1954 and has been used by the Court of Justice as from 2014.

Range of topics in EU law

As far as the choice of topics included in the book is concerned, this is becoming slightly more difficult as EU law extends its scope and degree courses change to reflect this or to reflect the particular topics of interest to those teaching and/or examining the course. There is, however, an irreducible minimum largely because EU Law is presently still a core subject for the Law Society and the Bar. So, whilst the subject matters contained in this volume cover all of the now reduced and more general Law Society and Bar Council requirements, this book may not cover all the topics on your particular course or, indeed, the particular approach taken.

Treaty references

The Treaties are abbreviated to the TEU and TFEU and to avoid confusion these will always be employed after the Article number, and where appropriate the predecessor European Community (EC) and European Economic Community (EEC) Treaties may be referred to using those abbreviations. As previously with the entry into force of the Treaty of Amsterdam on 1 May 1999, the original Treaties have been renumbered following the Lisbon Treaty. Although new numbering now applies, it is necessary to be aware of the old numbering as previous case law will refer to old numbering only and, as some cases take up to 13 years or even longer to final judgment on appeal before the CoJ, the problem will remain a current one for a while yet. The policy adopted in this book is to refer predominantly but not exclusively to the new numbers only and occasionally, where this is relevant, to include the old numbers in brackets, e.g. Art 267 TFEU (ex 234 EC), and very occasionally back to the old EEC Treaty (ex 177 EEC). For the most part, even when referring to pre-Lisbon or Amsterdam case law or legislative provisions, the new number will be given first, although this may not be technically correct. Occasionally, when close attention to the old numbers and content of provision is essential, the old numbers will be retained but this will be made clear, e.g. old Art 12 EC (now 18 TFEU). It is hoped confusion may be avoided. Similarly, the terms 'Union' and 'EU' will be employed unless discussing old case law where the court itself, of course, used the terms then valid of Community and EC law. In those instances the new terms will normally be placed in brackets. Quotes will use the terms current at the time without adding the new terms afterwards. I realise this may give rise to some confusion but this is the consequence of the changes agreed by the Member States and we just have to live with it and through it, until the years bring some familiarity and stability with the new numbering and terms (by which time, they will probably go and change it again).

The use of statutory materials in EU law examinations

Most institutions allow reference to statutory materials during the examination. One real advantage is that there is no need to concentrate too heavily on memorising statutory provisions whilst revising. It leaves you more time to consider the application and interpretation, rather than having to waste time on the regurgitation of particular provisions. It also makes it pointless to reproduce the whole of a legislative provision in an answer if the examiner knows that you have it in front of you during the examination. Indeed, there is no need for the reproduction even if statutory materials are not allowed to be used in the examination. However, to ignore completely the legislative provisions prior to the examination means you will be unfamiliar with them and will probably waste time finding the relevant provisions; e.g. some candidates, when provided with material, seem to spend an inordinate amount of time browsing or flicking through them during the examination. If you can, try to treat these materials as a last resort or a mental crutch to which you can refer should your memory fail you. There is no compulsion to look at them at all, but you may still need to cite specific parts of provisions to support your answer.

Open-book examinations

Open-book examinations, where you are able to take in other materials as well, are less common and vary considerably as to the materials that the candidate is allowed to use during the examination and the time allowed to complete the examination. You still have to revise and prepare thoroughly for the examination and not try to rely on finding the information whilst in the exam hall. They are a hybrid between the closed-book examination and assessed work in the form of extended essays or dissertations, but still require a structured answer at the end of the day.

To end this chapter on general information, tips, and advice, I'd like to make two points, which may be repeated in some of the chapters following. First, many of the questions, whether essay or problem type, contain fictitious Directives and Regulations; some, though, use actual ones. It is possible that only actual legislation is used on your particular course, which may resemble the fictitious ones used in a question. Whichever are used, these are designed to test your knowledge of the principles learned in your studies and the answer method suggested here remains the same.

Secondly, be aware of dates. When you see dates in a problem, this should set alarm bells ringing; they are not put into a question by chance or to signify my birthday. It means some sort of deadline or period may have or has expired, the consequences of which may affect the outcome of the solution.

The OUP Q&A series Online Resource Centre: www.oxfordtextbooks.co.uk/orc/qanda/ will contain links to EU portal web pages and further useful information.

The latest edition of Blackstone's EU Treaties & Legislation contains the consolidated versions of the EU and TFEU Treaties as revised and amended by the 2007 Lisbon Treaty and a collection of useful secondary EU legislation.

Finally, and I hope this advice is not too late, the best preparation for an examination is to have worked consistently over the period of your course. If you have, some of the questions and answers suggested here might actually make sense to you and not be the first time you have come across the issues, cases, or law involved. Apart from that, I wish you 'all the best' in the examination.

The Origins, Institutions, and Development of the Union and the Legislative Processes

2

ARE YOU READY?

In order to attempt questions in this chapter, you must have covered all of these topics in both your work over the year and in revision:

- The history and development of the Communities and how it has developed into the Union; direct questions on this would be rare but not ruled out.

- The principal institutions of the Council, the European Commission, and the European Parliament, and in particular the inter-relationship of these institutions in the legislative and other processes of the Union.

- The role and legality of the delegated legislation procedures under **Arts 290 and 291 TFEU**, the legislative procedures contained in **Arts 288 and 289 TFEU**, or the budget procedures in **Arts 310–319 TFEU** may be questioned in further detail or questions may focus on the powers and rights of the European Parliament (EP), the Council, or the Commission separately.

KEY DEBATES

Debate: Lisbon changes

Following the considerable institutional reform brought about by the **Lisbon Treaty**, many questions have been raised focusing on the changes brought about by the Lisbon Treaty and whether they represent further progress on the path to integration or a break on that progress.

Debate: The division and change to EU competences

Concerns raised by the Member States about the EU assuming too many competences has also been a hot topic as have the challenges made by Member States to halt the so-called 'competence creep'.

QUESTION 1

'European integration is initially a wholly political concept whose implementation proceeds by the formulation of economic policies and decisions.'

Comment on this statement by the European Commission from the 1960s.

CAUTION

- Try to achieve a balance of coverage of the various elements in your answer and do not over-concentrate on one particular aspect such as the historical beginnings or present-day changes.

- Do not be sidetracked by the fact this is a quote from the 1960s; it is as relevant today as it was then but does need to addressed both historically and currently.

DIAGRAM ANSWER PLAN

Outline the reasons for establishing the European Communities

Consider whether there was an ultimate goal of integration.

Stress the objectives of the original **EEC Treaty**

Consider developments since the 1950s

Stress these are no longer just economic but also social policies

Evaluate the significance of recent reforms

Conclusion

SUGGESTED ANSWER

[1] This title and first part of the answer addresses the questions of why the Communities, and now Union, were set up and how they were designed to achieve their aims.

[2] Commence with a review of reasons, which must be addressed in contrast to suggesting that the reasons were based purely or merely on economic grounds, although it is difficult to distinguish the two terms completely.

[3] Consider the process by which the implementation of the political concept was to be achieved, including considerations of the theories of European integration of federalism and functional integration.

Reasons for establishing the Communities[1]

The term 'European integration' is taken to refer to the European Communities which were set up in the 1950s. We can ask then, what were the reasons for setting up these Communities by treaties between nation states?[2] The Communities were a political response to the Second World War and the massive destruction that had taken place in Europe as a consequence. They represented both an attempt to ensure that such a war could not occur in Europe again and to provide a better and hopefully more stable means by which the reconstruction of Europe could take place. They aimed to remove the rivalries between nation states by legally binding them together in economic communities. So, the reason for setting up the Communities was the result of entirely political motives to eliminate war and provide a new basis for economic reconstruction of Europe. Thus, the primary motivations were political but economic tools were employed to achieve that integration.

How was integration to be achieved?

What was the political concept of European integration? At the time the Communities were being contemplated and even after the establishment of the Treaties, different views were adopted on the form and extent of integration.[3] These ranged from the view that a European Federal State was envisaged to the view that the Member States were only participating in the erection of a common market concerned only with economic cooperation. It was, however, originally widely considered that because there was success in certain policies this would automatically lead to a spillover from one area to another to lead to increasing integration and that the whole process of integration was a dynamic and not a static process. This process is termed functional integration. In fact, it was considered that in order for the original policies to work properly there must be continuing integration. Thus, sector-by-sector integration and the process of European integration were regarded as inexorable. For example, common tariffs and the establishment of the Common Market would lead to exchange rates being stabilised to ensure that production factors and costs in the Member States were broadly equal. This in turn requires monetary union to be established to ensure exchange rates do not drift apart and this requires full economic union to be achieved so that the value of different components of the common currency is not changed by different policies in different countries. This economic integration would also mean that the political integration would eventually follow. Whilst the above is a rather simplistic account of the theories of integration, it also helps understand the suggestion that any decision on the part of the Community, and now Union, to go no further in terms of integration would in fact not maintain a stable position but would ultimately be regressive as it would start to undermine or undo the previous successes and integration achieved.

Federalism or some form of federal state may therefore be the argued goal of the Communities, and now Union, if the aims are not limited to the distinct policies thus far agreed. In order to make the goal of the Communities and Union more acceptable the term 'a closer union' has been used in both the old **EC and EU Treaties**. The **post-Lisbon TEU** expresses this again as the Member States being 'Resolved to continue the process of creating an ever closer union'. Its exact meaning is unclear as to whether it refers to federalism or something short of that. The UK's view on this during the negotiations for the **Treaty of European Union** was that it falls somewhat short and whilst the EU does operate on the supra-national level, the UK maintained that it does not signify an inevitable move to federalism, a view now shared by other countries such as Denmark, Poland, and the Czech Republic.

The economic activities of the EU[4]

[4]Look at how the implementation was to be achieved by considering the overall objectives of the original **EEC Treaty** and the way in which further laws and decisions could be reached to assist integration.

The way in which these fundamental political objectives were to be converted into economic and social ones was initially by the agreement to establish a treaty providing the legal basis for economic and further integration. The aims and objectives of the Community were clearly set out in the **EC Treaty**. The **Preamble** and **Arts 2 and 3 EC** (now Arts 2 and 3 TEU) set out in general terms the type and range of policies the Community was to pursue to achieve the general objective of European integration.

Article 2 EC, for example, set the general goals as the establishment of a common market and an economic and monetary union. This was to be achieved by the implementation of the common policies or activities referred to in **Arts 3 and 4 EC**. **Article 3 EC** notably included policies on customs duties, a common commercial policy, free movement of goods, persons, services, and capital, agriculture and fisheries, transport, and competition. Newer developments include[5]

[5]Since the quotation arises from the 1960s you will be aware it predates the various treaty revisions so don't limit your answer to an intention as viewed in the 1950s and 1960s.

activities and policies in the social sphere, economic and social cohesion, the environment, research and technological development, trans-European networks, health protection, education and training, culture, development cooperation, overseas policies, consumer protection and energy, civil protection, and tourism.

Those objectives and policies were expanded upon in specific parts of the Treaty, for example, free movement of workers in now **45 TFEU** and competition law in **now 101–102 TFEU**. The Treaty Articles were not to be the only source of legal provisions formulating the economic policies and decisions. The Community institutions, notably the Council, Commission, and, at first to a very limited extent, the European Parliament, were also empowered by the Member States with their own law-making powers to establish further laws to achieve European integration and the objectives of the Treaties. These powers are summarised in **now 293–294 TFEU**. Furthermore, a European Court of Justice (CoJ) was established for the Community to adjudicate on Community law and provide rulings binding on the Member States. These further help to implement the concept of European integration.

[6] You could consider the further question of whether the arguable eventual goal of the Communities, and now Union, of political union to be achieved by progressive economic integration will ever be reached.

Concluding remarks[6]

Thus, whilst it would be true to agree that the original concept was a political one, which has and is being implemented by economic policies, the debate continues and it is clear from the intense discussions surrounding the **Single European Act** (SEA), the **Treaty on European Union**, and the further changes in the 1990s to date that the eventual goal of the Union is far from clearly or definitively determined. European integration is still dependent on further political impulses. Implementation of European integration can only proceed by further political policy and not just by economic decisions. Indeed it can be observed from the very modest scope of social policy in the original **EEC Treaty, Art 119 (now 157 TFEU)** that considerable advances or inroads have been made into other non-purely political or economic areas of the Member States' economies. The underlying political nature of the EU was clearly seen during the negotiations at the Nice 2000 IGC and in gaining the ratification of all 28 Member States for the **Lisbon Treaty**, where only after very hard political bargaining was sufficient agreement reached to provide for continued European expansion and integration. The political impetus for new policies to assist integration and indeed the wide-ranging political debate as to the future of the EU continues. These events show quite clearly that European integration is indeed a wholly political concept because without the political agreement, there will be no further economic integration. It remains to be seen how Brexit will impact on the integration process. [7]

[7] Due to the continuing uncertainty about the Brexit process, whatever you might say here must be short, along the lines of stating that there is a debate about whether Brexit will be a catalyst for disintegration or encourage the remaining 27 states to pull together in greater integration.

✚ LOOKING FOR EXTRA MARKS?

■ You could point to the various and numerous changes brought about by the institutional reform of the Lisbon Treaty as an example of political change.

■ Just to give one example here: the formalising of the European Council with a European President as a main institution as political head which gives further impetus to economic integration.

■ A brief mention of Brexit and its possible consequences could be included as outlined under point 7 above.

Q **QUESTION** **2**

'As far as its legislative procedures are concerned, the EU is neither efficient nor democratic.'

a Discuss this statement in the light of the powers and the decision-making procedures of the Council, Commission, and European Parliament.

b What reforms would you advocate which would overcome these criticisms?

! CAUTION

■ This question is quite complex because it is in three parts. The first sentence can be broken down to determine what issues must be considered.

■ This final section is probably the hardest to prepare for in that it really requires you to have read particular advocated reforms during your course on top of those already put into effect following the entry into force of the **2007 Lisbon Treaty.**

■ Although good original suggestions will pick up a few extra marks it is not the major part of the answer. If you have not considered possible reforms, it is not worth spending an excessive amount of time trying to think up reforms; it would probably be better to find another question to answer.

☐ DIAGRAM ANSWER PLAN

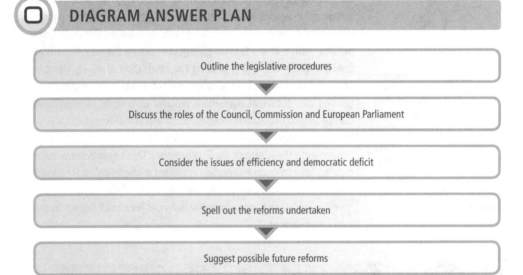

Outline the legislative procedures

▼

Discuss the roles of the Council, Commission and European Parliament

▼

Consider the issues of efficiency and democratic deficit

▼

Spell out the reforms undertaken

▼

Suggest possible future reforms

A SUGGESTED ANSWER

[1] The legislative procedures must be described as concisely as possible because specific features of these procedures should be considered further in the answer.

Introduction to the legislative procedures[1]

At present all the legislative procedures commence with a proposal from the Commission although following the entry into force of the **Lisbon Treaty**, suggestions and recommendations for legislative acts may also come from the EP, the European Council, the Member States, the ECB, the CoJ, the EIB, and EU citizens. Following the **Lisbon Treaty** there are now effectively just three procedures: the ordinary legislative procedure, the special legislative procedure, and the consent procedure. In addition, the Commission and the Council have limited delegated or go-it-alone powers.

[2]Set out the original position.

Under the EP's initial advisory role[2] a limited number of **EEC Treaty Articles** (17) provided that the Council was required to consult the EP as to its opinion before coming to a decision on Community secondary law; see e.g. **old Arts 54 or 56 EC**. The *Isoglucose (Roquette Frères)* **cases (Cases 138–9/79)** confirmed that the EP had to be consulted. However, on receipt of that opinion the Council could proceed to ignore it and override any view given by the EP. In two cases, *EP* v *Council* (C-65/91) and *Parliament* v *Council* (C-392/95), the Court annulled two Regulations which had been substantially amended by the Council without a further consultation of Parliament taking place when the Council had amended its draft legislation. This still exists within the special legislative procedure but only in limited instances as will be considered further.

The ordinary legislative procedure[3]

[3]Outline the ordinary legislative procedure and changes made to it by Treaty amendment.

Article 289 TFEU has been amended over the years to provide that the EP act more extensively with the Council and Commission in the legislative process, notably by the introduction of the co-decision procedure and its renaming as the ordinary legislative procedure, detailed in **Art 294 TFEU**. It provides for the enhanced participation of the EP to the extent that ultimately, the EP can reject a legislative proposal at a second reading. The EP cannot impose its own will on the content of a legislative proposal, and equally the Council cannot force unwanted legislation on the EP. Note that in the procedure, the Council votes mainly by QMV but at times, according to some Treaty Articles and parts of the procedure itself, it must vote unanimously. The following description takes into account the amendments made to the procedure by the **Treaties of Amsterdam and Lisbon**.

The ordinary legislative procedure provides a process by which both the Council and EP may consider and approve a legislative proposal or amend it, in which case, the other institution must further consider the proposal. Ultimately, the institutions must either agree on the proposal or either the Council or the EP or both reject it.

Special legislative procedures[4]

[4]Then, briefly set out the two remaining procedures, the special legislative procedure followed by the consent procedure.

This second category is really a bundle of procedures that may be referred to in the Treaties variously as 'the' or 'a' special legislative procedure, and essentially groups together a number of procedures that differ in one or more elements from the ordinary legislative procedure. Instead of QMV, the Council may vote by unanimity or the EP may just be consulted or asked for its consent rather than co-deciding. Other bodies, such as the EESC, CoR, or ECB, may also be included in the process. It incorporates the original consultation procedure. Under this procedure, the Commission proposes legislation that it deems necessary to fulfil a Union aim; the EP is then consulted and it offers its opinion; and the Council decides on the matter, sometimes by QMV, but usually unanimously. However, on receipt of the opinion of the EP, the Council could proceed to ignore it and override any view given by the EP.

The consent procedure

The consent (previously referred to as 'assent') procedure was introduced by the SEA and extended under the **TEU and Lisbon Treaty**, so that the EP's consent is required by the Council in respect of membership and withdrawal applications to the EU, the Union's membership of international agreements and organisations, and association agreements with third countries (**Arts 49 and 50 TEU, and 218 and 217 TFEU**): in total, in 15 instances. In the event of disagreement, the EP has effectively a right of veto, but there are no formal mechanisms built in by which a dialogue between the two institutions can be initiated in the event of a disagreement on any aspect or an entire Agreement. In reality, though, any such dispute would have been subject to debate and discussion behind the scenes. Consent may also be employed to confirm serious and persistent breaches by a Member State (**Art 7 TEU**) and in establishing a procedure for the revision of the Treaties (**Art 48 TEU**). The procedure has not been made subject to time limits.

[5]Address the issues in the second sentence of the question that the EU is neither efficient nor democratic in respect of the powers and activities of the three political institutions.

Evaluation of the procedures[5]

The efficiency and democracy of these procedures must be considered in the light of powers of the institutions which support or contradict the view expressed in the question.

The powers of the Council are basically set out in **Arts 16 TEU and 238 TFEU**. The Council disposes of EU legislation which must be initiated by the Commission. The power of the EP is set out in **Art 14 TEU** which provides that the EP shall exercise legislative functions which are detailed in **Arts 289 and 294 TFEU** and by giving consent (previously known as assent).

The Commission's powers are to initiate the legislative procedure by making proposals and to act under powers delegated to it by the Council. The Commission's right to act under delegated powers is extremely restricted by the revised management committee structure by which the Council retains overall much of its original powers.

A feature that that supports the first statement was the limited role played by the EP in the legislative procedure although that has changed considerably over the years and the EP has now effectively an equal say with the Council. It might be argued that the main ordinary legislative procedure is quite convoluted and slow although the reality is that most EU legislation is now passed at an early stage of the procedure thus relatively efficiently. Finally, the most fundamental feature is that even with the ordinary legislative procedure, the Council and EP's ultimate power is only that of a negative veto but again to temper that consensus and agreement is reached in the vast majority of cases.

Addressing the criticism concerning the lack of efficiency, the delays that were often and still are experienced in the legislative procedure can be cited, and also that there are still a number of different procedures according to the Treaty. The procedures became more complex and, as evidence, the stagnation of the legislative process in the 1970s and 1980s could be highlighted. Further evidence is that the Council could not cope with the amount of work necessary and has had to devise ways in which decision-making power could be delegated but control could nevertheless be retained by setting up a number of complex management committees. The Council by its nature acts in the interests of the Member States and not the Union, hence compromises must be reached, which has delayed some legislation by very many years. The **Lisbon Treaty reforms**, though, have reduced the number of procedures and appear to allow law-making to be more efficient. Reports show that the Council decides on legislation by finding an acceptable consensus rather than pushing each time for a vote, thus making law-making easier to achieve.

The question of democracy is easier to address and clearly points to the role of the EP as the only directly elected body and originally only having a lesser role in the legislative process, and the question of delegation to Committees controlled by the Council and not the EP. This whole argument is described as the democratic deficit in the EU, i.e. because the EP is the only directly democratically elected element, in order to maintain the democratic right or justification of EU laws, the legislative process must be more in the hands of elected bodies. If this democratic deficit is real then something needs to be done.

[6]Review the reforms already put into effect under the **Maastricht, Amsterdam, Nice, and Lisbon Treaties** to determine whether these have answered the criticisms before suggestions for further reform are made.

The Reforms[6]

The criticisms of the Maastricht Treaty and subsequent reforms are that the power of co-decision could be argued to give the EP a negative power of veto and **Art 294 TFEU** is not comprehensive and still only applies to limited specific areas, although this has been expanded significantly by the Treaties, especially the **Lisbon Treaty**, to some 40 more Treaty Articles. The ability under **Art 225 TFEU** to request the Commission to make legislative proposals in areas of EU policy is also unclear as to whether it can insist that a proposal is made. Whilst the amendments by the **Nice and Lisbon Treaties** were more limited in scope than hoped and planned for, particularly in view of the changes proposed originally for the Constitution for Europe, which originally would have provided for one single legislative procedure featuring the co-decision process, they have considerably improved matters. However, the cooperation procedure, which was used less and less, was scrapped in favour of the co-decision procedure, which became the 'ordinary' procedure under **Arts 289 and 294 TFEU**. This procedure was extended again into new areas, although certain areas such as Tax and Social Security retained the use of unanimous voting, as have, indeed, over 50 other legal bases. Whether this addresses the concerns about democracy and efficiency will only be measurable after the passage of time. The **Lisbon Treaty** also introduced a role for the National Parliaments in the legislative process, which is now referred to in **Art 12** of the **amended EU Treaty** and is contained in a Protocol on the role of National Parliaments. This requires that draft legislative acts of the Union are forwarded to National Parliaments for their opinion. Whilst this could be argued to increase democracy, it might be at the expense of efficiency, as another body (or collection of bodies) is introduced into the law-making process and, apart from the in-built extra time required, may simply slow or prevent the Council from reaching a consensus on a particular issue if hindered by unfavourable national Parliaments' opinions. In relation to this change the 2008 article by Barratt[7] on the involvement of national Parliaments is instructive.

[7] Cited in the 'Taking Things Further' section at the end of the Chapter.

Any reforms have to try to increase democracy, which could be achieved by giving the EP a completely equal role to the Council's and/or increasing the participation of the national parliaments. The former would not be at the expense of efficiency, whereas the latter probably would.[8] However, any increase in the powers of the EP is to be at the expense of some other organisation, not the National Parliaments but the Councils of Ministers and/or the Commission. Imposing time limits on the legislative process might help efficiency but may undermine democracy if participants are not given adequate time to consider and comment on proposals.

[8] Reforms you suggest depend on your views as to whether the Union is inefficient or undemocratic or, whether previous reforms have improved the situation. State how they are to be achieved and the consequences for the other institutions.

✚ LOOKING FOR EXTRA MARKS?

■ Make a longer comparison with the past procedures to show that the principal procedure today, the ordinary legislative procedure, is in fact far more democratic and indeed efficient.

■ Some University courses will have considered statistics of law-making to show that a clear majority of laws are enacted at first reading by the Council and the EP, so providing these would be very profitable.

■ If you had time and space, a consideration of why the procedures changed would be very positive (facilitating further integration, taking account of more Member States, the democratic deficit).

Q QUESTION 3

In the light of the roles of the Advocates General and the Court of Justice of the European Union and with reference to the jurisprudence of the Court, consider whether the Court of Justice possesses law-making powers in the EU legal order.

! CAUTION

- This appears to be a relatively straightforward question dealing with the CoJ and the Advocates General and their impact in the EU legal order, but you need to make sure you answer the actual question and not just provide a general answer.

- The amount of detail you include for the first part of the answer will depend on the coverage in your course and whether, for example, you have considered in detail the Protocol on the Statute of the Court of Justice **or** the Rules of the Court of Justice. If not, then supply as much detail as you can.

☐ DIAGRAM ANSWER PLAN

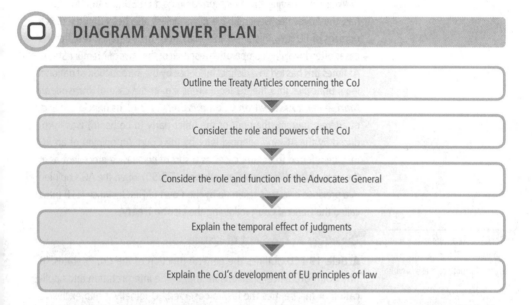

Outline the Treaty Articles concerning the CoJ

⌄

Consider the role and powers of the CoJ

⌄

Consider the role and function of the Advocates General

⌄

Explain the temporal effect of judgments

⌄

Explain the CoJ's development of EU principles of law

A ▶ SUGGESTED ANSWER

[1] The question can be broken into easier sections, starting with a general description of the Court, judges, and Advocates General. Brexit will, of course, reduce the number of judges but not necessarily the number of Advocates General.

[2] You need to outline the position and function of the Advocate General (AG) and how that may play in answering the question.

Introduction[1]

The CoJ presently consists of 28 judges and 11 Advocates General, nominated and appointed by unanimous agreement by the governments of the Member States. They must be chosen from persons whose independence is beyond doubt and who possess the qualifications required for appointment to the highest judicial office in their own countries (**Arts 251–253 TFEU**).

The position of the Advocates General[2] is established under **Art 252 TFEU**. The role of an AG is to assist the Court by giving an opinion, in complete independence and impartiality, on the issues of a case. In doing so the AG will examine the legal issues in depth and critically review the jurisprudence of the Court on the subject. The reasoned submissions of the Advocates General are to be made in open court. It is a general requirement that the opinion of the AG be heard before judgment is given unless the case raises no new point of law (**Art 20** of the **Statute of the Court of Justice**). The AG can therefore take the public view of things and consider the submissions of all the parties but cannot be bound to present or represent any particular view. Additionally, the opinion of the AG is not binding on the Court but it acts like a sort of persuasive precedent. Alternatively, it can be considered that the opinion of the AG acts like a first instance decision subject to an automatic and instant appeal. The AG plays no part in the actual decision of the Court and once the AG has delivered an opinion it brings to an end his or her role in the case.

Whilst not having the direct formal impact on EU law that the Court has, the Advocates General have nevertheless also helped in the development of EU law. This arises indirectly from their detailed research for cases often involving comparative research of the laws of Member States. At times this has led to a distinct influence by the introduction of national legal principles into the EU legal order, e.g. in the case of *Transocean Marine Paint Association* v *Commission* (**17/74**), the principle of *audi et alterem partem* (the right of the other party to be heard) was introduced by the AG and adopted later by the Court. An opinion of an AG may be referred to in later cases as a sort of persuasive precedent as in the case of *Prodifarma* v *Commission* (**T-3/90**) when the AG's opinion in a previous case was taken up by the Court of First Instance (CFI) (now called the General Court following the **Lisbon Treaty**).

[3] Then you must turn to the role and powers of the CoJ. The place to start for both of these is with the Treaty.

The duties of the Court of Justice[3]

Article 19 TEU outlines the general function of the CoJ. It states: 'It (the Court of Justice) shall ensure that in the interpretation and application of the Treaties the law is observed.' Originally it had exclusive jurisdiction over EU law but was joined by the Court of First Instance and judicial panels (now the General and Specialised Courts under **Arts 256–257 TFEU**). The Court has been divided into chambers to help expedite the business of the Court. The jurisdiction and tasks of the Court are laid down in **Arts 258–281 TFEU**.

As a result of the fact that the European Treaties and some of the secondary legislation are framework measures, they often require considerable amplification and interpretation. This, coupled with the style of interpretation which has been adopted by the Court to give effect to the aims of the Treaties, has given a wide scope to the CoJ to engage in judicial activism.[4]

[4] Decide whether the role played by the CoJ in the decisions it reaches constitute a law-making power and, thus, whether it adds to the body of EU law, or whether it merely interprets and applies existing EU law.

A primary form of interpretation is described as teleological in that the Court tries to determine in the light of the aims and objective of the Treaties and legislation what was intended and what result would assist those goals. These methods are applied in addition to the usual array of methods of interpretation found in the Member States' legal systems. The Court often refers to the spirit of the Treaty and Community (now Union) to come to a particular conclusion.

[5]The reference to the jurisprudence of the CoJ is simply asking you to refer to the case law of the CoJ where necessary to support your arguments and answer.

See in particular the leading case[5] of *Van Gend en Loos* **(26/62)** at para 71 and the case of *CILFIT Srl* v *Ministro della Sanita* **(283/81)**, concerned with the necessity of national courts to refer a question under **Art 234 EC (now 267 TFEU)**. This form of interpretation allows the Court to be more adventurous in its decision-making than could be assumed from a literal reading of the legal provisions. For example, in certain circumstances it has been held that persons who are unemployed or studying can be classified as workers under EU law; see the case of *Lair* v *Universität Hannover* **(39/86)**.

Precedent in the EU legal order?

Past decisions are often cited in Court, however, they are only persuasive rather than having any formal authority. For example, the *Da Costa* case **(28/62)** can also be observed to give rise to a form of precedent in that the CoJ stated that it was possible for national courts to refer to previous judgments of the CoJ in identical cases to achieve a solution without the need for reference to the CoJ. However, it must be stated that there is no formal system of precedent but the Court, as do courts in civil law jurisdictions, tries to maintain consistency in its judgments. An example of a reversal of the Court's decisions is in the case of *EP* v *Council* in the *Comitology* case **(302/87)** in which the EC was denied the right to take action under **Art 230 EC (now 263 TFEU)**, but it was later allowed in the case of *EP* v *Council* **(C-70/88)** concerned with a Euratom decision Treaty base by Council to protect Parliament's prerogatives.

One aspect which may hinder a law-making role is the requirement to give a single judgment of the Court. This is because a single judgment is at times difficult to interpret later because it does not reveal whether the decision was reached on a unanimous or majority verdict. Hence it can be confusing and terse and thus difficult to apply in future cases as 'established' law.

[6]This demonstrates just how judicially inventive the Court has been in establishing leading principles of EU law.

The establishment of EU principles of law[6]

It can be observed that the Court has played a crucial role in the establishment and development of the EU legal order by the establishment and development of leading principles of EU law. Notable judgments are those concerned with what are now fundamental decisions of the Court including direct effects (*Van Gend en Loos* case **(26/62)**) and supremacy (*Costa* v *ENEL* case **(6/64)**) and case rulings in actions concerning the rights of the EU institutions, notably the EP. In the case of *Les Verts* v *EP* **(294/83)**, an action against the EP under **Art 230 EC (now 263 TFEU)** was admitted despite the lack of any mention in the Article that the EP could be a defendant and in *EP* v *Council* **(C-295/90)**, concerned with the Treaty base, the extension of the rights of the EP to take action under **Art 230 EC (now 263 TFEU)** was confirmed despite not being given the right under the provision of the Article itself.

A number of cases could then be cited to provide evidence that the CoJ enjoys some form of law-making role but it would be best to rely on leading cases in which the CoJ has established the fundamental principles of EU law of direct effects and supremacy of EU law: *Van Gend en Loos* **(26/62)** and *Costa* v *ENEL* **(6/64)**. Quotations from these cases could be employed to great effect.

In *Van Gend en Loos* the CoJ held:

the Community constitutes a new legal order of international law for the benefit of which the States have limited their sovereign rights, albeit in limited fields, and the subjects of which comprise not only Member States but also their nationals.

From *Da Costa* it was held:

By contrast with ordinary international treaties the **EEC Treaty** has created its own legal system which became an integral part of the legal systems of the Member States and which their courts are bound to apply. By creating a Community of unlimited duration, having its own institutions, its own personality, its own legal capacity and more particularly real powers stemming from a limitation of sovereignty or a transfer of powers from the states to the Community the Member States have limited their sovereign rights and have created a body of law to bind their nationals and themselves.

Also:

It follows . . . that the law stemming from the treaty, an independent source of law, could not because of its special and original nature, be overridden by domestic legal provisions, however framed, without being deprived of its character as Community law and without the legal basis of the Community itself being called into question.

These cases demonstrate more than the simple interpretation and application of law as there is nothing in the Treaty to expressly establish these two fundamental principles of EU law. Furthermore, the introduction of new principles to the EU legal order also establishes new principles and rules of EU law. The question that remains is whether this is law-making.[7] During the Intergovernmental Conference (IGC) of 1996–7, some Member States had expressed their dissatisfaction with the high degree of judicial activism exercised by the CoJ in cases such as *Barber* **(C-262/88)**, which defined pension payments, in certain circumstances, as pay. No changes resulted from this but it may be regarded as evidence that the Member States consider the CoJ to be doing more than just interpreting law.

[7] Reaching a conclusion depends on how 'law-making' is defined. It is at least arguable that it would not be incorrect to describe it as having law-making powers.

➕ LOOKING FOR EXTRA MARKS?

- Take a more detailed look at the reasoning behind such cases as *Van Gend en Loos* and *Von Colson*.

- A lot more case law could be used as examples of how the court has been judicially active to the point of describing it as law-making. Such case law would include: *Defrenne*, *Marshall*, *Mangold*, amongst others.

QUESTION | 4

The **2007 Lisbon Treaty**, having eventually being ratified by all of the Member States, is a much poorer substitute for the **2004 Constitutional Treaty** whilst essentially making the same institutional and other changes to the EU.
Discuss.

CAUTION

- Avoid a simple description of events.
- Equally avoid a purely descriptive answer on what the **Lisbon Treaty** and/or **Constitutional Treaties** contained.

DIAGRAM ANSWER PLAN

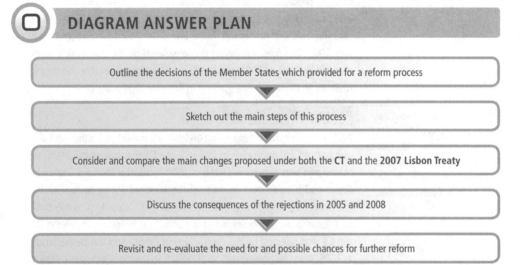

Outline the decisions of the Member States which provided for a reform process

Sketch out the main steps of this process

Consider and compare the main changes proposed under both the **CT** and the **2007 Lisbon Treaty**

Discuss the consequences of the rejections in 2005 and 2008

Revisit and re-evaluate the need for and possible chances for further reform

SUGGESTED ANSWER

[1]This question is one which is designed to highlight not only the changes which were proposed but also the difficulties the Member States have experienced in trying to reform the EU.

[2]Consider why significant changes were proposed in both the **CT** and the **2007 Lisbon Treaty**. Go back to the previous decisions of the Member States which launched the Union on the reform path.

The background to reform[1]

In preparation for the planned future expansion of the EU, in 1999,[2] the then 15 Member States convened an intergovernmental conference to discuss institutional change which concluded with the signing and eventual ratification of the **Nice Treaty**. The Nice Council Summit saw the agreement of the Member States as to how to move on to the next stage of Treaty amendment and further integration. It was further agreed to do this in a different way to make Treaty reform more inclusive and transparent. The Nice Council Summit provided a 'Declaration on the Future of the Union' which was to address a number of issues for the next IGC, planned for 2003. The details were finalised at a later summit of the Member States in Laeken in December 2001, which saw the start of an ultimately unsuccessful attempt to put the EU on a new constitutional footing. The Laeken Summit formally set up and prepared the agenda for a 'Convention on the Future of Europe' which was headed by a Praesidium of 12 members, led by Valéry Giscard d'Estaing, a former French President. It further consisted of representatives of the heads of state and government of the 15 Member States and the 13 candidate countries, 30 representatives of the National Parliaments and 26 from the candidate countries, 16 members of the EP and two members from the Commission. It laid out in a declaration the goals for making the EU more democratic, transparent, and efficient. In particular, attention would be paid to the governance of the Union, institutional preparations for the forthcoming expansion, the division of competences, and democratic participation in decision-making processes of the Union. The Convention worked until June 2003 when it wrote up its report and a draft Constitutional Treaty (**CT**) was finalised and presented to the European Council in Greece on 18 July 2003. This was subsequently considered by the IGC which commenced in October 2003 and the draft **CT** was presented to the Heads of State and Government Summit in Rome in December 2003.

What the CT contained[3]

[3]Make a comparison of what the **2004 Constitutional Treaty (CT)** and its substitute, the **2007 Lisbon Treaty**, contain. You must outline why these Treaties were considered desirable or necessary in the first place.

After some very hard bargaining on voting numbers in Council and the number of Commissioners in 2003–4, the **CT** was put to the Member States and was signed in October 2004 by all the Member States in Rome and handed over to each of the Member States to ratify it by parliamentary approval or referendum or both according to the constitutional or legal requirements of each state. However, in referenda, the **CT** was rejected by the electorates of France and the Netherlands in 2005. After an agreed period of reflection during which some states continued the ratification process, taking the total to 18, in June 2007 a further summit was held to see if the **CT** could be rescued or replaced. The German Presidency had the task of either making the **CT** more palatable or coming up with something in its place which nevertheless addressed the institutional challenges of enlargement. However, after another late night of Summit discussions, it was agreed to abandon the **CT** entirely and replace it. Even though the **CT** was abandoned, it is worthwhile listing the agreements[4] reached in that Treaty because most of these matters ended up in the **Lisbon Treaty** although in slightly altered or different form:

[4]Lists may not be preferred by your law school but sometimes they are easier to use where there is quite a long list of points to be made.

1   the transfer of a number of Article bases from unanimity to qualified majority

2   making the **Charter of Fundamental Rights** a legally binding part of the Treaty

3   providing the EU with the status of a legal person

4   establishment of the European Council as a main institution and the appointment of a President for the European Council (with a two and a half year term of office)

5   a smaller Commission comprising two-thirds of the number of Member States

6   creation of a common EU foreign minister to lead a joint foreign ministry with ambassadors

7   an express statement that Union law shall have primacy over national law

8   procedures for adopting and reviewing the Constitution, some without the need for another IGC

9   an exit clause for Member States.[5]

[5] You could mention that the exit clause in Article 50 TEU has now been triggered for the first time by the UK after the Brexit referendum.

The Lisbon Treaty

The **2007 Lisbon Treaty**, which did not replace the existing Treaties but amended them, has retained the following features of the **CT**. The Union did get its legal personality; the proposed Union Minister for Foreign Affairs is instead called the High Representative of the Union for Foreign Affairs and Security Policy (the High Representative). The European Council with President was established as envisaged by the **CT**. The Commission size was also to be reduced as planned, but this was revised again as a part of the deal to get Ireland to hold a second referendum on the **Lisbon Treaty**. The names and types of secondary law—'Regulations', 'Directives', and 'Decisions'—will be kept.

[6] Noting the changing status of the EU Fundamental Rights Charter is particularly important.

The **Charter on Fundamental Rights**[6] will become legally binding but only through a Declaration attached to the Treaties and with an opt-out for the UK and Poland and later the Czech Republic. Primacy of Union law was removed as an express statement in the Treaty and instead placed in a declaration which merely affirmed the settled case law establishing primacy. The transfer of a number of Articles to QMV and the co-decision procedure proceeded largely as planned.

The aspects of the **CT** which were not retained in the **Lisbon Treaty** were those more of a symbolic nature which were perceived by the Member States to be a large part of the reason for the rejection by the French and Dutch electorates, although studies have failed to establish this with any authority. The items completely abandoned were the references to a European flag, an anthem, a motto, and reference to a Europe day celebration which were argued to suggest too strongly of statehood. Note, though, that 16 Member States agreed Declaration 52 attached to the treaties that the flag, anthem, motto, euro, and Europe Day would continue as symbols to express the community of the people in the EU and their allegiance to it.

The **Lisbon Treaty** was supposed, by stripping away the offensive parts of the **CT** and retaining most of the institutional changes, to make the changes more palatable to the Member States and their electorates. However, as the question suggests, the end result is less than satisfying despite making most of the changes considered necessary to allow the Union to operate effectively in the future. This is because of the way the changes were made. Rather than contained in a single document, as with the **CT**, the **Lisbon Treaty** does this by complicated and extensive amendments to the **EC and EU Treaties**. The **TEU** was turned more into an overview Treaty with the **EC Treaty** being converted into a treaty dealing with substantive issues, called the **Treaty on the Functioning of the European Union**, and the term 'Community' has been replaced throughout by 'Union'. Both Treaties, however, concern the institutions and a number of Articles in both Treaties are concerned with the same subject matter. In addition, rather than tidying up and reducing the protocols and declarations attached to the Treaties, more have been added. Useful articles on the changes are Craig, P, 'The Lisbon Treaty: process, architecture and substance' (2008) and Dougan, M, 'The Treaty of Lisbon 2007: winning minds, not hearts' (2008).[7]

[7] Cited in 'Taking Things Further' at the end of the Chapter.

At this stage[8] it is clear that the **Union Treaty** architecture remains complicated but, having been ratified by all Member States, it is progress. As the question suggests, it is arguable that this could have been done better, perhaps in a single document, and still have removed those elements considered offensive and which did not contain the word 'Constitutional' or similar, by just calling it, for example, the **'Consolidated EU and EC Treaty'**.

[8] State a view at this stage of whether you think **Lisbon** represents progress.

It is to be noted that not only was the **CT** rejected by the electorates in two Member States, but its supposed much more palatable replacement, the **Lisbon Treaty**, was rejected by the Irish electorate in June 2008.[9] Indeed, all but one state considered that the changes were insignificant enough not to have to subject the Treaty to a referendum at that time. It was generally assumed it would be ratified with less difficulty than the **CT**. Following a period of consideration and negotiation after the Irish rejection, in exchange for the agreement by Ireland to hold a second Referendum, EU leaders agreed to provide legal guarantees respecting Ireland's taxation policies, its military neutrality, and ethical issues. More controversially they also agreed that each state should maintain one Commissioner each, contrary to the Treaty itself. Constitutional challenges in other states such as Germany, the Czech Republic, and Poland were resolved and the deliberate delay by the Czech President in completing the Constitutional ratification process was withdrawn. The Treaty was finally ratified by all 27 States in November 2009 and entered into force on 1 December 2009.

[9] You need to address the fact that both attempts to reform the EU have been undermined by rejection in one or more states at some stage.

In conclusion, I would suggest that with only, for the most part, the symbolic aspects having been removed and because most substantive changes remained, the **Lisbon Treaty** is a poorer substitute, especially because of the way that the changes have been made.

LOOKING FOR EXTRA MARKS?

- Try to sum up the latest position on the consequences of these developments for the future of the reform of the EU.

- You could link the changes to the competences division to a discussion about the control on future integration by the Member States.

TAKING THINGS FURTHER

- Barratt, G, 'The King is Dead, Long Live the King: The Recasting by the Treaty of Lisbon of the Provisions of the Constitutional Treaty concerning National Parliaments' (2008) 33 EL Rev 66.
  This article is good in looking at the changes brought about by the Lisbon Treaty in the involvement of national parliaments in the scrutiny and enactment of EU secondary law.

- Craig, P, 'The Lisbon Treaty: Process, Architecture and Substance' (2008) 33 EL Rev 137.
  A general article on the changes brought about by the Lisbon Treaty.

- Dougan, M, 'The Treaty of Lisbon 2007: Winning Minds, not Hearts' (2008) 45 (3) CML Rev 609.
  Another view on the changes introduced by the Lisbon Treaty.

- Horsley, T, 'Subsidiarity and the European Court of Justice: Missing Pieces in the Subsidiarity Puzzle' (2012) 50 JCMS 267.
  A closer look at how the CoJ viewed the attempt by Member States to challenge EU law on the grounds of a breach of Subsidiarity.

Online Resources   www.oup.com/uk/qanda/

Go online for extra essay and problem questions, a glossary of key terms, online versions of all the answer plans and audio commentary on how selected ones were put together, and a range of podcasts which include advice on exam and coursework technique and advice for other assessment methods.

3

The Sources, Forms, and Individual Remedies of EU Law

ARE YOU READY?

In order to attempt questions in this chapter, which contains a number of interconnected topics, you must have covered all of these topics in both your work over the year and in revision:

- The sources of EU law.
- The development of the system of individual remedies which include:
  1 Direct effects
  2 The concept of an 'emanation of the state'
  3 Indirect effects
  4 State liability
  5 Incidental horizontal effects
  6 The direct effects of general principles.

KEY DEBATES

Debate: The continuing discussion on the horizontal direct effects of Directives

Although this is an old debate it continues to occupy both academic writers and the Court of Justice (CoJ), along with how both seek to get round the limitation of denying such effects.

QUESTION | 1

Identify the sources of law (other than Treaty provisions and EU secondary law) invoked by the Court of Justice. What is the justification for the recognition and application of such sources in the EU legal order?

! CAUTION

- This question bypasses a consideration of the internal sources of EU law, namely the Treaties, Regulations, Directives, and Decisions, to consider other sources of law and legal rules which have a presence or an impact in the EU legal order.
- Concentrate on the provisions of international agreements, general principles of law, and fundamental rights provisions and consider the justifications given by the CoJ to employ these other sources in its judgments.
- By all means mention the Treaties and Secondary Legislation but do not spend much time on them as they are not the focus of attention of this question.

◯ DIAGRAM ANSWER PLAN

Introduce the Treaty and non-Treaty based sources of EU law.

▼

Consider the status of and position in EU law of International agreements, fundamental rights, and general principles

▼

Consider the contribution of the CoJ

▼

Explain the rationale for the acceptance of non-Treaty-based sources

▼

Conclusion

A ⟩ SUGGESTED ANSWER

[1] This is your chance to delineate what you are going to write about and what you are not, to demonstrate to the examiner you have understood and interpreted the question correctly.

Introduction[1]

The EU Treaties, complete with the EU Charter of Fundamental Rights and the Protocols and the secondary forms of EU law sanctioned by those Treaties—in particular Regulations, Directives, and Decisions under **Art 288 TFEU**—are not the only sources of law or legal rules which have an impact in the EU legal order. Whilst the Treaties and secondary EU legislation are clearly the most important and abundant sources, other external sources have been recognised and employed by the CoJ.

[2] These other sources are the subject matter of this question and thus the ones to concentrate on.

The sources external to the Treaties and secondary legislation

These other sources[2] can be broadly classified into three categories.

One additional source of law arises from the international agreements entered into by the EU on behalf of the Member States, or those, such as the European Road Transport Agreement or the North-East Atlantic Fisheries Convention, where the EU has taken over the competence of the Member States as agreed. Most notable are the WTO and GATT agreements on import duties and trade, association agreements with other European states, and the Lomé and Cotonou Conventions between the Member States and many emerging and former dependent nations. Some of these have been considered in cases[3] and have been held by the CoJ also to give rise to direct effects in the same way as EU sources of law.

Other major sources of external law include the categories of fundamental rights and general principles.

Fundamental rights[4] now feature prominently in EU law, and in particular now **Art 6 TEU** provides that the Union shall respect fundamental rights, as guaranteed by the ECHR, and those human rights common to the Member States as general principles of EU law. Furthermore, any applicant states joining the European Union are now obligated by **Art 49 TEU** to have respect for human rights. The actual articles of the ECHR are often referred to directly as in the *Hauer* **(44/79)**, *Kirk* **(63/83)**, and numerous later cases. The European Charter of Fundamental Rights which has been attached by Declaration (No 1) to the Treaties by the 2007 Lisbon Treaty is now an additional internal source of law and is binding in the European Union with the exception of the internal application[5] in the Czech Republic, Poland, and the UK, which have negotiated an opt-out Declaration and Protocol. Whilst this would not prevent the CoJ from continuing to look at other sources of fundamental rights, clearly the rights Charter should be its first port of call.

Fundamental rights therefore, in their various forms and from various sources, play and will continue to play a very important role in the EU.

General principles of law have been used to assist the Court of Justice in the interpretation and application of EU law and by the parties to assist them in challenging the EU institutions or law and the actions of the Member States in the application of EU law. General principles from external sources can arise from particular provisions of other legal systems, in particular the constitutions of Member States, or principles of natural law or justice found in common law or in written form in some Member States or international law and agreements. The public law and legal systems of Germany, France, and now the UK have all had a considerable impact on the supply of general principles for the EU legal order. The principles which form a source of EU law need not be present in all of the Member State legal systems nor indeed in a majority. The CoJ will often conduct a comparative review of whether or in what form the principle exists in some or all of the Member States with regard to human rights. Often too, the Advocate General (AG) or judges in the case may be particularly influential in the introduction of a certain principle into the EU legal order. The Advocates General from particular countries are more easily able to identify the principles, which may be common in one form or another in a number of the Member States and thus more likely to introduce these principles to the CoJ. For example, the Latin maxim *audi alterem partem* was introduced by the AG in *Transocean Marine Paint Association* v *Commission* (17/74). He argued that in the absence of Transocean being allowed to present their views on the matter, the Commission's Decision would be in breach of a general principle of law, clearly applicable in the UK and other legal systems.

[6]Having established what the additional sources are, you should now outline why and how they are justified.

Justification[6] for the introduction of further sources

When it comes to considering the rationale for these additional sources of EU law, it is to be noted that the justification for the recognition and application differs according to the type of other source.

The conclusion of agreements with countries associated with the Member States and agreements with other third countries is specifically catered for under **Arts 217–218 TFEU**. In the *Haegemann* v *Belgium* (181/73) case, an agreement between the Community (now Union) and Greece was held to be binding on the Member States even though such agreements are not envisaged by what is now **288 TFEU**. Furthermore, although there is no statement in the Treaty that such agreements entered into by the Union or by the Member States can give rise to direct effects, the CoJ has held that they may give rise to direct effects providing they satisfy the criteria established in the leading case of *Van Gend en Loos* (26/62). These criteria tend, however, to be more strictly applied. To this extent an investigation of one of the GATT provisions in the case of *International Fruit* (No 3) (21–22/72) was held not to be directly effective. However, provisions of the Yaoundé Convention and the EEC-Portugal association agreement were held to be directly effective in the cases of *Bresciani* (87/75) and *Kupferberg* (104/81).

Whilst some general principles are clearly imported into the legal system from external sources, others have been developed by the Court of Justice from the Treaty.[7] There are three principal Treaty Articles which provide some justification for the CoJ to introduce general principles into the EU legal order.

[7]Whilst these are not external, they were not provided expressly by the Treaties or secondary legislation either, hence their inclusion in the answer. They include, of course, direct effects, indirect effects, state liability, and the supremacy of EU law.

Article 19 TEU is a general guideline set by the Treaty for the functioning of the CoJ. It provides that the CoJ shall ensure that in the interpretation and application of the Treaties the law is observed. This is taken to mean the law outside of the **Treaty**. **Art 19 TEU** has been invoked to introduce very many different general principles of law, as well as human rights, noted above. More specifically, two further articles of the Treaty mandate the court to take account of general principles of law. **Article 263 TFEU** refers to the infringement of any rule of law relating to the application of the Treaty as one of the grounds for an action for the challenge to the validity of EU law and **Art 340 TFEU**, concerned with damages claims, specifically allows the settlement of claims against the EU institutions on the basis of the general principles of the laws of the Member States. The latter two are specific to the claims raised under those Treaty Articles but they do serve to reinforce the Court of Justice's claim that it can rely on general principles as a source of law in the EU legal order.

The **EC Treaty (Arts 12 and 141) (now 18 and 157 TFEU)** has also supplied the basis for non-discrimination which applies both in relation to nationality and sex and has been further developed into a general principle of equality and non-discrimination.

More widespread and logical arguments for the inclusion of general principles are that the EU and the Court were morally and socially, if not legally, obliged to observe fundamental human rights especially those upheld in the constitutions of the Member States. No self-respecting legal system in Europe could ignore, or be seen to be ignoring, such ideologically important rights such as these. Failure to observe them might lead to serious clashes with Member States' constitutional law, which might have led to severe strains on the EU legal system. The *Internationale Handelsgesellschaft*[8] ([1974] 2 **CMLR 540)** case before the German court showed the potential for conflict and ultimate harm to the EU legal order if the EU fails to uphold human rights provisions.

Another argument stems from the fact that the Treaties are only framework Treaties and require completion by reference to other laws. For the most part this is done by the specific secondary legislation of the EU, but this only provides the substantive law rules, which also often require interpretation by the CoJ. The EU legal order was established anew and does not have the traditions of the Member States' legal systems to rely on, which are rich in developed principles of law. Therefore, something is needed to assist the CoJ in its task, and general principles, many of which are borrowed from the Member States' legal systems, do just that.

Conclusion

There is a rich vein of other legal sources in the EU legal order, which have been justified mainly by the CoJ both generally and impliedly by reference to Treaty Articles, but also now expressly in the **Treaty**; see **Art 6 TEU**. The most notable as identified in the body of this answer are fundamental rights from a number of sources, general principles, and the various international agreements the EU has entered into.

[8] This case, concerned with supremacy of EU law, showed that Member State courts might not comply with EU law which failed to respect their constitutions' respect of human rights.

➕ LOOKING FOR EXTRA MARKS?

- Whilst headings are not compulsory, adding them, as in the answer above, will show you have planned your answer.
- Mention that whilst presently not a member of the Council of Europe and the ECHR, the EU has committed itself to Accession by Art 6 TEU and is negotiating with the Council of Europe for accession. This will boost the fundamental rights protection in the EU.

ⓠ QUESTION | 2

While the TFEU suggests that Regulations and Directives are very different types of legislative instrument, the doctrine of direct effects has partly blurred the distinction between them.

Discuss.

❗ CAUTION

- This question concentrates on the debate which ensued following the CoJ's gradual development of the doctrine of direct effects.
- In answering the question you clearly need first to outline both forms of law from their Treaty base and then to explain that they were intended as having different functions.
- The question itself indicates that you should concentrate your answer on the influence of the doctrine of direct effects on this; this requires therefore a definition and explanation of direct effects.

▢ DIAGRAM ANSWER PLAN

> Investigate **Article 288 TFEU**: Regulations and Directives

▼

> Outline the definition and functions of Regulations

▼

> Outline the definition and functions of Directives

▼

> Compare Regulations and Directives

▼

Explain the eroding of the distinction

▼

Stress the impact of direct effects on Regulations and Directives

 SUGGESTED ANSWER

Article 288 and Regulations and Directives

[1] Here you are addressing, what is the question getting at?—what am I supposed to be answering?

The question concerns[1] Regulations and Directives, which are at present the two most important forms of secondary law that can be enacted by the institutions of the EU under the power granted by **Art 288 TFEU**.

It was considered that the establishment and development of direct effects by the CoJ was undermining the clearly intended distinction between the two forms of secondary EU legislation as set out in the **Treaty**. Essentially the concern was that if both Regulations and Directives could give rise to direct effects then no real difference any longer existed between the two. This answer will explore that argument.

Article 288 TFEU provides the following:

A regulation shall have general application. It shall be binding in its entirety and directly applicable in all Member States.

A directive shall be binding, as to the result to be achieved, upon each Member State to which it is addressed, but shall leave to the national authorities the choice and form and methods.

Regulations

Regulations are general or normative provisions of legislation applicable to all legal persons in the EU rather than to specific individuals or groups. They are usually very detailed forms of legislation to ensure that the law in all Member States is exactly the same.

Regulations become legally valid in the Member States without any need for implementation and this process is sometimes described as self-executing. It was held in the case of *Commission v Italy* **(Slaughtered Cows) (39/72)** that Member States cannot subject the Regulation to any implementing measures other than those required by the act itself. There may, however, be circumstances where the Member States are required to provide implementing measures to ensure the effectiveness of the Regulation, as in the case of *Commission v UK* **(Tachographs) (128/78)** where originally the UK had not provided sanctions for companies not fitting tachographs to lorries in contravention of the EU Regulation.

Directives

Directives, in contrast, set out aims which must be achieved but leave the choice of the form and method of implementation to the Member

States. This was done to ease the way in which national law could be harmonised in line with EU law and give the Member States a wider area of discretion to do this. If, for example, a Member State considers that the existing national law is already in conformity with the requirements of a new Directive then it need not do anything, apart from the standard additional requirement in Directives that the Member State inform the Commission how the Directive has been implemented. Member States are given a period in which to implement Directives which can range from one year to five or more, depending on the complexity of the subject matter and the urgency for the legislation. Two years is usual. The 2011 article by Dickson considered the status of Directives in the EU legal system[2].

[2]Cited in the 'Taking Things Further' section at the end of the chapter.

Comparison of Regulations and Directives[3]

[3]At this stage, try to summarise the notable differences in the forms of legislation.

Directives are normally aimed at the Member States, whereas Regulations apply to everyone. Regulations were designed to be directly applicable but it would seem from **Art 288 TFEU** that Directives require some form of implementation in order to take effect or have validity in the EU legal order. Directives were designed with the harmonisation of different national rules in mind whereas Regulations were aimed to be prescriptive by providing one rule for the whole of the EU. Hence Regulations would be detailed and precise and Directives more likely to be framework provisions laying down general guidelines and therefore less precise by nature.

[4]The answer can now consider why the distinction seems to have been blurred in practice.

Thus, by design, these are very different forms of legislation.[4] In practice a less rigid or distinct division has been observed.

Eroding the distinction[5]

[5]This can be covered in two parts, first generally and then with specific attention to direct effects.

It is not always the case that Regulations are precise and complete, as noted above in the case of the Tachographs, and further action was required on the part of the Member States. Regulations should be normative but they are often used in respect of specific individuals: for example, the anti-dumping Regulations and others in the area of competition law. On the other hand, Directives can often be very detailed: see e.g. **Directive 2004/38** concerning now quite detailed provisions in support of the free movement of workers and members of the worker's family, which has consolidated a lot of previous case law on the topic.

The impact of direct effects on the distinction

The biggest assault on the distinction arose when the CoJ held that it was not only Treaty Articles and Regulations which could give rise to rights which could be directly enforced by individuals before the national courts, but also other forms of EU law could also give rise to direct effects. This is the term given to judicial enforcement of rights arising from provisions of EU law which can be upheld in favour of individuals in the courts of the Member States. The term 'directly effective' may also be used and it describes the right to rely directly on EU law in the absence of national law or in the face of conflicting national law. The cases of *Grad* **(9/70)** and *Van Duyn* v *Home Office* **(41/74)** confirmed that other forms of law, including Decisions and Directives, could also give rise to direct effects. They must also satisfy the criteria required of Directive effects as initially laid down in the case of *Van Gend en Loos* **(26/62)** and that the time limit given to the Member State has expired (*case* **148/78** *Pubblico Ministero* v *Ratti*). Therefore, although Directives are not directly applicable in that they are not automatic and general in application and give rights without further implementation, they have been held to give rise to directly enforceable rights in specific circumstances, i.e. where they have not been implemented or have been incorrectly implemented (*case* **51/76** *Verbond van Nederlandse Ondernemingen*). The argument then arises as to whether the distinction has been eroded in that both Regulations and Directives can be enforced by individuals in the national courts and in practice there is really not a great deal of difference between them.[6]

[6] This is where the very important *Marshall* case comes in.

This might have been, or become, more likely if the CoJ had not decided in the case of *Marshall* **(152/84)** that Directives could not give rise to rights which could be enforced against other individuals, the so-called 'horizontal direct effects'. Thus a distinction remains as Regulations are capable of horizontal direct effects.

To date, the Court has upheld this position, although there is a line of case law developing which suggests that in an action between private parties, a Directive may be relied on incidentally. In the case of *CIA Security* v *Signalson* **(C-194/94)**, CIA was able to rely on the Directive's requirement that Member States notify the Commission to get clearance for national technical standards, in an action by a competitor accusing them of not meeting legal requirements. Belgium had not notified the Commission, thus their standards were held to be inapplicable. These incidental direct effects cases do not, however, blur the fundamental distinctions between Regulations and Directives.

Conclusion

Whilst it may be argued that in practice the gap between Regulations and Directives has narrowed, clear distinctions remain and they are still used for different purposes as the occasion demands, i.e. either a harmonising rule to accommodate different previous positions or laying down a new rule or sets of rules entirely. Furthermore, even when it comes to considering direct effects, Directives are only enforceable by individuals in a limited number of cases where approved by the CoJ and not universally and they do not provide rights directly enforceable between individuals. Thus a distinction remains.

➕ LOOKING FOR EXTRA MARKS?

▪ If there is time you could suggest that despite calls from the AG general from time to time, and in particular in the case *Faccini Dori* (C-91/92), to allow horizontal direct effects of Directives, the CoJ has declined to follow this advice.

▪ You could also mention the development of cases starting with the case of *Mangold* (C-144/04), in which general principles were held to have direct effects, thus diverting attention away from any erosion of the difference between Regulations and Directives.

Q QUESTION | 3

Does the distinction between vertical and horizontal direct effects cause difficulties for individuals in actions involving EU law? If so, what has been done to mitigate these difficulties?

❗ CAUTION

▪ You need to concentrate on the consequence of the CoJ ruling in *Marshall* (152/84) and subsequent case law which denied individuals the ability to enforce Directives against other individuals.

▪ Don't overdo coverage on the general aspects of the direct effects of Treaty Articles, Regulations, and Directives.

▪ Don't rehearse the arguments for and against having horizontal direct effects of Directives as these go beyond the required answer for this question.

◻ DIAGRAM ANSWER PLAN

Define direct effects as developed through case law and in application to Treaty Articles, Regulations, and Directives

▼

The limitations of direct effects the *Marshall* case placed on Directives

▼

The principle of 'indirect effects': *Von Colson* and *Harz* cases (14 and 79/83)

▼

The principle of 'state liability': *Francovich* (C-6 and 9/90)

▼

Incidental indirect effects cases

▼

Direct effects of general principles

(A) SUGGESTED ANSWER[1]

[1] This question picks up where the last one left off; it asks you to consider the arguments in respect of horizontal direct effects and whether this causes problems for individuals in certain circumstances.

What are direct effects?[2]

Direct effects is the term given to judicial enforcement of rights arising from provisions of EU law which can be upheld in favour of individuals in the courts of the Member States. To be capable of direct effects a provision must satisfy the criteria established by the CoJ, initially in the case of *Van Gend en Loos* **(26/62)**, that the provision:

[2] The answer requires a definition of what is meant by both types of direct effect and requires you to know and explain that it is impliedly referring to the direct effects of Directives which cause the difficulties.

- should be clear and precise
- should be unconditional
- should not require implementing further measures by the state or Union institutions
- should not leave room for the exercise of discretion by the Member State or Union institutions.

In *Van Gend en Loos* it was held that the institutions of the Community (now Union) are endowed with sovereign rights, the exercise of which affects not only Member States but also their citizens, and that Community (now EU) law was capable of conferring rights on individuals which become part of their legal heritage.

[3] The distinction was highlighted by the *Marshall* case, which should be discussed.

Vertical and horizontal direct effects[3]

Direct effects have been found to arise from many Treaty Articles, which often obligate not just organs of the state as in a vertical relationship, and it was confirmed by the CoJ that employers are obligated to comply with the requirements of a Treaty Article and other individuals may enforce corresponding rights directly against the obligated party who has failed to comply with EU law, termed horizontal direct effects. Confirmation came in *Defrenne* v *Sabena (No 2)* **(43/75)** in which the rights of an air hostess for equal pay under **now 157 TFEU** were upheld against the

[4] Although state owned the airline enjoyed registered company status and was thus in a horizontal relationship with its staff.

employing state airline,[4] Sabena, who were in breach of the obligation. That Directives could also give rise to direct effects was confirmed by the CoJ in the cases of *Van Duyn* **(41/74)** and *Ratti* **(148/78)**.

The question of whether Directives could be held further to give rise to horizontal direct effects and be enforceable against other individuals was open to speculation. However, the CoJ decided in the case of *Marshall* **(152/84)** that Directives could only be enforced against the state or arms of the state and not against individuals. Even though the

Health Authority was held to be a part of the state, the Court of Justice nevertheless sued the occasion of the case to settle the matter. A claim against private employers would fail in the same circumstances.

The consequences of the *Marshall* decision[5]

[5] Here you must display your knowledge of the consequences of the *Marshall* decision.

Marshall decided there could be no horizontal direct effects of Directives because Directives are not addressed to individuals, therefore individuals should not be obligated by them. The result of this decision is that the scope of the concept of public service as opposed to a private body is crucial. This results in no uniform application of EU law either in a Member State or between Member States or between public and private and employers, because there are different concepts of what is the state and what are private and public employers. Furthermore, this position can be further complicated by the movement of utilities and companies in and out of public ownership. Certain individuals are thus denied rights that employees in the public sector can enforce in the face of non-compliance by Member States. The uniformity of the EU law is undermined in important areas of law dealing with employment rights, where many Directives are relevant to private employers and the protection of individuals and their rights; e.g. **Art 157 TFEU** on equal treatment can create horizontal direct effects but the Directive providing other rights cannot (**Directive 2006/54**). An example of the consequences for individuals is the *Duke* case ([1988] 1 CMLR 719) in the UK, which considered the same question as in the *Marshall* case (152/84). However, in *Duke* a private employer was involved and the House of Lords held that Mrs Duke could not uphold her claim for equal treatment in retirement because Directives could not give rise to direct effects which could be relied on horizontally. The decision has thus led to an arbitrary and uneven protection of individual rights.[6]

[6] You have thus identified that the consequences following the ruling concerning Directives is unfortunate.

Case law addressing the consequences: the concept of the state[7]

[7] The final part must concentrate on how the difficulties have been avoided or circumvented by reference to case law which has provided alternative solutions.

One way pursued by the CoJ is by expanding the concept of public sector in the case law and thus including more individuals capable of protection of EU law; see e.g. the cases of *Johnson* v *RUC* (222/84) and *Foster* v *British Gas* (C-188/89) which showed that, although the concept was wide enough to include nationalised industry and includes any form of state control or authority, a distinction nevertheless remains between public and private employers. It still allows a variation as between public and private employees and between the Member States. The difficulties of and limits to this approach are demonstrated in the UK case of *Rolls Royce plc* v *Doughty* ([1992] 1 CMLR 1045), in which the Court of Appeal considered that the nationalised Rolls Royce was not a public body for the purposes of the claim to direct effects. Privatisation of once nationalised companies also affects the rights of individuals. In *Rieser Internationale Transporte GmbH v Autobahnen- und Schnellstraßen Finanzierungs AG* (C-157/02), it was held that the provisions of a directive capable of having direct effect may be relied upon against a legal person governed by private law where the state has entrusted to that legal person the task of levying tolls for the use of public road networks and where it has direct or indirect control of that legal person. Thus, private companies undertaking a public duty also come within the scope of the *Foster* ruling.

Indirect effects

Another line of case law has developed, however, which may provide an alternative for individuals defeated by the absence of horizontal direct effects. In the cases of *von Colson* (14/83) and *Harz* (79/83), both cases concerned **Art 6 of the old Equal Treatment Directive (76/207)**[8] respectively involving a public and private employer; thus the contrast of available remedies was starkly visible. Rather than highlight the unfortunate results of the lack of horizontal direct effects of Directives, which would have helped *von Colson* but not *Harz*, the CoJ concentrated on **Art 5 EC (now 4(3) TEU)** which requires Member States to comply with Union obligations. The Court held that this requirement applies so that courts are obliged to interpret the implementing national law in such a way as to ensure obligations of a Directive are obeyed. The *von Colson* line of argument requires there to be national law to interpret, or rules which the national court can, and is willing to, construe to achieve the correct result. Further cases which develop the boundaries of this principle are *Marleasing* (C-106/89), which required the national courts to apply Community law regardless of whether the national law was based on any particular Directive and regardless of the intent or even existence of national law, and *Kolpinghuis* (80/86), which held that a Member State which has not implemented a Directive cannot use direct effects to worsen the position of an individual. Neither goes as far to protect the rights of individuals to the same extent as would be achieved by the extension of horizontal direct effects to Directives. In *Pfeiffer v Rotes Kreuz* (Cases C-397–401/01), the CoJ has confirmed that national courts are bound to interpret national law so far as possible to achieve the result sought by a Directive taking into account national law as a whole, as opposed to narrowly looking at a particular national provision.

[8]Old cases will refer to old and often replaced legislation; you simply have to learn this.

State liability[9]

[9]The development of the principle of state liability has come to the aid of individuals who might otherwise have suffered from a lack of legal redress against other individuals.

A significant alternative development by the CoJ is the use of general provisions of the Treaty, **Arts 5 and 189 EC (now 4(3) TEU and 288 TFEU)**, originally in the *Francovich* case (6 and 9/90), to impose liability on the state for the non-implementation of Directives.

In *Francovich*, the relevant Directive was held to be not capable of giving rise to direct effects, but the requirements of the effective and uniform application of Community (now EU) law gave rise to a liability on the part of the state to compensate for its failure to implement the Directive where the Directive had conferred rights on individuals and there was a link between the breach and the damage caused. It does, however, take the emphasis away from the difficulty caused by the lack of horizontal direct effects of Directives. *Francovich* has now been followed by the *Brasserie du Pêcheur* and *Factortame III* (46 and 48/93) cases in which the CoJ held that all manner of breaches of Community (now EU) law by all three arms of state could lead to liability to individuals. Thus it expands the circumstances which might give rise to liability in cases where there would be no rights because either there are no horizontal direct effects or even no direct effects at all. The focus though has been moved to the seriousness of the breach.[10] These later cases require that, in order for liability to arise on the part of the Member State, there must have been a sufficiently serious breach of a rule of law intended to confer rights on individuals. This has provoked further case law to help decide how serious a breach is required for Member States to incur liability. *British Telecom* (C-392/93) takes a less generous view of what constitutes a breach but this can be contrasted with the *Hedley Lomas* case (C-5/94) where a mere infringement will invoke potential liability. The difference is explained by the degree of discretion the member state had in implementing EU law: the less, the more likely a liability would ensue. Thus, if there is a breach, Member States must compensate according to the principles established in *Francovich*. In other words, a *von Colson* failure under EU law should not be the end of the litigation line. The *Francovich* judgement was considered by Bebr to be *Van Gend en Loos* come full circle in his 'Case Note on *Francovich*' (1992).[11]

[10] Mention that *Factortame III* introduced the revised criteria that the breach must be analogous to liability of the EU institutions under Art **340(2) TFEU**; see *Bergaderm* case (C-352/98P).

[11] Cited in the 'Taking Things Further' section at the end of the chapter.

[12] This is the final, thus far, development which gets round the difficulties caused by the distinction introduced by the *Marshall* case.

General principles[12]

Cases which appear to introduce horizontal effects are *Mangold* (Case C-144/04) and *Adeneler v ELOG* (Case C-212/04) and *Kükükdeveci* (Case C-555/07). These provide that general principles of EU law can also give rise to direct effects. Alternatively, the *von Colson* sympathetic interpretation principle can also be applied to general principles of the EU, which in these cases involved the general principle of no discrimination, rather than looking closely at the Directive, which may have problems of either not applying horizontally or that the implementation period had not expired or both.

Conclusion

It may be concluded that the difficulties caused by the *Marshall* (152/84) decision, whilst not changed, have been mitigated in most circumstances.

LOOKING FOR EXTRA MARKS?

- Mention the possible use of Treaty Articles as an alternative to relying on Directives which may cause the problems generated by the *Marshall* case.

- As was mentioned in the answer itself the inclusion of a discussion of the least important post-*Marshall* development of incidental/triangular effects may gain marginal additional marks, particularly as time and space for this will be short.

QUESTION | 4

As part of its social programme, under Art 157 TFEU, the Council adopted two (fictitious) Directives on 1 January 2017. The first Directive 2017/1 provides *inter alia* that 'Member States shall take such steps as they consider appropriate to encourage employers to adopt the same pension arrangements for men and women doing the same kind of work'. The second Directive 2017/2 provides that 'Member States shall ensure that employers do not discriminate between men and women in respect of holiday entitlement.'

Member States were given two years in which to implement both Directives. At the present time (January 2019) the UK has taken no steps to implement either Directive and there are no national laws covering these issues.

In July 2018, a Local Authority Purchasing Department engaged Mrs Evans and Mr Rees as clerks. Their work is the same and they are paid the same. However, Mr Rees' contract of employment provides that he is entitled to five weeks' holiday a year and is included in the company's own pension scheme, whereas Mrs Evans' contract of employment provides that she is entitled to three weeks' holiday a year and can only join the Company's pension scheme after one year.

In January 2019, the Local Authority Purchasing Department engaged a further clerk, Mrs Jones, who is employed on the same terms as Mrs Evans.

Mrs Evans and Mrs Jones are unhappy with their contracts of employment. Advise Mrs Evans, who made a claim in December 2018, and Mrs Jones, who now claims, whether there are any provisions of EU law on which they could rely in an action brought before an British Court or Tribunal.

How would your advice be different if the place of employment at which they were working had been privatised?

CAUTION

- Do not answer this question as if it was a general question on direct effects and equally do not write just about direct effects and leave out the alternatives.

- As with all problem questions pace your answer; don't spend too much time on one aspect to the deficit of other parts, which may have warranted greater coverage.

- You may ignore the fact that there may be real Directives covering the same ground or providing the same or similar rights.

■ You must have studied and revised all the possible remedies available to individuals because: 1) they are so interconnected; and 2) often you may not be able to secure a remedy through direct effects alone and will be forced to consider other alternatives in order to assist the parties you are asked to advise. So look at the following checklist and make sure you can indeed check off the following list of prerequisite knowledge blocks before attempting to answer.

DIAGRAM ANSWER PLAN

Identify the issues	■ State the material facts ■ Two claims of discrimination by Mrs Evans and Mrs Jones
Relevant law	■ Outline the law: statutory, general principles, and case law, in particular: ■ the two Directives providing for equality in Pensions and Holiday entitlement ■ Outline the principle of direct effects
Apply the law	■ The possible problems with its application to Directives
Application of the alternatives	■ Indirect effects *(Von Colson)* ■ State liability *(Francovich)* ■ General principles *(Mangold)*
Part II and conclusion	■ If private, the possibility of the use of **Art 157 TFEU** ■ Conclusion

SUGGESTED ANSWER[1]

[1] For this first problem question in the book, I have provided a more extensive breakdown of the question and answer.

[2] In order to provide a solution you should identify the issues or particular problems arising as a result of the facts of the case.

The facts[2]

There are two Directives which have not been implemented by the UK which provide pension and holiday entitlement rights for workers, which should have been implemented by 1 January 2019. One complaint relates to discrimination from July 2018 and the other from January 2019. Mrs Evans and Mrs Jones claim they have suffered discrimination relating to pension arrangements and paid holiday entitlement.

[3]Law can include statutory law, general principles, and case law. EU law means Treaty provisions or provisions of secondary EU law, i.e. the Regulations, Directives, and Decisions.

EU statutory law[3]

The legal basis for these claims is **Art 288 TFEU** which sets out the secondary laws of the EU and in particular, obligates Member States to achieve a required result when implementing Directives.

General principles and case-developed law

The doctrine of direct effects will allow individuals to enforce EU rights before their national courts. The further developments by the CoJ of indirect effects and state liability also need to be considered, as well as the case of *Mangold* (**C-144/04**) and subsequent cases. These provide that in certain circumstances Directives, where implementation periods have not expired, may nevertheless help determine the outcome of a case in favour of individuals before the national courts by the reliance on general principles instead.[4]

[4]These latter three developments will only need to be considered if you are unable to secure the claimants, rights under direct effects.

Directives can give rise to direct effects[5] providing they satisfy the criteria as laid down in *Van Gend en Loos* (**26/62**): i.e. are the relevant provisions clear, precise, and unconditional? The special concerns of Directives and the time limits given for their implementation were considered in *Publico Ministero v Ratti* (**148/78**) which concerned the prosecution by the Italian authorities for breaches of national law concerning product labeling. Mr Ratti had complied with two Directives; however, the expiry period for implementation of one of these Directives had not been reached. The Court held he could rely on the one for which the time period had expired provided it satisfied the other requirements, but not for the Directive whose implementation period had not expired. So, when the time period has expired an individual can rely on the Directive if it fulfils the criteria. In the case of *Marshall (152/84)*, the CoJ held, however, that Directives could not be enforced against other individuals but could only be enforced vertically against the state to whom they were addressed. The more recent cases of *Mangold* (**C-144/04**), *Adeneler v ELOG* (**Case C-212/04**), and *Kükükdeveci* (**Case C-555/07**)), provide that under certain circumstances it may not be necessary to wait for the implementation period to have expired because individuals may rely on general principles of EU law which were held to give rise to direct effects.

[5]It would be useful to briefly define direct effects and the particular considerations applicable in respect of Directives.

So, with the facts and law established the claims of the two workers must be considered.

[6]Apply the legal rules to the issues and come to conclusions on each issue. Where helpful or necessary you should introduce any relevant case law to come to a conclusion on the problems or aspects of it.

Application[6]

The claims

Mrs Evans and Mrs Jones seek to rely on both Directives, Mrs Evans from July 2018[7] and Mrs Jones from January 2019. To determine this, the criteria adopted by the CoJ must be applied. Three questions arise, all of which must be addressed. They are: 1) are the claims vertical against the state? 2) have the time limits for the implementation of

[7]It is necessary to know whether in the absence of the UK implementing legislation at the material time they can rely directly on the Directives.

the Directives expired? and 3) are the relevant provisions directly effective?

Vertical or horizontal direct effect?

It is clear that as these are claims against the local authority, the claims are vertical and thus are permissible under the direct effects of Directives according to the *Marshall* case, noted above.

Directives and time limits[8]

[8]Here the *Ratti* limitations are outlined subject to the case of *Mangold* and the possibility that the direct effect of general principles can effectively override this restriction.

Only if the time limit has expired can the Directives be relied on. So, in respect of any claim to rely on either of the Directives before January 2019 the time limits will not have expired and the claim will fail. The UK should have implemented the Directives by 1 January 2019. Therefore, applying the *Ratti* **(148/78)** case, when the first claim by Evans was made the time limit had not expired and therefore the Directive cannot give rise to direct effects at that time. The time limit had expired for the second claim made in January 2019, i.e. Mrs Jones' claim, so we can move on and consider whether both Directives can give rise to direct effects.

Are the Directives directly effective?[9]

[9]Here the basic criteria are applied to determine whether the actual provisions of the Directives are clear, etc.

The claim in respect of equal pensions is covered by the first Directive, but does it satisfy the criteria for direct effects? Is it clear, precise, and unconditional, etc.? The answer to this is that it is probably not clear enough given the words 'Member States shall take such steps as they consider appropriate to encourage'. Therefore, there will not be direct effects and the Directive cannot be relied upon before the national courts; see generally the cases of *Van Gend en Loos* **(26/62)** and *Van Duyn* **(41/74)**.

The second Directive relates to the holiday entitlement. Does it satisfy the criteria of direct effects? Yes, the Directive is clear, precise, legally perfect, complete, and requires no further legislative intervention or implementation. It imposes a clear and unconditional obligation on Member States to ensure that employers do not discriminate between men and women doing the same kind of work in respect of holiday entitlement. The word 'shall' is a clear obligation. The provision therefore meets the requirements for direct effect, and can be relied on before a national court, but only as outlined above when the implementation period has expired, subject to *Mangold*.

Alternative remedies[10]

[10]As only Evans has succeeded this far on holiday pay but not on pensions, it is necessary to consider what, if any, alternatives there are.

Indirect effects

If direct effects were not established, other remedies may be available using the *von Colson* **(14/83)** line of case law. The CoJ held in *von Colson* that, although a Directive may not be directly effective, the Member States' courts should take the provisions of the Directive into account when applying national law. However, there are no rights in national law, so a national court cannot make an interpretation according to EU law. In these circumstances the *Marleasing* (C-106/89) and *Koplinghuis* (80/86) cases should be applied to state that there are general obligations under **Arts 4(3) TEU and 288 TFEU** for the Member States to ensure compliance with EU law but it is up to the national courts and they are not obliged to go against national rules of interpretation. Therefore, it is unlikely indirect effects will help and a further alternative is required to assist both Evans and Jones.[11]

[11] It helps to keep a running conclusion if time and space permit.

State liability

If, for whatever reason, the national courts cannot or will not interpret national law to read in compliance, the case of *Francovich* **(C-6 and 9/90)** might apply. If an individual suffers damage as a result of the failure of a Member State to implement a Directive, the Member State may be liable to pay damages, providing the Directive itself defined and conferred a right on individuals, the content of which was clear and not open to differing interpretations (*British Telecommunications* **(C-392/93)**). The fact that the UK has not taken any steps to implement the Directives by the prescribed time has been held by the CoJ to be sufficient to find a sufficiently serious breach of EU law (*Dillenkofer* **(C-178, 179, 189, and 190/94)**). Therefore Mrs Jones and Mrs Evans may have a claim for compensation against the UK. Any damages must compensate them in full for losses directly incurred because of the breach (*Bonifaci* **(C-94 and 95/95)**) but subject to the national court determination of national rules. Therefore Evans is probably helped by state liability but the claims for Jones are still problematic.

Direct effects of general principles[12]

[12] This is the third alternative if the others have failed to help.

Later cases lend support to the sympathetic interpretation of *von Colson*, but mark a further development by the Court of Justice. The cases of *Mangold*, *Lindorfer* **(C-144/04 and C-227/04)**, and *Kükükdeveci* **(Case C-555/07)** encourage national law to take any measures they can to provide for the rights in EU law regardless of the state of national law. However, they also provide, in particular in the *Mangold* and *Kükükdeveci* cases, that despite the fact that a Directive's implementation period had not expired it may be possible nevertheless to achieve the requirements of the Directive. In these cases, the CoJ held that despite the fact that the Directive was not past its implementation date, the principle breached by the Member State was discrimination, which was a general principle of EU law. Hence, then, it could not be affected by the unexpired transposition period of a Directive which provided the framework in which the general principle was applied. Thus, the general principle applied, not the Directive. The argument in the case was that both a strict application of **Art 6 of Directive 2000/78** and the application of the general principle would have the same result; therefore, in order to get over difficulties of transition period or the lack of direct effects, it was better to use the general principle. This would help claims which were premature but also where the Directive for whatever reason gave rise neither to direct effects nor indirect effects and damages were not possible. In this case, equality of treatment between men and women is most certainly a general principle stated of **EU law** which would lead to the claim by Mrs Jones succeeding.

Private employer[13]

[13]This is the alternative question addressed but you need to recognise that this is a minor part and does not need as much coverage.

It can be generally stated that the CoJ has repeatedly emphasised that direct effects of Directives only arise as against the Member States, and not against private individuals (see *Marshall* **(152/84)** and *Dori* **(C-91/92)**), thus none of the claims would succeed here. However, whilst Directives cannot give rise to horizontal direct effects, Treaty Articles can. It may be argued that as pensions have been held to constitute pay which is covered by **Art 157 TFEU**, a claim is therefore not dependent on the Directive and can be lodged relying on **Art 157 TFEU** itself, which is clear and precise and has been held to give rise to direct effects in the case of *Defrenne* v *Sabena (No 2)* **(43/75)** and applied to pensions in the case of *Barber* **(C-262/88)**. Whether holiday entitlements could also be interpreted to be pay is uncertain as there is no previous case which has considered this. The case of *Garland* **(12/81)** held that low fare travel facilities for the family of ex-workers could be considered to be pay, but whether this would extend to holiday entitlement is not guaranteed, although it is likely in view of the fact that even sick pay has been held to come within the meaning of pay in *Rinner-Kuhn* v *FWW* **(171/88)**. So a claim for equal pensions provisions is very likely to succeed if lodged under **Art 157 TFEU**. In this case the application of the indirect effects principle would equally succeed or the *Mangold* and *Lindorfer* cases could also apply to achieve the same result. As a final resort, should these other claims fail, a claim for damages under the state liability principle could be made.

Conclusion

In conclusion, there is such an array of remedies available to individuals under EU law today, that both claims would in all likelihood succeed either in being upheld to establish discrimination or in obtaining compensation from the Member State if not. Evans will in all probability succeed in the holiday pay claim under direct effects and under indirect effects for the pension claim. Jones will probably succeed under general principles for both. If private, **Art 157 TFEU** could come to the rescue of both.

LOOKING FOR EXTRA MARKS?

- You don't have to include headings; only do so if you have time. In other words if when including some headings you fail to finish the answer or miss some points you will lose more marks than the marginal mark or two you might gain.
- Use clear concise writing without unnecessary repetition and a concise summary at the end.
- Recognise the relative importance of the alternative ending.

TAKING THINGS FURTHER

- Bebr, G, 'Case Note on *Francovich*' (1992) 29 CML Rev 557.
  Explanation of how the Francovich case plugged the gap left by earlier developments.
- Dickson, J, 'Directives in EU Legal Systems: Whose Norms Are They Anyway?' (2011) 17 ELJ 190.
- Cabral, P, and Neves, R, 'General Principles of EU Law and Horizontal Direct Effect' (2011) 17 EPL 437.
  Looking at this more recent development concerned with general principles.
- Easson, A, 'The Direct Effect of EEC Directives' (1979) 28 ICLQ 319–53.
  Setting the basics of direct effects.
- Prechal, S, 'Member State Liability and Direct Effect: What's the Difference After All?' (2006) 17 EBL Rev 299.
  Comparison of remedies.
- Schiek, D, 'The ECJ Decision in Mangold: A Further Twist on Effects of Directives and Constitutional Relevance of Community Equality Legislation' (2006) 35 ILJ 329.
  Considers the development of the direct effects of general principles as another way of getting around the limitation with the direct effects of Directives.

  Special Report of the EU Commission of 15 July 2009 on the 'Case law of the Court of Justice of the European Union connected with claims for damages relating to breaches of EU law by Member States,' available at http://www.ec.europa.eu/eu_law/infringements/pdf/jur_09_30385_en.pdf.
  What it says on the label: it is a report of the cases in which the Member States have been sued under the state liability principle, which may be used as examples.
- Winter, J, 'Direct Applicability and Direct Effect: Two Distinct and Different Concepts in Community Law' (1972) 9 CML Rev 425.
  This clarifies and explains the at times confusing overlap of these two concepts.

Online Resources
www.oup.com/uk/qanda/

Go online for extra essay and problem questions, a glossary of key terms, online versions of all the answer plans, and audio commentary on how selected ones were put together, and a range of podcasts which include advice on exam and coursework technique and advice for other assessment methods.

The Supremacy of EU Law and its Reception in the Member States

4

ARE YOU READY?

In order to attempt questions in this chapter, you must have covered all of these topics in both your work over the year and in revision:

● The relationship between the EU and the Member States, which will involve a consideration of the reasons for the supremacy of EU law before looking at the reception of EU law in some of the Member States. Some questions, however, may look at these two aspects independently as suggested in the next heading.

● The reception in one or two or more Member States may be undertaken and examined.

● The legal arguments for supremacy and the political and legal logic may both be considered in establishing the reasoning for EU law supremacy.

● In the topics noted above, the main cases encountered are very likely to be *Van Gend en Loos*, *Costa* v *ENEL*, *Simmental*, *International Handelsgesellschaft*, *Factortame*, and then the principal cases of the particular Member States which may be considered in your course, as highlighted in the following answers.

● The topic of Brexit may now feature in some University courses but understandably, given the high degree of uncertainty in the negotiations and outcomes, many may also avoid it at this stage until things are clearer.

● A direct question and answer on Brexit will be included in online resources accompanying this text to be found at www.oup.com/uk/qanda/

KEY DEBATES

Debate: the key debate in this area is one that, to a greater or less extent, concerns all of the Member States.

Simply and essentially, that is, the extent to which the Court of Justice view on the supremacy of EU law is accepted by the Member States.

QUESTION | 1

Is it the case that 'the doctrine of the supremacy of EU law is a logical if not a necessary inference from EU Treaties'?

CAUTION

■ This is a very cryptic question which may confuse you as to how you go about answering it. The crucial sentence is posed as a question which, of course, has to be answered. So you have to address that.

■ Do not then answer this as 'write all you know about the supremacy of the EU' and thus simply write the history or case law development of EU law supremacy. That would be to miss the more subtle aspects of the question. The annotated tips along the way will make everything clear.

DIAGRAM ANSWER PLAN

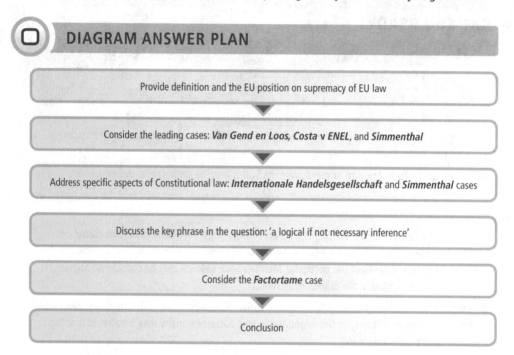

Provide definition and the EU position on supremacy of EU law

▼

Consider the leading cases: *Van Gend en Loos, Costa* v *ENEL*, and *Simmenthal*

▼

Address specific aspects of Constitutional law: *Internationale Handelsgesellschaft* and *Simmenthal* cases

▼

Discuss the key phrase in the question: 'a logical if not necessary inference'

▼

Consider the *Factortame* case

▼

Conclusion

SUGGESTED ANSWER[1]

[1] This clearly concerns the now well-established doctrine or principle of supremacy of EU law.

[2] A definition of the subject matter of the question is required. You need to state what you understand by the phrase 'the doctrine of the supremacy of EU law'.

Definition[2] and Treaties' position on supremacy of EU law

Supremacy of EU law means quite simply that when it comes to a clash between valid EU law and valid national law the EU takes priority. The question has suggested that the **EU Treaties** do not expressly provide for supremacy, i.e. there is at present no Treaty article which clearly states that EU law is supreme. If the **Constitutional Treaty** had entered into force, the supremacy of EU law would have been expressly stated (in **Art I-6**). However, it is still the case that by a direct reading of either of the **EU** or **TFEU Treaties** you might not necessarily infer that EU law is supreme. However, whilst there is no express statement of supremacy in the Treaties, it can be argued that some of the articles of the **Treaties** impliedly or logically require supremacy.[3] Thus, a conclusion as to whether EU law supremacy is to be inferred from the **Treaties** depends upon a consideration of some of their provisions.[4] For example, see: **Art 4(3) TEU**, the good faith or fidelity clause; **Art 18 TFEU**, the general prohibition of discrimination on the grounds of nationality; **Art 288 TFEU** in respect of the direct applicability of Regulations; **Art 344 TFEU**, the obligation of Member States to submit only to Treaty dispute resolution; and **Art 260 TFEU**, the requirement to comply with rulings of the Court of Justice. From these Treaty Articles, you could conclude that EU law infers supremacy but cannot state that the Treaty expressly or categorically imposes it.[5]

[3] The question suggests that it 'is the case that it is a logical if not a necessary inference' and you have to determine exactly what this cryptic part of the question is demanding and must address both these contentions.

[4] Although the word 'logical' appears first I would address the part about the inference first, because this refers you to the Treaty provisions.

[5] Outline how the Treaties logically provide for supremacy, by reference to the Treaty and from the jurisprudence of the CoJ in which statements on supremacy are made.

The position of the Court of Justice

It is more through the decisions and interpretation of the Court of Justice (CoJ) that the reasons and logic for the supremacy of EU law were developed. The CoJ's view on this is quite straightforward. From its case law, notably *Van Gend en Loos* **(26/62)**, *Costa v ENEL* **(6/64)**, and *Simmenthal* **(106/77)**, it is first of all clear that EU law is assumed to be an autonomous legal order which is related to international law and national law but nevertheless distinct from them.

The *Van Gend en Loos* case affirmed the Court's jurisdiction in interpreting EU legal provisions, the object of which is to ensure uniform interpretation in the Member States. The CoJ held that the Community (now Union) constitutes a new legal order of international law for the benefit of which the States have limited their sovereign rights.

Further elaboration of the new legal order in *Van Gend en Loos* was given in *Costa v ENEL*. The case raised the issue of whether a national court should refer to the CoJ if it considers Community (now EU) law may be applicable or, as was the view of the Italian Government, simply apply the subsequent national law. The CoJ stressed the autonomous legal order of Community (now EU) law in contrast with ordinary international treaties. It held that the **EEC Treaty** has:

created its own legal system which became an integral part of the legal systems of the Member States and which their courts are bound to apply. By creating a Community of unlimited duration, having its own institutions, its own personality, its own legal capacity and more particularly real powers stemming from a limitation of sovereignty or a transfer of powers from the states to the Community the Member States have limited their sovereign rights and have created a body of law to bind their nationals and themselves.

The Court also established that Community (now EU) law takes priority over all conflicting provisions of national law whether passed before or after the Community (now Union) measure in question:

The integration into the laws of each Member State of provisions which derive from the Community, and more generally, the terms and spirit of the Treaty, make it impossible for the states, as a corollary, to accord precedence to a unilateral and subsequent measure over a legal system accepted by them on the basis of reciprocity. Such a measure cannot therefore be inconsistent with that legal system.

[6] These back up the argument that supremacy can be inferred by some Treaty Articles.

That is, a later national law does not overrule an earlier EU law. As additional justifications,[6] the CoJ also invoked some of the general provisions of the Treaty: **Art 5 EEC (now 4(3) TEU)**, the requirement to ensure the attainment of the objectives of the Treaty, and **Art 7 EEC (now 18 TFEU)**, regarding discrimination, both of which would be breached if subsequent national legislation was to have precedence. Furthermore, the CoJ considered that **Art 189 (now 288 TFEU)**, regarding the binding and direct application of Regulations, would be meaningless if subsequent national legislation could prevail. The Court summed up its position:

It follows . . . that the law stemming from the treaty, an independent source of law, could not because of its special and original nature, be overridden by domestic legal provisions, however framed, without being deprived of its character as Community law and without the legal basis of the Community itself being called into question.

Therefore, EU law is to be supreme over subsequent national law.

[7] Whilst not strictly required to answer the question, I would suggest adding a paragraph that EU supremacy applies even in the case of constitutional law.

In the **Factortame (No 2) (C-213/89)** case,[7] the CoJ, building on the principle laid down in **Simmenthal (106/77)**, i.e. that a provision of EC (now EU) law must be implemented as effectively as possible, held that a national court must suspend national legislation that may be incompatible with EC (now EU) law until a final determination on its compatibility has been made. In the case of doubt national law should be suspended. The **Factortame (No 2)** case represents another confirmation that national constitutional practices or rules, in this case the doctrine of parliamentary sovereignty in the UK, must not be allowed to stand in the way of a Community (now EU) law right. In the case, it was the clear understanding of the UK national courts that they had no power to set aside or not apply an Act of Parliament. The CoJ held that even if the Community (now EU) law rule was still in dispute, the national procedure should be changed so as not to possibly interfere with the full effectiveness of the Community (now EU) law right.

Overall conclusions on supremacy

The CoJ in the cases of **Van Gend en Loos**, **Costa v ENEL**, and **Simmenthal**, amongst others, has held that EU law supremacy is a logical conclusion. It can also be inferred from the EU law doctrine of direct effects that EU law should be supreme both because of the transfer of powers from the Member States and by having its own law-making machinery. It must, therefore, have precedence if the Union is going to work. The voluntary limitation of sovereignty and the need for an effective and uniform EU law requires supremacy. To give effect to subsequent national law over and above the Union legal system which Member States have accepted would be inconsistent and illogical.

LOOKING FOR EXTRA MARKS?

- Supremacy in the Constitutional Treaty was toned down for the **2007 Lisbon Reform Treaty** which added a **Declaration (No 17)** referring to the well-settled case law on primacy as confirmed by an **Opinion of the Legal Service of the Council (11197/07 of 22 June 2007).** The declaration on primacy therefore is still not a bold express statement contained within the Treaties but tucked away in an oblique reference. The answer needs to reflect this.

- It is worth mentioning the consequences of a Member State not giving primacy to EU law when it should have done. Liability on the part of the state will be incurred, as first established by the CoJ in the *Francovich* **(C-6/90)** case and later confirmed in *Factortame III* **(C46 and 48/93).**

QUESTION │ 2

How does the European Communities Act 1972 ensure that EU law which is directly effective or directly applicable has that status in the UK and prevails over conflicting UK law?

What problems, if any, have been experienced in practice in attaining the aims of the Act?

! CAUTION

- With Brexit still hanging over the UK for this edition of this book, this question has not been removed. If and when Brexit actually happens, which at the time of writing is far from clear with talk of a two- or three-year extension or transition period on top of the initial two years envisaged by Article 50 TEU, EU law will continue to prevail over UK law. Hence prudence, on my part, leads me to retain this until the UK's exit from the EU is certain and accomplished. The EEC Act of 1972 will then, of course, be repealed.

- To return to preparing the answer, for the first part, make sure you do not write a general 'The UK in the EU' answer or wander into a discussion on UK current Brexit discussions. The question focuses on the legal technicalities.

- The second part of the question actually requires you to focus on the judicial interpretation and application of the Act rather than any political discussion about the effects of EU membership on UK sovereignty, although in view of the Brexit issue this will be toned down.

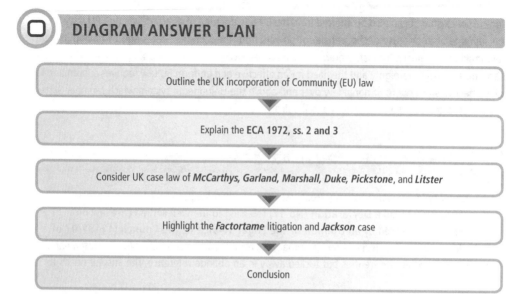

DIAGRAM ANSWER PLAN

> Outline the UK incorporation of Community (EU) law

> Explain the **ECA 1972, ss. 2 and 3**

> Consider UK case law of *McCarthys, Garland, Marshall, Duke, Pickstone*, and *Litster*

> Highlight the *Factortame* litigation and *Jackson* case

> Conclusion

SUGGESTED ANSWER[1]

[1] This question requires you to consider the legal argument of how membership was accommodated in the UK legal system and the reception of Community (now EU) law in the UK courts.

EU law implementation in the UK is primarily concerned with how the **1972 Act** observes and takes account of such well-established EU law concepts or doctrines of direct effects and supremacy of EU law and the difficulties in respect of sovereignty.

How EU law was incorporated in UK law[2]

[2] First, you should look in detail at the Act and how it sets out to achieve its aims.

In contrast to the earlier practice of incorporation of international law treaties which followed the dualist approach to international law, the **ECA 1972** did not reproduce the whole of the Community Treaties or subsequent secondary Community and now EU legislation as Acts of Parliament. If this was so, the words of any future UK Act could impliedly override and thus repeal the inconsistent part or parts of the Treaty, as it would simply have the status of any other UK Act of Parliament.

All prior Community (EU) legislation was adopted by a simple Act of Accession, except for those Directives which required national law implementation. The Act therefore impliedly recognised the unique new legal system and is now regarded as a very special form of UK legislation by its attempt to bind future Parliaments.

The ECA sections 2 and 3[3]

[3] This is the core of the answer to the first part: taking a detailed technical look at how the **ECA 1972** achieved its aims.

Section 2(1) recognises the direct applicability and thus validity of Community (EU) law Treaty provisions and Regulations and arguably the doctrine of direct effects. This is termed in the Act as 'enforceable Community right and similar expressions'. Thus those rights or duties which are, as a matter of Community (EU) law, directly applicable or effective are to be given legal effect in the UK. It also provides that all such future Community (EU) legal provisions shall also be given legal effect and enforced and followed in the UK.

Section 2(4) recognises the supremacy of Community (EU) law and therefore concerns sovereignty. It states that any such provision and any enactment passed or to be passed (that refers to any Act of Parliament past or future) shall be construed and have effect subject to the foregoing provisions of this section. That is a reference back to the entire section, in particular s 2(1), and means any future Act of Parliament must be construed in such a way as to give effect to the enforceable Community (EU) rights in existence. This is achieved by denying effectiveness to any national legislation passed later which is in conflict. This is further controlled by the directions to the UK courts. **Section 3(1)** instructs the courts to refer questions on the interpretation and hence the supremacy of Community (EU) Law to the CoJ if the UK courts cannot solve the problem themselves by reference to previous CoJ rulings. This follows the *Costa* v *ENEL* **(6/64)** ruling and is backed up by s 3(2) which requires the courts to follow decisions of the CoJ on any question of Community (EU) law. Therefore, it can be argued the combination of s 2(1) and (4) with the control of s 3(1) and (2) achieves the essential requirements of the recognition of direct effects and the supremacy of EU law for past and future UK legislation.

[4]By looking at the UK case law on the Act, you can show how it works in practice, i.e. looking at how the UK courts have interpreted and applied it.

[5]Whilst it would be better to concentrate on the latest cases which provide a truer reflection of the present situation, a brief review of earlier case law demonstrates your more comprehensive knowledge.

Case law on the ECA 1972[4]

The views of the courts in decided case law is thus now paramount here because the application of EU law is dependent on the national judiciary.

The most important of the earlier cases[5] is *McCarthys Ltd* v *Smith* ([1979] ICR 785) in which Lord Denning MR expressed the view that it was the court's bounden duty to give priority to Community law under s 2(1) and (4) of the **ECA 1972** in cases of deficient or inconsistent national law, i.e. unintentional inconsistency. Lord Denning thought that with regard to an express or intentional repudiation of the Treaty or expressly acting inconsistently, the courts would be bound to follow the express and clear intent of Parliament to repudiate the Treaty or a section of it by the subsequent Act. The Court of Appeal ([1981] QB 180 at 199) later confirmed Community (EU) law is now part of UK law and whenever there is any inconsistency Community (EU) law has priority.

In *Garland* v *BREL* ([1983] 2 AC 751), UK and Community (EU) law were regarded by the House of Lords as clearly inconsistent. A reference was made to the CoJ (12/81), which ruled that Community law covered the situation in the case. The House of Lords considered themselves bound in view of the CoJ ruling and **ECA 1972** to interpret the national law in such a way as not to be inconsistent with the UK obligations under Community law. They concluded (obiter) that UK courts should interpret UK law consistently, no matter how wide a departure from the words of the UK Act the interpretation needed to be.

In *CR Smith Glaziers (Dunfermline) Limited* v *Commissioners of Customs and Excise* ([2003] UKHL 7), the House of Lords held that 'It was the duty of a UK court to construe a statute, so far as possible, in conformity with European law.' The case considered the construction of provisions adopted by the Commissioners which did not conform with the terms of the **Sixth VAT Directive (77/388)**. Accordingly, the CoJ held that it was necessary to adopt an alternative interpretation which did conform to it.

Two cases known as *R* v *Secretary of State for Transport, ex parte Factortame Ltd* (**C-213/89 and C-221/89**) are particularly important cases in respect of the supremacy of Community (EU) law. A party seeking to rely on Community (EU) law sought an interim injunction against the crown not to apply a disputed national regulation issued under a UK Act whilst the merits of the case were being referred to the CoJ. This was something not previously acceptable as courts could not set aside UK law. The House of Lords considered that if Community law rights are to be found to be directly enforceable in favour of the appellants those rights will prevail over the inconsistent national legislation, even if it has been passed later. It was said (obiter) that:

This [**s 2(4)**] has precisely the same effect as if a section were incorporated into [the national statute] which in terms enacted that the provisions [of an Act] were to be without prejudice to the directly enforceable Community rights of nationals of any Member State of the EEC.

Upon the return of the procedural aspect from the Court of Justice, the House of Lords held that, if a national rule precludes a court from granting an interim relief, in order to determine whether there is a conflict between national law and Community (EU) law, the court must set aside that rule: in effect to ignore national law. Lord Bridge considered that if the supremacy of Community law over the national law of Member States was not always inherent in the **EEC Treaty**, it was certainly well established in the jurisprudence of the CoJ long before the UK joined the Community. He concluded that under the terms of the **1972 Act** it has always been clear that it was the duty of a UK court to override any rule of national law found to be in conflict with any directly enforceable rule of Community law. Therefore, national courts must not be inhibited by rules of national law from granting interim relief in appropriate cases because it is no more than a logical recognition of supremacy.

In a 2005 case, *R (Jackson)* v *Attorney General* ([2005] UKHL 56), Lord Hope suggested that even an intentional or express repudiation of EU law might not be followed by the new Supreme Court and expressed the view that whilst Parliament did not actually say that it could not enact legislation which was in conflict with Community law, in practice his opinion was that was the effect of **s 2(1)** when read with **s 2(4)** of the **ECA 1972**.

Conclusions

The view now of **s 2(4) ECA 1972** is that it is a direct rule to give priority, rather than a rule of construction. As far as the House of Lords is now concerned **s 2(4)** of the **ECA 1972** has led to the modification of the doctrine of parliamentary sovereignty because implied repeal of previous Acts of Parliament, as far as EU law obligations are concerned, would not be heeded by the courts. Indeed, in the *Metric Martyrs case* (*Thoburn* v *Sunderland City Council* ([2002] 1 CMLR 50)), the High Court expressed the view that the **ECA 1972** had acquired a constitutional quality which prevented implied repeal. Whether this overrides the *dictum* in *McCarthys Ltd* v *Smith* ([1979] ICR 785) is open to question. It remains open for Parliament to expressly repeal the Act. In such a case the courts would of course have to observe this faithfully. Thus far, the **EU Act 2011** merely appears to confirm supremacy of EU law over the UK, albeit by virtue of the **ECA 1972** itself or by any other act which confirms it.

LOOKING FOR EXTRA MARKS?

- Whilst actually not changing the answer in any significant way, mentioning newer case law such as *R (HS2 Action Alliance Ltd)* v *Secretary of State for Transport* ([2014] UKSC 3), would demonstrate that you are keeping up to date with case law.

- If time and space, you could briefly contrast the position of the UK with the courts of other Member States to show that, judicially, the UK through the **ECA 1972** and case law on it has been able to recognise both the direct effects and supremacy of EU law.

QUESTION 3

How have the courts of Member States other than the UK reacted to the Court of Justice's view on the supremacy of EU law?

CAUTION

- To be capable of answering this question, you must have at least taken account of the position in other Member States in your course on EU law. This is not always the case, or the depth of treatment may vary considerably.

- This is a dangerous question as it gives little guidance and allows free range so make sure you stick to answering the question.

- Do not write just a small amount about a large number of states, better to do it the other way round.

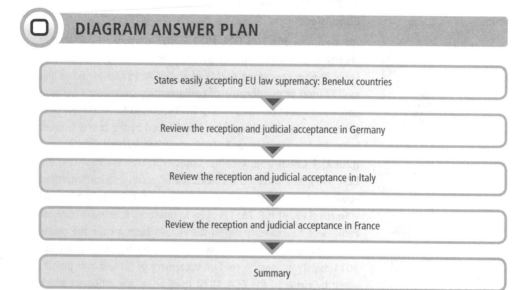

DIAGRAM ANSWER PLAN

> States easily accepting EU law supremacy: Benelux countries

> Review the reception and judicial acceptance in Germany

> Review the reception and judicial acceptance in Italy

> Review the reception and judicial acceptance in France

> Summary

SUGGESTED ANSWER[1]

[1] This question focuses on other Member States and how they have accommodated and accepted EU law.

EU law, of course, applies in all 28 Member States and according to the CoJ is supreme over all laws in those states. EU law has not, though, been accepted on that understanding in all Member States.

States easily accepting EU law supremacy: Benelux countries[2]

[2] Choosing these countries is not dynamic but is a good way of setting the scene and contrasting with more controversial states if chosen.

A number of states have not experienced any problems so far; see e.g. Luxembourg, Netherlands, and Belgium.

In Belgium, the constitution was amended to allow for the transfer of powers to institutions governed by international law (**Art 25a**). However, Belgium was a dualist country whereby later laws would prevail over earlier laws including international treaties if simply converted into national law. The courts in Belgium have no role in respect of judging the validity of international agreements but accepted Community (EU) law supremacy as if it were a monist country and not by dependence on a Belgium statute (see *Minister for Economic Affairs* v *SA Fromagerie 'Le Ski'* (**[1972] CMLR 330**)). It was held that in the case of conflict between national law and the directly effective law of an international treaty, the latter would prevail, even if earlier in time.

Reception and judicial acceptance in Germany[3]

[3] The states which may have been chosen in EU law courses are often those whose courts may have been reluctant to accept EU law supremacy. Germany is a prime example.

In Germany, in contrast, some difficulties were experienced, especially in respect of the provision of fundamental rights in the German constitution (*Grundgesetz*) and in the Community (EU) legal order.

[4]First, look at the Constitution to see how it regards non-domestic law.

Article 24 of the German constitution[4] allows for a transfer of powers and membership of international organisations and was used to establish membership of the European Communities. **Article 25** declares general rules of public international law to be an integral part of federal law and to take precedence over national law but it is silent as to the effect of international law on the German constitution.

[5]Then consider the judicial reaction, in particular of the Constitutional courts in those countries which have such a body.

The view of the Federal Constitutional Court (FCC)[5] is paramount because of its constitutional position in the German state.

In the ***Wunsche Handelsgesellschaft* decision ([1987] 3 CMLR 225)**, the Federal Constitutional Court accepted that Community recognition and safeguards of fundamental rights through the case law of the CoJ were sufficient and of a comparable nature to those provided for by the *Grundgesetz*. Thus, as long as EU law ensures the effective provision of fundamental rights the Federal Constitutional Court will not review EU law. It also stated that it would not be prepared to accept constitutional complaints from lower courts on this basis. The basis for the decision is not, however, the inherent supremacy of EU law but the fact that **Art 24** of the *Grundgesetz* allowed a transfer of powers to the Union and the subsequent accession act obliges the German courts to accept the supremacy of EU law.

Following these cases there would seem to be no procedural difficulty in getting Union rights at least considered in the proper forum in Germany. Any court which refuses either to follow a previous ruling of the CoJ or make an **Art 267 TFEU** ruling may be subject to the review of the Federal Constitutional Court for an arbitrary breach of **Art 101(1)** of the *Grundgesetz*.

The Federal Constitutional Court held in the ***Brunner case* ([1994] 1 CMLR 57)** that the **German Accession Statute to the Treaty on European Union** was compatible with the German constitution and thus rejected claims that it was unconstitutional, although again there was a statement to the effect that a review function of the Constitutional court would still be maintained to ensure Community (EU) law complied with the provision of fundamental rights. This was confirmed in the **Lisbon Judgment (2008)** by the same court. The 2010 *Honeywell decision* (2 BvR 2661/06) by the FCC, though, held that review could only be contemplated in the most obvious cases and only after the CoJ had been given the chance to review the case by a reference from the Federal Constitutional Court only.

[6]Cited in the 'Taking Things Further' section at the end of the chapter.

The 2011 article by Pavendah and the 2013 article by Giegerich[6] gives a very good overview of the mood swings taken by the Federal Constitutional Court and its attempt to play a review role over EU law.

[7]As with Germany, consider Italy in the same way as it is also a good state to choose.

Reception and judicial acceptance in Italy[7]

In Italy the position both constitutionally and judicially was and is very similar to Germany. Both constitutions allowed a transfer of power to international organisations but were silent as to the effect on constitutional law (see **Art 11** of the **Italian Constitution**).

As in Germany, the focus in Italy is on the Constitutional Court. Given that two of the leading cases on supremacy, *Costa* v *ENEL* **(6/64)** and *Simmenthal* **(92/78)**, arose from Italy, it should certainly have been clear to the Italian Constitutional Court what was expected of it. Again there has been a mixed reaction, also along the lines of the German Constitutional Court.

In *Granital SpA* v *Administrazione delle Finanze* ((1984) 21 **CML Rev 756–72**) the supremacy of Community (EU) law was accepted on the basis of an interpretation of **Art 11** of the **Italian Constitution** allowing for the limitation of sovereignty in favour of international organisations, and by reason of the case law of the CoJ. The case did, however, make the reservation that Italian law should only be cast aside where directly applicable Community (EU) law exists, similar in effect to the judgment of the House of Lords in the *Duke* case (**[1988] AC 618**).

A later decision in *Fragd SpA* v *Amministrazione delle Finanze* ((1990) 27 **CML Rev 93–5**) suggests the Italian Constitutional Court is still prepared to review Community (EU) law in the light of the fundamental rights provision in the **Italian Constitution**. This stance was confirmed in *Admenta* v *Federfarma* (**[2006] 2 CMLR 47**) in which the Italian State Council held that fundamental rights, as protected by Italian law, could not be reviewed in the light of EU law and were therefore to be reviewed exclusively in the light of Italian constitutional law.

Thus far, this remains the situation in Italy with the possibility for outright rejection of EU law supremacy.

[8]And do the same for France which is also regarded as a problematic state.

Reception and judicial acceptance in France[8]

The French courts are divided into two hierarchies with their own significantly different attitudes to EU law, despite the fact both are subject to **Art 55** of the **French Constitution** which is monist and gives international law a rank above municipal law, but is silent as to the effect on the Constitution. This is the point that has led to discrepancies between hierarchies.

The courts of ordinary jurisdiction have felt no hesitation in making **Art 267 TFEU** references to the CoJ and giving supremacy to Community law on the basis of **Art 55** of the **Constitution**. The French Supreme Court of Ordinary Jurisdiction, the *Cour de Cassation*, has in fact gone further and found for the supremacy of Community (EU) law without direct reference to **Art 55** of the **Constitution** and more on the basis of the inherent supremacy and direct effects of Community (EU) law itself. See the *Café Vabre* case (**[1975] 2 CMLR 336**) in which **Art 95 EEC (now 110 TFEU)** was held to prevail over a subsequent national statute. These rulings have been consistently followed by the lower courts and reference to either **Art 55 of the Constitution** or even the decisions cited here is rarely made (see e.g. *Garage Dehus Sarl* v *Bouche Distribution* (**[1984] 3 CMLR 452**)).

The Supreme Administrative Court, the *Conseil d'État*, has from time to time completely denied the supremacy of Community (EU) law or the need to make reference to the CoJ, relying heavily on the French principle of law, known as the *acte clair* (see e.g. *Minister of the Interior* v *Cohn-Bendit* (**[1980] 1 CMLR 543**)). The French court held individuals could not directly rely on Directives to challenge an administrative act. The court declined to follow previous CoJ rulings or make a reference itself.

However, some cases have demonstrated a much more cooperative attitude on the part of the French administrative courts. In *Nicolo* (**[1990] 1 CMLR 173**), the *Conseil d'État* reviewed the supremacy of international law including **EEC Treaty Articles** and held the latter to take precedence over subsequent national law, largely on the basis of **Art 55** of the **Constitution**. In *Boisdet* (**[1991] 1 CMLR 3**), incompatible national law was declared invalid in the face of a Community (EU) Regulation. In doing so the *Conseil d'État* followed the case law of the CoJ. The *Rothmans* case (**[1993] CMLR 253**) confirms the supremacy of Community (EU) Directives over subsequent national law and that public authorities cannot enforce the incompatible national law.

In *Dangeville* (**[1993] PL 535**), the Paris Administrative Court of Appeal upheld the ruling of the CoJ in *Francovich* (**C-6 and 9/90**) and imposed a liability to pay damages for the failure to implement a Community (EU) Directive.

The **Treaty on European Union** has been declared compatible with the constitution after amendment to the constitution and has been ratified and thus takes priority over French national law (**Art 88**). As a result of that change the French Constitutional Court (**Decision 2004/496 of 10 June 2004**) has declared that it will no longer review Community (EU) law in the light of the Constitution, save in relation to express elements, which is taken to mean those protecting fundamental rights in a way similar to the German Constitutional Court.

However, despite the change to the Constitution and the rules more sympathetic to the supremacy of EU law, cases taking a less cooperative position are still being decided by the *Conseil d'État*. In *Compagnie Generale des Eaux* (**2009**), the Court once again confirmed its earlier position of denying the direct effect of Directives when in conflict with a national administrative act.

Summary

A consensus appears to be emerging from the national and consti-tutional courts that EU law supremacy is accepted only in so far as it does not infringe the individual rights protection of the national constitutions, in which case the constitutional courts will exercise their reserved rights over national constitutions to uphold them over

[9] Cited in the 'Taking Things Further' section at the end of the chapter.

inconsistent EU law. The 2013 article by Komerek[9] takes a closer look at the position of some of the Constitutional Courts in member states. Only a few states appear to be accepting EU law unconditionally, such as Belgium. Whether this is a trend which will continue and lead to an outright rejection is, though, at this stage, unclear.

✚ LOOKING FOR EXTRA MARKS?

- Contrasting the position of the states chosen with the UK would be good, in particular by highlighting that a seemingly very reluctant state, the UK, nevertheless has a good track record of acceptance, whereas Germany, an enthusiastic Member State, has had judicial difficulties with full acceptance.

- Considering one or more of the later eastern European entrant states would be good, if covered in your course or module of EU law. Poland, Hungary, and the Czech Republic would be good candidates.

- Considering one or more of the later Scandinavian states would be good, if covered in your course or module of EU law. Denmark, Finland, and Sweden would be good candidates.

Q QUESTION 4

The transfer of power to the EU and control of competence in the EU is now firmly regulated by the Treaties following the Lisbon Treaty reforms.
Please discuss.

! CAUTION

- There is a lot to this question so getting a good structure is key to getting a good mark.

◻ DIAGRAM ANSWER PLAN

Outline how powers and competences are transferred and the different types of competences

Explain the various ways in which competences have been extended

▼

Explain what is meant by the 'competence creep' and how it is controlled

▼

Explain, in particular, subsidiarity and proportionality and the protocol on those principles

▼

Summarise the changes made by the **Lisbon Treaty** and involvement of the national parliaments

▼

Conclusion

SUGGESTED ANSWER

[1] This question aims to get you to look at why and how powers and competences were transferred both before the **Lisbon Treaty** came into effect and following.

[2] You should start by looking at how powers were and are transferred from the Member States to the EU.

Introduction and the transfer of powers and competences

When the Union was first established,[2] to be able to achieve the goals set for it, the Member States had to pool their resources in the new entity and transfer some of their sovereign rights to the Union and its institutions. The Member States provided the competences for the Communities (Union) to make their own laws, a process as acknowledged by the CoJ in *Van Gend en Loos*, but with the proviso that the power transfer or transfer of sovereignty was carried out only within limited fields. There was not a general transfer of power, which would include the ability to redefine competences without reference to any other body. The competences have grown hand in hand with the complexity of the Union and, whilst this transfer of competences should be a clear-cut process whereby any exercise of these powers by the institutions of the Union can only be within the terms granted by the Member States, that has not been the case. Further, what is attributed to the Union by the Member States is necessarily removed from Member States' competence. In other words, the Member States no longer have competence in the fields transferred. Therefore, there has been growing concern about the extension of competences especially where these have not been express, hence the term 'competence creep'.

[3] Then explain the meaning of competences and how they are divided into different types.

Division of competences[3]

There is a division of the degree of competences transferred from exclusive to shared and complementary competences.

Exclusive

The Union enjoys exclusive competences in a few areas only, such as commercial policy to third countries (as upheld by the CoJ in its

Opinion 1/75), and parts of the Common Fishing Policy. These are now set out in **Art 3** of the **TFEU** and include customs union, competition policy for the internal market, monetary policy for the Eurozone, parts of the **Common Fisheries Policy,** and commercial policy.

Concurrent/shared

In other areas—that is, in most areas—the dividing line is not so clear and competence is shared or concurrent between the Member States and the Union. Following the Lisbon Treaty reforms, it is set out in **Art 4 TFEU**.

Complementary

Areas of law outside those exclusive and concurrent competences remain the competence of the Member States, although, following Lisbon, the Union may support or complement Member States' activities in these areas as sanctioned by a new **Art 6 TFEU**.

It is in the area of shared competences that most difficulties arise, where it can still be unclear whether the Union or the Member States have the competence for a particular action. Furthermore, the degree of sharing also alters according to the subject matter: e.g. in areas such as the internal market, as soon as the Union acts under its competence, it assumes exclusive power to act and the Member States are then deprived of the power to act in conflict. If, however, the Union chooses not to act, the Member States retain the power to act. As a result, it is possible for there to be a genuine grey area between what is within the Union competence and what is still within the Member State competence.

This is a matter that has troubled the EU time and again, in particular as it became clear from the progressive judgments of the CoJ that the Community (and now Union) had taken over from the Member States even in areas to which the Member States were not sure they had agreed, or indeed to which they were of the conviction that they had not agreed, or even where they considered that they had excluded that particular matter from EU competence. As a result, there has been a reaction by some of the Member States.

The extension of competences: Treaty amendment[4]

The first of these ways, Treaty amendment, is deliberate and clear-cut. The areas of Union competence have expanded greatly as a result of the Member States assigning additional competences to the Union, with successive Treaties. The second and third ways are not express and have led to the use of the term 'competence creep' to describe the manner in which the institutions' competences have advanced incrementally.

Residual/general law-making powers

The second way by which competences have been expanded is via the residual or general law-making powers, which include both specific and general kinds.

Specific residual powers are those that grant subsidiary law-making powers to complete goals in specific areas, in particular to complete the internal market. **Articles 114 and 115 TFEU** provide for the approximation of laws affecting the establishment or functioning of the internal market and measures for the completion of the internal market. **Article 114 TFEU** provides that to achieve the objectives of the internal market, set out in **Art 26 TFEU**, where powers are not otherwise provided by the Treaty, action can be taken by qualified majority voting (QMV). In other words, action can be taken outside of the express and exclusive granting of powers to the Union by a majority and not by the agreement of all of the Member States.

Article 115 TFEU is an exception to the powers granted in **Art 114,** which is a general power to enact harmonising legislation. It does, however, contain safety measures so that Member States and institutions do not go too far: the Council must act by unanimity and must consult only and not co-decide with the European Parliament (EP).

It has been held, though, by the CoJ that these Articles should not be used where other Articles are more appropriate.

The general kind of residual power is **Art 352 TFEU,** which provides that, where in furtherance of any of the objectives of the Treaty and where no specific power exists, the Union may act by means of the Council acting unanimously with the consent of the EP. Note that previously it was only necessary to consult the EP.

Implied

The exercise of implied powers is the third means of extending competences. This was recognised by the CoJ in cases dealing with both internal and external powers of the Commission, where, in the absence of express powers in the Treaty, powers are nevertheless required to achieve a Union goal and are thus implied. Furthermore, implied powers to carry out internal competences can also be used to support external powers, although no such external powers are provided in the Treaty. The CoJ confirmed the validity of implied powers in the Union legal order as early as in the *Fedechar* case (8/55) and in subsequent cases.

The ways the competence creep can be controlled[5]

The increase in the competences of the Union, without those not expressly sanctioned by the Treaties, has been increasingly criticised and challenged, including challenges before the Court of Justice[6] to some proposed and completed Community and Union actions, and more formally by amendments to the Treaties to try to curb this

[5] Particularly after the changes made by the **Lisbon Treaty**, the suggestion is that they are now firmly regulated, which suggests that they were not before.

[6] Cited in the 'Taking Things Further' section at the end of the chapter.

development. See the 2005 article by Weatherill[7] exactly on this dual topic of creep and control.

Restrictive drafting

Legal bases have been drafted restrictively so that the Commission cannot use the base for further legislative intervention. See e.g. **Art 168(5) TFEU**,[8] which provides for action to promote cooperation in public health matters, but 'excluding any harmonisation of the laws and regulations of the member states'.

Subsidiarity and proportionality

The principle of subsidiarity requires that decisions be taken at the most appropriate level and, in the EU context, this focuses on whether a decision should be taken at the level of the Union or Member States. The wish to regulate activities within the Union should not insist on action at the Union level when it is not necessary. Essentially, it provides that the Union should take action only where objectives could be better attained at the Union level than at the level of individual Member States. It was subsequently introduced generally into the Union legal order by the TEU.

Article 1 of the **TEU** provides that decisions are to be taken as closely as possible to the citizen; **Art 5(1) TEU** provides that 'The use of Union competences is governed by the principles of subsidiarity and proportionality' and further provides in **Art 5(3) TEU** that:

in areas which do not fall within its exclusive competence, the Union shall act, only if and in so far as the objectives of the proposed action cannot be sufficiently achieved by the member states, either at central level or at regional and local, but can rather, by reason of the scale or effects of the proposed action, be better achieved at Union level.

Proportionality is also contained in **Art 5 TEU** and is linked to the subsidiarity principle, because both are concerned with the control and exercise of powers by the institutions.

Article 5(2) TEU provides: 'Under the principle of proportionality, the content and form of Union action shall not exceed what is necessary to achieve the objectives of the Treaties.'

Like subsidiarity, it too is subject to **Protocol 2** and Union Acts are open to possible challenges if breaching proportionality.

Protocol on the principles and national parliaments' involvement[9]

The Protocol requires the Commission to consult widely before formally proposing legislation and, in an amendment brought in by the **Lisbon Treaty**, its draft legislative Acts shall be forwarded to the national parliaments at the same time as to the EP and Council, and the Commission must accompany drafts with detailed statements as to how the proposal complies with the principles of subsidiarity and proportionality, and must provide evidential support to demonstrate that Union action is required and the general and financial impact of the proposed legislation.

Articles 6 and 7 TEU further outline the Council members, national parliaments' ability to object to the proposal and the procedure involving how those objections are further considered by the Union institutions in the legislative processes, and how the Commission must issue a reasoned opinion if it wishes to maintain the proposal for further consideration in the legislative process. All in all, it is quite a convoluted process. As a last resort under **Art 8** of the **Protocol,** legislative Acts may be challenged under **Art 263 TFEU** for infringing the principle.

[10]Most important is considering any case law which has visited these issues and in particular considered subsidiarity or proportionality.

Challenges for non-compliance with the principles[10]

In *UK* v *Council* **(Working Time Directive) (Case C-84/94)** and *Netherlands* v *European Parliament and Council (Biotechnology Directive)* **(Case C-377/98)**, arguments raised by the Member States in the cases that subsidiarity had not been observed were roundly rejected by the Court of Justice. In the *Working Time Directive case*, the CoJ dismissed this part of the action with little discussion, merely to confirm that the Council had a clear power to act on working hours as an issue of the health and safety of workers. In other words, if it had the competence to act, it could not be prevented from acting.

However, in *Germany* v *Parliament and Council (Tobacco Advertising Ban Directive)* **(Case C-376/98)**, the harmonising **Directive 98/43/EEC** banning most forms of tobacco advertising was enacted under what was then **Art 95 EC (now Art 114 TFEU)** as an internal market measure. This was challenged by Germany, who argued that the measure was more closely allied to a public health measure and, thus, should have been enacted under the then **Art 152 EC (now Art 168 TFEU),** which expressly prohibited harmonising legislation. The CoJ held that measures under (the then) **Art 95** must have the primary object of improving conditions for the establishment or functioning of the internal market and that other Articles of the Treaty may not be used as a legal basis in order to circumvent the express exclusion of harmonisation. It held further that to construe the internal market Article as meaning that it vests in the Union legislature a general power to regulate the internal market would be incompatible with the principle embodied in (the then) **Art 5 EC** that the powers of the Union are limited to those specifically conferred upon it. The CoJ thus held that, as a measure doing little to enhance the internal market, the use of the legal market Treaty base was inappropriate and it therefore annulled the measure entirely.

The judgments are not a clear endorsement that subsidiarity is a clearly justiciable issue; more that it is another confirmation that where an incorrect legal base is used, or where no powers have in fact been conferred, this provides grounds for the annulment of the measure. The tobacco judgment is regarded as a reply to national courts, in particular the German Constitutional Court, which might have been minded to take Union law into its own hands, by showing that the CoJ is prepared to police incursions into the Member States' competences by the EU's institutions. In the 2012 article by Horsley,[11] a closer look at how the CoJ viewed the attempt by Member States to challenge EU law on the grounds of a breach of subsidiarity is taken.

[11] Cited in the 'Taking Things Further' section at the end of the chapter.

Proportionality was raised in *UK v Council (Working Time Directive)* **(Case 84/94)** by the UK under the argument that the restrictions imposed on working time were not minimum requirements, but were excessive—that is, disproportionate. This view was rejected by the CoJ on the grounds that unless there had been a manifest error or misuse of powers, the Council must be allowed to exercise its discretion in law-making involving social policy choices.

Finally, in the attempt to counter the competence creep, the **Lisbon Treaty** has introduced a new requirement in **Art 296 TFEU** that relates to the competence and legal base issues, and states that: 'When considering draft legislative acts, the EP and the Council shall refrain from adopting acts not provided for by the relevant legislative procedure in the area in question.'

Summary

The changes made by the **Lisbon Treaty** include a clearer division of competences, a revised Protocol on subsidiarity and proportionality, and involving the national parliaments in EU law-making. So whilst there is greater Treaty regulation, legal challenges for a breach of subsidiarity or proportionality will remain difficult to win in view of the complexity of those principles and the degree of discretion enjoyed by the EU institutions.

✚ LOOKING FOR EXTRA MARKS?

- Better candidates will indicate that the case law has shown that legal challenges have actually not been very effective in trying to get to grips with the protocol on subsidiarity and proportionality.

- Discussing the involvement of national parliaments and whether their participation is helpful would be beneficial. You could note that they have intervened only rarely, and with limited success; for example, the Commission proposal for a Posted Workers Directive was objected to by two national parliaments. The Commission subsequently amended the proposal and a watered-down version (Directive 2014/67) was adopted. The Commission Proposal to establish a European Prosecutor's Office was opposed by fourteen national parliaments, yet the Commission elected to proceed.

TAKING THINGS FURTHER

- Avbelj, M, 'Supremacy or Primacy of EU Law—(Why) Does it Matter?' (2011) 17 ELJ 744.
  A general view on the supremacy of EU law.

- Craig, P, 'Britain in the European Union' in Jowell, J and Oliver, D (eds), The Changing Constitution, 6th edn (Oxford: Oxford University Press, 2007).
  A view on the UK acceptance of EU law.

- Dashwood, A, 'The Relationship between the Member States and the European Union/ European Community' (2004) 41 CML Rev 355–81.
  Although a bit dated now, this article does discuss the overall picture rather than concentrate on one Member State and its relationship with EU law.

- Gaja, G, 'New Developments in a Continuing Story: The Relationship between EC Law and Italian Law' (1990) 27 CML Rev 83.
  A view on Italian acceptance of EU law.

- Giegerich, T, 'The German Federal Constitutional Court's Misguided Attempts to Guard the European Guardians in Luxembourg and Strasbourg' (2013) 1232 Der Staat im Recht, 49.
  Looking at the attempts by the FCC to conduct an oversight over EU legislation.

- Horsley, T, 'Subsidiarity and the European Court of Justice: Missing Pieces in the Subsidiarity Puzzle' (2012) 50 JCMS 267.
  A closer look at how the CoJ viewed the attempt by Member States to challenge EU law on the grounds of a breach of Subsidiarity.

- Komerek, J, 'The Place of Constitutional Courts in the EU' (2013) 9 ECL Rev 420.
  Looking at the trend of Constitutional courts to take a closer interest in EU law supremacy.

- Manin, P, 'The *Nicolo* Case of the *Conseil d' État*: French Constitutional Law and the Supreme Administrative Court's Acceptance of the Primacy of Community Law over Subsequent National Statute Law' (1991) 28 CML Rev 499.
  A view on French acceptance of EU law.

- Payandeh, M, 'Constitutional Review of EU Law after Honeywell: Contextualising the Relationship between the German Constitutional Court and the EU Court of Justice' (2011) 48 CML Rev 9.
  A view on German acceptance of EU law.

- Weatherill, S. 'Competence Creep and Competence Control' (2005) 24 YEL 1.
  Doing exactly what it says on the tin.

Online Resources   www.oup.com/uk/qanda/

Go online for extra essay and problem questions, a glossary of key terms, online versions of all the answer plans and audio commentary on how selected ones were put together, and a range of podcasts which include advice on exam and coursework technique and advice for other assessment methods.

In particular a question and answer on Brexit will be included in the online material.

5

The Jurisdiction of the Court of Justice

ARE YOU READY?

In order to attempt questions in this chapter, you must have covered all of these topics in both your work over the year and in revision:

- The range of procedural actions in Arts 258–260, 263, 267, and 340 TFEU.

- Alternative actions or procedures which may need to be considered in the event that the most obvious or first action proves to be too difficult or unsuccessful for the applicant. These are alternative Articles to the one highlighted in the question and also appear in the list above.

- The procedure of each of the actions and the difficulties for applicants in these actions (which are the ones listed above in the first bullet point); often feature in difficult problem questions which also often require a consideration of more than one action.

KEY DEBATES

Debate: the efficacy of the enforcement actions

A particular key debate in this chapter concentrates on the rights of *locus standi* under **Art 263 TFEU** and also the standard of liability to be applied in actions for damages under **Art 340 TFEU** against the EU Institutions. The chapter though commences with a question on a less controversial action: the enforcements action by the Commission against failures of the Member States to comply with EU law in some way.

Q   QUESTION | 1

Discuss the effectiveness of the Art 258 TFEU procedure in ensuring compliance of EU law on the part of Member States.

⚠ CAUTION!

- Don't write an 'all I know about **Article 258 TFEU**' answer, and address the question itself, which will be made clear in the answer and comments.
- Don't limit your answer just to **Art 258**; a discussion of **Art 260** is also necessary.

☐ DIAGRAM ANSWER PLAN

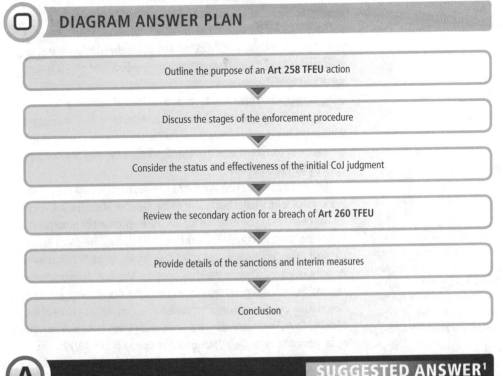

Outline the purpose of an **Art 258 TFEU** action

Discuss the stages of the enforcement procedure

Consider the status and effectiveness of the initial CoJ judgment

Review the secondary action for a breach of **Art 260 TFEU**

Provide details of the sanctions and interim measures

Conclusion

Ⓐ SUGGESTED ANSWER[1]

[1] The question concerns the Commission's ability under **Art 258 TFEU** to prosecute Member States for a failure to comply with their obligations under EU law.

The outline of Art 258 actions

The **Art 258 TFEU** procedure is provided to allow the Commission to pursue its task of policing the application and compliance with the Treaties and secondary EU law obligations. In order for a procedure to commence, a breach of an obligation by a Member State must be suspected by, or brought to the attention of, the Commission. A breach or failure to act is most often observed in the forms that a Member State has failed to implement EU legislation, mainly Directives, or that the implementation was incomplete or dilatory, or the Member State has failed to remove national legislation which is now in conflict or inconsistent with EU legislation or obligations. This includes decisions of the Court of Justice (CoJ). A breach may also be the action of a Member State in enacting or maintaining legislation or national regulations incompatible with the Treaty or secondary EU law. The failure can be attributed to all organs of the state, not just the government.

[2] The answer requires a brief description of the procedure for the actions under **Art 258 TFEU**.

The stages of the enforcement procedure [2]

If the Commission thinks a breach is probable, **Art 258 TFEU** requires certain administrative procedural steps to be taken before a court action can result. The first part of **Art 258 TFEU** states: 'If the Commission considers that a Member State has failed to fulfil an obligation under the Treaties, it shall deliver a reasoned opinion on the matter.' This means the Commission must have reached a conclusion that the Member State is in breach of an obligation before it can commence an action before the Court. The matter can be brought to its attention by its own investigations and supervision of implementation by Member States, by the Member States, the EP, other institutions, or bodies of the EU. Before the action formally commences the Commission will have attempted to bring the perceived breach to an end by informal discussions.

Having decided a state has breached its obligations the Commission will inform the state and give the state the opportunity to answer the allegation or correct its action or inaction before the formal procedure of **Art 258 TFEU** begins.

Not every suspicion of infringement by the Commission will even result in the initial formal letter being sent to the Member State. The initial letter has been held to be essential for the commencement of proceedings before the Court (*Commission v Italy (274/83)*). In 2006, as an example year, [3] the Commission sent out 1,536 formal notice letters stating its point of view. Following the reply from the Member State, or after a reasonable time where no reply is received, the Commission will then deliver a reasoned opinion which records the reasons for the failure of the Member State. The reasonable time is generally taken to be two months as in *Commission v Italy (Slaughtered Cows)* (Case 39/72). This is delivered to the Member State and is registered by the Court of Justice. Many of the original complaints will have been settled informally by this stage and the resulting number of reasoned opinions in 2006 was 680. [4]

[3] Here the year is not important as the figures are just illustrative. It may be that in your EU law course or module different reference years have been used. This is fine, and as noted the figures are just to provide evidence in answering the question.

[4] In describing the procedure, give an idea of how many cases reach the Court of Justice. The year selected is not crucial as the percentages have been fairly consistent over the years.

If the state should then fail to comply with the reasoned opinion of the Commission within a reasonable time, also generally taken to be two months, the Commission then has the discretionary right to bring the matter before the CoJ. One hundred and eighty-nine cases were brought in 2006. These figures are produced each year in a Report on monitoring the application of EU law. The final stage of the procedure is action before the CoJ and its judgment, which is merely declaratory. It is possible, however, for the Court to order interim measures, as it did, for example, in the *Factortame* case (C-213/89). I will also consider interim measures under effectiveness. After the judgment the state is required to take the necessary measures to comply with the judgment. The CoJ delivered 90 judgments in 2006.

[5] Having provided a description, you are required to consider whether this procedure is effective in ensuring Member States' compliance with EU law.

The status and effectiveness of the Court of Justice judgment

The effectiveness of the action in securing compliance must now be considered. [5] Other international tribunals, for example, the International

Court of Justice at the Hague or the European Court of Human Rights in Strasbourg, are unable to directly enforce their judgments against miscreant Member States, and the best that can really be achieved is the issue and discussion of a report on the failure or breach and the hope that the ensuing political pressure will encourage compliance.

Whilst the initial judgment of the Court of Justice is only declaratory and carries no specific sanctions, except in specific circumstances outlined below, Member States are placed under a further obligation under **Art 260 TFEU** to comply with the judgment by taking the necessary measures. If they do not do this a further action by the Commission under **Art 258 TFEU** for a breach of **Art 260 TFEU** may lie against them. This has taken place a number of times and increasingly so; for example, in 1989 it was used on 26 occasions and in 1998 the Commission commenced 39 actions for a breach of **Art 228 EC (now 260 TFEU)**. The leading instance of this is *Commission v Italy* **(second Art Treasures case) (48/71)**. The Commission discerned that because Italy had not complied with the Court's judgment in the first *Art Treasures* case **(7/68)**, judgment should be given that Italy had also failed in its obligation under **Art 228 (now 260 TFEU)**. Despite the fact that Italy complied with the original decision prior to judgment, the Court agreed.

Prior to the **Treaty on European Union**, the judgment was, however, only declaratory but other methods to secure the eventual compliance of the Member States were possible in the Community legal order. However, even prior to the **TEU** coming into force it was rarely necessary to rely on other methods of enforcement. Despite the lack of direct sanctions the **Art 260 TFEU** procedure can be regarded as effective, in that in most actions the Member States complied with the judgment in good time. The 2008 Monitoring Report noted that over 3,400 complaints and infringement procedures were being handled, but that 68 per cent were settled before the formal stage had commenced and that 94 per cent had been settled prior to the CoJ giving a ruling.

Sanctions[6]

[6]The sanctions are now the most important element in securing compliance and thus effectiveness: do not leave them out.

Articles 260–261 TFEU provide that sanctions can be requested by the Commission in an action to establish that the Member States have failed to comply with a previous judgment of the Court of Justice. This has already occurred in a number of requests by the Commission for penalty payments to be levied. For example, Spain was fined in **Case C-278/01** for not complying fully with the **Bathing Water Directive (76/160)**. The fine was set at €624,000 per year for each per cent of beaches not meeting the standards set. At the time of judgment 15 per cent of beaches had not met the standard. *Commission v France* **(C-304/02)** is a very instructive case both in terms of what the court can do in fining Member States and for the comments made in the case. The case highlights the unique nature of this fining possibility which does not exist in the national or indeed international legal systems against states. It also established that the CoJ could impose both a lump sum and periodic payment to encourage compliance, regardless of what the Commission requested.

The conclusion is that with fines, the revised **Art 260 TFEU** is having an effect in securing compliance. The **Lisbon Treaty** has amended **Art 260**[7] to provide first of all that a second reasoned opinion is not required, thus speeding up the action requesting a fine, and also for a one-step process for the situation where Member States fail to notify measures transposing a Directive. Instead of taking two actions, the Commission can take just one action and request a fine at the same time. Hence then the first judgment of the CoJ results in a ruling and the sanction simultaneously. The considerable saving of time this would achieve should further encourage compliance on the part of the Member States.

There are also interim measures under **Art 279 TFEU** which are an additional tool to encourage compliance and which have been used to prevent the continued breach of EU law by the Member States (see e.g. *Commission v UK* **(Pig Producers) (Case 53/77)**, and the *Special Road Tax for Lorries in Germany* **(C-195/90R)**). The Commission successfully applied for interim measures in both cases to suspend the application of the national measures alleged to breach EU law whilst the substantive question in each case was being considered by the Court of Justice.

[7] These amendments might well prove to be very effective in securing compliance and must therefore be referred to.

Conclusion

An action under **Art 258 TFEU** only proceeds as far as judgment in a minority of cases, hence it is already effective in most cases prior to that stage. If not conclusive at the administrative stage, then with the threat of fines looming or at the judicial stage with the imposition of fines, the action almost certainly will be. The vast majority of Commission actions (c 95 per cent) are settled though, and secure compliance before the judicial stage. Although Wennerås in his 2012 article suggested Art 260 TFEU would make little difference in securing compliance, the reality is that Art 260 TFEU combined with the Commission success rate in securing compliance before judicial action is necessary has gone a long way to ensure an effective enforcement procedure. Overall, it may be argued, the system does work reasonably effectively.

⊕ LOOKING FOR EXTRA MARKS?

- If you are not comfortable with headings, don't worry about them, they will only bring marginal extra marks.

- Whilst not an express requirement for the answer, and only if you have time, having completed the essential answer, it would be useful to suggest other ways in which compliance may be required or encouraged, especially if your conclusion is that Art 258 is not very effective in securing Member States' compliance. See the suggested additional sentences:

Alternatives

Alternatively, actions by individuals in the national courts to defend or establish their individual rights based on EU law, which are referred to the CoJ under Art 267, also serve to bring to the attention of the Commission and the CoJ a failure by the Member State. In most circumstances the Member States amend their laws to comply with their EU obligations without the need for an **Art 258 TFEU** action by the Commission. Many examples could be cited here but leading cases are *Van Gend en Loos* **(26/62)**, *Marshall* **(152/84)**, or any similar case where direct effects have upheld individuals' rights under EU law in the face of conflicting national law.

One development which may spur on Member States to comply, far more than any of the above actions, is the prospect of having to compensate in each case where an individual has suffered damage as a result of the failure of the Member State to comply with an EU obligation. In the case which decided this, *Francovich* **(C-6 and 9/90)**, the provision of law was a Directive. There are three conditions to such an action:

■ The Directive must provide an individual right.

■ It must be determined by the provisions of the Directive alone.

■ There must be a link between the breach and the damage caused.

Q **QUESTION** | **2**

In June 2016 the Council of Ministers issued a (fictitious) Directive 20176/1 on washing machine specifications which was to be implemented by all Member States by 1 June 2018. The controversial nature of the Directive, which would have opened the ailing British washing machine industry up to competition from other Union Member States, and the pressure on parliamentary time meant that the UK Government did not alter its own regulations on the specifications which must be met by washing machines marketed in the UK. However, the UK Government did issue a note in October 2018 to all customs officers, advising them of the existence of the Directive and informing them that all washing machines which met the specifications in the Directive were to be granted access to the UK market, even if they did not meet the stricter requirements of the UK regulations.

In December 2018, Danny, an importer of washing machines, had a consignment of French washing machines held up at customs at Dover because, although they met the requirements of the Directive, they did not meet the specifications contained in the UK regulation. The washing machines were not released until mid-June when customs received the government note.

In January 2019, the Commission instituted proceedings under Art 258 TFEU and, following the issue of a reasoned opinion in May 2019, the UK Government introduced a regulation to implement the directive.

The UK Government, in response to the reasoned opinion, observes:

a   that it was unable to comply with the Directive because of the lack of parliamentary time

b   that the note issued in June was sufficient to comply with the requirements of the Directive

c   that, in any event, the Directive had now been implemented by the new regulation, and the proceedings under Art 258 TFEU no longer served any useful purpose and

d   that France had also failed to implement the Directive within the time limit.

⊙

1. Advise the EU Commission as to the validity of these arguments by the UK Government and its chances of successfully enforcing EU law.
2. Briefly outline if there are any other parties who could take action against the UK.

CAUTION

- Whilst the question does involve the free movement of goods, it is not a question about this and should not therefore be answered as one—this would miss the focus or point of this question.

- As with other problems, you should address the specific issues in the problem and not write a general answer about **Art 258 TFEU**.

- Some Universities will designate percentages they consider appropriate to each part to assist you in deciding how much you write for each part, whereas others will leave that to your discretion, which itself forms part of the assessment of your knowledge, skills, and abilities in constructing excellent answers to questions.

- Make sure you address all parts (a–d) and answer both 1) and 2); failure to do so will mean you can't gain those marks.

DIAGRAM ANSWER PLAN

Identify the issues	■ Identify the facts which give rise to legal issues ■ The failure to implement a directive by the UK and impounding of imports
Relevant law	■ Outline the relevant law: **Art 258 TFEU**
Apply the law	■ Discuss the defences raised and the additional or alternative actions including a preliminary ruling under **Art 267 TFEU**, damages under **Art 340 TFEU**, or the possibility of an action by another Member State under **Art 259 TFEU**
Conclude	■ Conclusion

¹As with other problem questions, the answer should follow the structure of FLAC/IRAC: Facts (Issues), (Relevant) Law Application, and Conclusions.

²Start with a brief introduction to the area of law.

³This question concentrates on the ability of Member States to resist a conclusion under **Art 258 TFEU** that they have breached EU law obligations.

⁴You must consider each of the particular defences in turn which were raised by a Member State to avoid being found in breach of EU law obligations.

1. In the EU legal order, **Art 258 TFEU** provides an enforcement action² whereby ultimately the Commission can take a Member State before the CoJ to establish a breach of an EU law obligation. Member States, though, have raised various defences³ to justify their non-compliance with obligations, which may be acceptable in international law, but without success in the EU legal order under **Art 258 TFEU**. In this problem, the UK's failure to implement a Directive has led to the impounding of washing machines. The Commission has taken action under **Art 258 TFEU** and the UK has raised various defences.

Article 258 and Defences⁴

(a) The first reason given by the UK is similar to the argument of force majeure or overriding necessity raised in the case of *Commission* v *Belgium* **(Re: Duty on Timber (77/69))**. Belgium failed to implement a Community (EU) Directive and was taken before the CoJ by the Commission. The Belgian Government pleaded that it should not be held responsible for the negligence of the Belgium Parliament in not completing the implementation. This was rejected by the CoJ. Similarly, the argument raised by Italy in the *Art Treasures* case **(7/68)**, that the delay in implementing Community (EU) measures was the consequence of political difficulties, was rejected by the CoJ.

(b) The suggestion that the note, which only advised the appropriate authorities but did not actually bring UK law into compliance, would be an adequate defence is also likely to be held to be insufficient. See the case of *Commission* v *France (Re: the French Maritime Code)* **(167/73)** in which the formal rules were not amended but a change in practice was advised to the French authorities. The CoJ held that this was not sufficient to comply with Community (EU) law obligations.

(c) The defence that no legal interest remained was raised in *Commission* v *Italy* **(the Italian Pigmeat case (7/61))**. However, it was held that, as long as the Commission has an interest, it can bring a case before the Court of Justice and therefore the interest can continue even when the infringement no longer exists. Furthermore, in the case of *Commission* v *Italy* **(Slaughtered Cows case (39/72))** the CoJ held that where a legal issue remains unsettled an interest remains.

(d) An argument based on reciprocity, i.e. that another Member State's or EU institution's own failure to act justifies a defendant Member State's failure to comply with an obligation, was put forward as a defence in *Commission* v *Belgium and Luxembourg* **(90–91/63)**. The two states involved claimed they were merely taking reciprocal action in disregarding Community (EU) Directives because the Council had delayed in passing legislation. The CoJ held that the Community (EU) was a new legal order whose structure involves the prohibition of Member States taking justice into their own hands. Similarly, where other Member States have not complied with their obligations the CoJ has held (**Commission v France (232/78)**) that this does not entitle non-compliance on behalf of the defendant Member State, even where the Member State's constitution specifically allows for this (**French Constitution, Art 88**).

[5]It would be helpful to provide a conclusion whether you regard the UK to have raised a successful defence.

It is likely[5] therefore that all of these defences raised will be rejected by the CoJ and the UK will be found in breach of its (EU) law obligation.

Other parties capable of taking action[6]

[6]This part of the question is more open than the first part in that there are a number of possible alternatives to consider.

2. In addition to the action under **Art 258 TFEU** by the Commission, individuals either affected by a refusal to allow imports or suffering damages resulting from delays may consider attempting the following actions.

[7]Starting with an action by the importers to challenge the right of the UK to prevent imports taking place and requesting a reference under **Art 267 TFEU**.

An individual[7] who is affected by the action of the UK may point to the breach of an EU obligation or duty by a Member State as a defence to prosecution by that Member State or where they seek to challenge national rules which operate against their interest. It was early in the life of the Communities that the **Art 177 EEC (now 267 TFEU)** preliminary ruling procedure was seen to short-circuit or, alternatively viewed, to complement the use of **Arts 169 and 170 EEC (now 258–259 TFEU)**. This was objected to by the Dutch Government in the **Van Gend en Loos case (26/62)**, which thought that it was up to the Commission only and not individuals to take action or claim rights against Member States. This claim was firmly rejected by the Court and, by the establishment of the doctrine of direct effects, was able additionally to place the policing of Community (EU) law in the hands of private individuals, who often have more reason to bring actions. Danny might therefore consider an action before the national courts to get his machines released without too much delay.

Individuals may benefit from Member State compliance with **Art 258 TFEU** actions, as shown in **Commission v France (Advertising of Alcoholic Beverages) (152/78)**. It was held that a French ban on advertising foreign spirits was discriminatory and contrary to Community (EU) law. France failed to remove its legislation and prosecuted an importer for advertising. Waterkeyn, the advertiser, referred to the previous judgment as a defence. In **Procurieur de la République v Waterkeyn (314–316/81)** it was held that individuals could rely on such past judgments as a defence to protect their rights.

[8]Consider an action by the importers to claim damages if they have suffered as a result of the UK action.

Alternatively, an individual may attempt to obtain damages[8] from the Member States where the breach by the Member State is claimed to have caused damage to individuals who then make a claim against the Member State to recover. This form of action at the moment is now well established and proving to be extremely effective in encouraging Member States to comply with EU law obligations if they find themselves having to pay out significant damages in an increasing number of cases.

It was tried in the case of the French turkey producers who, following the Commission **Art 169 EEC (now 260 TFEU)** action against the UK in the *Poultry Meat* case **(40/82)** which held a British ban was contrary to Community (EU) law, sought an action for damages against the Ministry of Agriculture who applied the ban. The claim was dismissed as showing no good cause of action unless it could be shown that the Ministry acted in bad faith, in which case the proper action is that for judicial review and not a tort action for damages. However, in *Bourgoin SA* v *Ministry of Agriculture* **[1986] 1 CMLR 267 and [1987] 1 CMLR 169**, the case was settled out of court and the Government paid £3.5 million compensation to the French farmers.

The case of *Francovich* **(C-6 and 9/90)** had the result that the Italian Government were obliged to pay the claimants as a result of failure to implement Community (EU) legislation. There are three conditions to such an action:

(i)   the Directive must provide an individual right

(ii)   it must be determined by the provisions of the Directive alone

(iii)   there must be a link between the breach and the damage caused.

It is not necessary to show that the Member State has already been held in breach of its EU obligations in an **Art 258 TFEU** action by the Commission (*Hedley Lomas* **(C-5/94)**). In fact, it was held in *Dillenkofer* **(C-178, 179, 188–190/94)** that a failure by a state to take any measure to transpose a Directive in the prescribed time constitutes a sufficiently serious breach of Community (EU) law in order to found liability, as long as the other two conditions are also met.

In *Brasserie du Pécheur* v *Germany*; *Factortame* v *UK* **(C-46 and 48/93)**, the ECJ extended the principle of state liability to all violations whatever organ of the state causes the infringement.

In considering this, the ECJ would take into account:

(i)   whether the scope of the EU provision was clear and precise

(ii)   the extent of the margin of appreciation left to the Member States

(iii)   the intentional or voluntary character of the infringement

(iv)   whether the error of law was excusable or inexcusable

(v)   whether the attitude of the EU institutions had contributed to the breach.

In the *Factortame* case the Court considered that the UK Government was well aware of the Commission's attitude to the Merchant Shipping Act, as well as the views of national courts that these rules infringed Community (EU) law. Moreover, the UK Government had failed to implement the judgment of the CoJ of 10 October 1989.

Given the facts of the case to hand, it is likely there would be a similar result and the UK would be liable for any damage suffered by Danny as a result of the breach by the UK.

[9]Finally, a possible action by another Member State whose exporters may have suffered or who wish anyway to challenge the British measures.

Additionally, the French Government[9] might be interested in assisting the French manufacturers of washing machines whose products have been denied access for so long. It may consider taking an action under **Art 259 TFEU** to establish a breach by the UK. Such actions are, however, extremely rare (only a handful resulting in a judgment by the CoJ) and it is likely that a concerned Member State would leave it up to the Commission to take instead an **Art 258 TFEU** action.

Conclusion

An action by the Commission under **Art 258 TFEU** is very likely to be successful even in view of the various defences mounted by the Member State. Whether this is the case or not, there are alternatives which could be taken by individuals or other member states which would also help force the UK Government to act.

LOOKING FOR EXTRA MARKS?

- Highlight the fact that under the **Art 258** action by the Commission, individuals have no rights to insist on prosecution by the Commission.

- Mention that after a successful **Art 258** action by the Commission, a Member State may be liable to fines under **Art 260** for a continued failure to implement the Directive.

- Provide a summary at the end of likely chances of success under the various actions.

QUESTION | 3

Natural and legal persons face substantial obstacles in challenging the validity of EU secondary law under Art 263 TFEU. Outline the requirements which must be met by an individual seeking to challenge:

a   an act addressed to him

b   an act addressed to another person or to a Member State

c   a regulatory act not entailing implementing measures.

Do you consider the requirements of Art 263 TFEU to be unduly restrictive to individuals?

CAUTION

- Do not guess or make up arguments about whether it is restrictive or not.

- This question requires you to engage in a more general discussion of the purposes of such an action and will be possible only if you have undertaken wider reading than just from textbooks on the topic.

DIAGRAM ANSWER PLAN

> Outline the purpose and procedure of an **Art 263 TFEU** action

> Address the *locus standi* requirements which must be met by an individual seeking to challenge acts

> Consider if there is a restrictive individual *locus standi* under **Art 263 TFEU**

> Spell out the latest position, especially in respect of the amendment to **Art 263 TFEU**

> Consider the case law of the Court of Justice on conditions (b) & (c), especially *Plaumann v Commission*

> Consider whether the requirements as outlined are unnecessarily restrictive for individuals

> Conclusion

A) SUGGESTED ANSWER[1]

[1] This question concentrates on the admissibility element of the '*locus standi*' requirements of an **Art 263 TFEU** action and the particular difficulties encountered by the so-called non-privileged applicants.

[2] Provide a brief explanation of **Art 263 TFEU**.

[3] Consider the various categories of applicants but be brief.

Outline and purpose of Article 263 TFEU[2]

Article 263 TFEU provides for an action before the Court of Justice to review the validity of acts of the institutions of the Union. If those acts are found to be invalid, the CoJ including the General Court has the sole right to declare acts void. There are two elements in respect of the action: admissibility, which includes, most importantly, the issue of *locus standi*, and the merits or substance of the action. The first presents the greatest barrier to the non-privileged, legal or natural, individual applicants in practice.

The issue of *locus standi*[3]

Article 263 TFEU names the Member States, the Council, the European Parliament, and the Commission as privileged applicants, who have the right to attack any act. It further names the Court of Auditors, the European Central Bank, and the Committee of the Regions as institutions who may invoke **Art 263 TFEU** as a matter of course but only to protect their own prerogative powers. All other persons are termed non-privileged applicants with a more restrictive *locus standi*. **Article 263 TFEU** as amended by the **Lisbon Treaty** provides:

4 This requires you to know what the requirements are for individuals to challenge under **Art 263 TFEU**.

Any natural or legal person may institute proceedings against an act addressed to that person or which is of direct and individual concern to them, and against a regulatory act which is of direct concern to them and does not entail implementing measures.[4]

(a) To challenge an act addressed specifically to the applicant automatically gives standing according to **Art 263 TFEU** and is confirmed in any case concerned with a challenge by an individual to a Decision issued by the Commission. So, provided the applicant is the addressed person, the requirement is not restrictive at all. This is most clearly seen in the area of Competition law where a Decision will be addressed to companies who have breached the law and are fined in that Decision. The company concerned then has the automatic right to challenge that. As far as limb (a) is concerned, the new version appears to have increased the possibility of challenges which can be brought by individuals to all acts addressed to them and not just Decisions, although in practice individuals will be addressed with Decisions only and not other forms of general legislative or administrative acts.

(b) In order to challenge an act not addressed to them, i.e. to someone else or a Member State, the act must be shown to be of direct and individual concern to the applicant. If a Regulation can be shown to be of direct and individual concern, then it has been demonstrated that for that applicant, at least, it was not a Regulation but a Decision. As such then the change introduced by the **Lisbon Treaty** reflects previous case law. Whilst the jurisdiction of the Court is limited to the legally binding acts of the Council and the Commission and of the EP and European Council, it was held in the ***Noordwijks Cement Accord*** case **(8–11/66)** that other acts may be subject to review. The test to apply to a particular act is whether it has binding legal effects or changes the legal position of the applicant. Further, in ***Commission v Council*** **(ERTA) (22/70)** it was held that **Art 249 EC (now 288 TFEU)** is not exhaustive and special acts such as the minuted discussions of the Council, for the European Road Transport Agreement, could also be challenged. Thus the true nature of the measure is the determining factor. **Article 263** now makes it expressly clear that any act which alters the legal position may be the subject of a challenge.

5 This is the new and arguably radical change to **Art 263 TFEU** by the **Lisbon Treaty**, which may affect the discussion and conclusions in part 2.

(c) [5] In the case of challenging regulatory acts, they must be of direct concern and not entail implementing measures. The term 'regulatory act' was not defined in the amended Treaties, but it was held in the ***Inuit*** case **(T-18/10)**, that regulatory acts were general acts excluding legislative acts and confirmed in the ***Microban*** case **(T-262/10)**, and that implementing measures related to any intervention by either the Commission or Member States in the application of a general non-legislative act of the Commission. The challenge against regulatory acts will require only direct and not individual concern.

If the act is addressed to the plaintiff, then the plaintiff has *locus standi*. If the act is addressed to someone else, the question is then, is the act of direct and individual concern to the applicant?[6] If yes, the applicant has *locus standi*. If no, there is no *locus standi*. According to the previous case law, many applicants fail to gain admissibility, trying to show that the Act was of direct or individual concern to them. Therefore condition (b) is certainly restrictive and (c) may be, according to how it is and will be interpreted by the CoJ.

Case law on Art 263 TFEU in relation to conditions (b) and (c)

Although **Art 263 TFEU** limb (b) requires both direct and individual concern to be considered and according to the Treaty Article, in that order, the CoJ has often defined 'individual' first. If individual concern is not established, whether it was direct or not, the application would be rather academic and the claim would fail.

In the leading case of *Plaumann v Commission* (25/62), a Decision was addressed to the German Government refusing permission to reduce duties on clementines. The test was whether the decision affects the applicant by virtue of the fact that he is a member of the abstractly defined class addressed by the rule; for example, does it affect him because he is an importer of clementines, or because of attributes peculiar to him which differentiate him from all other persons. Plaumann was held to be one of a class of importers and not therefore individually concerned. In *Codorniu v Commission* (C-309/89), despite the CoJ confirming that the Regulation was a legislative measure applying to traders in general and not therefore individuals, it held that it could still be of individual concern to one of them. The Spanish company Codorniu had distinguished themselves by the ownership of a trademark for the term Crement from the year 1924, which term the Community (EU) had tried to reserve for French and Luxembourg producers.

Direct concern

'Direct' has been held to mean the effect of the decision on the interests of the applicant must not depend on the discretion or intervention of another person or Member State or Commission (see e.g. the *Alcan* case (69/69) and the *Zuckerfabrik Schöppenstedt* case (5/71)).

Condition (c)

The third condition provides individual applicants with a right to make an application against a regulatory act that is of direct concern to them and does not entail implementing measures. There was no definition provided in the Treaties for what is meant by a 'regulatory act'. If the second condition does, in fact, refer to a legislative act, then it is to be assumed that this refers to non-legislative acts—hence an arguably easier condition without the need to show individual concern for *locus standi*. Whilst legislative acts are described in new **Articles**

288–289 TFEU, regulatory acts are not. In *Inuit* (**Case T-18/10**), the General Court held that 'the meaning of "regulatory act" for the purposes of the fourth paragraph of Article 263 TFEU must be understood as covering all acts of general application apart from legislative acts'.

This means we have first to know what legislative acts are to be able to exclude them from a consideration under category (c). To determine whether an act is legislative, the GC in *Inuit* considered what decision-making process was used. In *Microban* (**Case T-262/10**), the General Court considered the legal basis under which the Directive was adopted. If the challenged Act was expressly adopted under **Art 289 TFEU** or any Article which refers to **Art 289** or the ordinary or general legislative process, it is a legislative act and thus not a condition (c) act. That leaves us with the conclusion that regulatory acts are indeed the general delegated and implementing acts of **Arts 290 and 291 TFEU**.

The regulatory act challenged must be direct and not entail any implementing measures but again there is no definition of 'implementing measures' in the TFEU. In *Microban*, the General Court confirmed the generally understood view that implementing measures related to any intervention by either the Commission or Member States in the application of a general non-legislative act of the Commission. Any intervention would thus remove or exclude a right to challenge. The 2014 article by Kornezo considers whether the reforms have made it easier for individuals to challenge.[7]

After the requirements of *locus standi* have been proved, the merits or substantive grounds of the action must be proved and these are provided in **Art 263 TFEU**.[8]

Are the conditions for *locus standi* too restrictive?[9]

The reasons for the difficulties[10] in demonstrating *locus standi* have been subject to much debate as to whether it is the policy of the CoJ concerned with 'floodgates' arguments. To some extent this has been answered by the establishment of the Court of First Instance (now General Court) to handle these cases which elevates the CoJ into the role of an appellate court in relation to these categories of cases. Also, the role of the CoJ, apart from competition law and anti-dumping cases, is not really a court for individuals. It is an EU court for the institutions and the Member States.

Those cases held to be admissible often arise from the application of retroactive legislation.[11] The applicants thus belonged to a fixed and identifiable group which could not be added to. Other arguments revolve around discussions about balancing the interests of the Union and individuals in the Union. The decision-making procedure in the EU is a much more complex procedure and often the result of compromise which makes legislation more difficult to enact. The inevitable economic choices of the Union are likely to affect individuals and must be allowed to be made, otherwise the ability of the Union and within it

[7] Cited in the 'Taking Things Further' section at the end of the Chapter.

[8] The question, though, does not require you to address this.

[9] The second part of this question raises the issue of whether the requirements are too restrictive and is the part which required wider reading.

[10] Addressing why there are restrictions will help you in deciding whether it is or is not unduly restrictive.

[11] The amount you are able to write in this part will depend on the reading you have done and how you have paced your answer or left time and room to address this part appropriately.

the Commission and Council and EP to operate would be undermined. Individuals' actions should not hinder the institutions' ability to operate.

In some areas, individuals find it easier to achieve standing, such as competition law, state aids, and anti-dumping measures; it may be argued that the very often closer involvement of particular individuals makes the difference. The applicants are likely to be the ones involved in the process by informing the Commission of certain situations or can be seen clearly to be affected by the measures complained about. This then sets them apart from the many other challenges arising most frequently against legislative decisions made under the Common Agricultural Policy. However, the overall picture remains that of a restrictive *locus standi* for applicants unless the recent developments become the norm.

Attempts have been made by both an Advocate General and the CFI to ease the ability of individuals to challenge acts which may be seen as evidence; certainly that they thought the restrictions were too restrictive. An adverse impact test previously suggested by an AG and upheld by the General Court was clearly rejected by the CoJ in **Unión de Pequeños Agricultores v Council (C-50/00P)** which means the position on individual access is as it was. Indeed, the CoJ confirmed this in the Commission appeal case of **Jégo-Quéré (C-263/02)** such that the test remains one of individual concern—which the company in the case did not prove, hence the application for annulment was denied and the previous judgment of the CFI (now the General Court) was overturned.

Finally, there is the provision of the indirect action via **Art 267 TFEU** or an action for damages under **Art 340 TFEU** as an alternative, which may also lead to EU law being challenged. This appears to be favoured by the Court and the Treaty by the provision of **Art 267 TFEU**. Consequently, it may therefore be argued, the requirements are not too restrictive.

Conclusion

Apart from acts addressed to applicants, challenging is still difficult. In particular, demonstrating individual concern was and remains very difficult. On balance, it might be argued that it is actually not too restrictive, as similar restrictions are found in the Member States and there are alternatives.

In the light of the new **Art 290 TFEU** definitions, legislative Regulations, Directives, and Decisions remain as they were and the new right of challenge applies thus to the delegated general acts of the Commission or Council, excepting those requiring implementing measures. This appears to make an action against general administrative acts less restrictive for individuals, but it remains, however, unclear as to whether the Member States actually intended the Treaty revision to make challenges to legislative acts by individuals easier. To reach firmer conclusions will require further interpretation by the Court of Justice.

LOOKING FOR EXTRA MARKS?

- You could point out that the restrictiveness is similar to actions for damages against the EU institutions under **Art 340 TFEU**, which you should or might have also encountered in your EU course or module. These are also ultimately not very successful.

- You might note that applications by legal and natural persons under **Art 263 TFEU** will be heard now by the General Court rather than the CoJ itself, although there are limited grounds of appeal to the CoJ.

- You might also note that case law by the General Court and opinions of AGs in the CoJ have not always been supported by the CoJ itself, which has maintained its previous position on limiting individual access. This should, however, form part of the discussion for the final part of the answer.

- Finally, it is important to get the balance right between the sections to ensure you answer the main part of the answer in sufficient detail but also address the follow-up part on whether the conditions are too restrictive appropriately.

QUESTION | 4

Following a widespread crop conversion to produce animal feed, there was a considerable over-production and consequent surplus of sweet lupins in the EU in 2018. As a result, (fictitious) Council and EP Regulation (1/2019) was enacted on 2 January 2019 which provided that exporters of sweet lupins during 2019 were entitled under the Regulation to incentives of €100 per tonne of sweet lupins exported. On 3 January 2019, R Hood Ltd applied for a licence to export 1,000 tonnes of sweet lupins. The company was granted the licence on the payment of a deposit of €5,000 which would be forfeited if the company did not comply with the requirements of the licence.

In April 2019, there was a sudden serious disruption in the sweet lupin crop which resulted in a considerable shortage of sweet lupins in the EU, and on 10 April 2019, the Council and EP enacted (fictitious) Regulation 4/2019 which eliminated without prior notice the refund subsidies of sweet lupins, making exporters liable instead for a levy of €5 per tonne exported. In enacting the Regulation, the Council and EP were specifically required to consider those who had already obtained licences to export sweet lupins in the 2019 marketing year and they did not provide reasons for its decision.

R Hood Ltd exported 400 tonnes of its quota before 10 April 2019 and is presented with a levy of €2,000. It must export the remaining quantity of its quota (600 tonnes) or lose the deposit of €5,000. Exporting the 600 tonnes will however make it liable to a further levy of €3,000.

Advise R Hood Ltd on whether, and on what grounds, if any, it can successfully challenge the second Regulation.

CAUTION

- There are dates in the problem: these should tell you that there is a time limit or period which is important and, depending on whether it has expired, may affect your answer.

■ The biggest task in answering problems on **Art 263 TFEU** is trying to resolve the often conflicting case law of the Court of Justice in considering the challenges to EU Regulations because of the restrictive *locus standi* requirements for individual, non-privileged applicants.

DIAGRAM ANSWER PLAN

Identify the issues	■ Identify the facts which give rise to legal issues; the Regulations which have affected the exporter
Relevant law	■ Outline the relevant law: **Art 263 TFEU** and the Regulations issued
Apply the law	■ Consider the merits of the action and suggest alternative possibilities to challenge the Regulation
Conclude	■ Conclusion

A ▶ SUGGESTED ANSWER[1]

[1] The question specifically requests you to advise the company as to whether they can challenge the second Regulation.

[2] This is the *locus standi* issue which will be relevant later in the answer.

[3] You need to consider both admissibility and merits.

This question concerns an action under **Art 263 TFEU,** which is the action to challenge the validity of EU acts before the Court of Justice and can be used by individuals who wish to challenge an act affecting them, but who are subject to restrictive rules on standing.[2]

The facts

On the facts given, if the second Regulation goes unchallenged R Hood Ltd face the situation where they either export the remaining 600 tons and become subject to a further levy of €3,000 on top of the €2,000 already levied, or do not export and lose the deposit of €5,000 for failing to comply with the earlier Regulation. Neither of these alternatives would be welcome. It would therefore be preferable for R Hood that the second Regulation should not apply to them so that they can rely solely on the first Regulation.

The law

Challenges to EU legislation can be undertaken under an **Art 263 TFEU** action to annul acts of the institutions but only if specific requirements are met,[3] particularly in terms of individuals who seek to challenge EU acts. For these so-called non-privileged applicants, admissibility has been the most difficult part of the action because of strict *locus standi* rules where they are not addressed by the act directly. There is, however, more than just one issue to consider in respect of admissibility.

The Challenge: Admissibility[4]

[4] Make sure you deal with admissibility entirely first. If not admissible for any reason, the Court will not—and therefore you cannot—consider the merits or substance of an action.

The institution challenged must be one envisaged by the Treaty—here it is the Commission, clearly named in **Art 263 TFEU**.

The Act challenged must also be one within the scope of **Art 263 TFEU**. In the present case it is a Regulation, which appears to be a legislative act of the EU institutions under **Art 288 TFEU**.[5]

[5] This is important and has to be discussed later as it may affect your answer.

However, because a Regulation is a normative act applicable generally, it carries more stringent requirements on the part of legal and natural applicants to challenge it. **Article 263 TFEU** provides that the applicant must show the act is of direct and individual concern to them and by doing so acknowledges the previous case law on challenges to Regulations. The third alternative under which an individual can challenge an act is if it is a regulatory act, such as a delegated act of the Commission under Art 291 TFEU, which appears not to be the case here.[6]

[6] As with the previous comment, this needs to be investigated and determined.

The final consideration in respect of applicability which is of vital importance is the time limit. **Article 263 TFEU** states that the challenge must be made within two months of the publication of the measure challenged. In the present problem, given that no further date or information is provided, it is assumed that the challenge is made within the required two-month period. If it is outside of this then the application is inadmissible and it is not possible then to proceed to the merits or substance of the issue.

Admissibility is thus dependent on the ability to challenge the Regulation. It has been held that because Regulations are normative acts of general concern they cannot individually concern applicants. As a result the CoJ has held that true Regulations cannot be challenged, see *KSH v Council and Commission* **(101/76)**, as they apply to categories or persons and not to individuals, although in the case of *Codorniu SA v Commission* **(C-309/89)** it would seem that the Court confirmed the true status of a Regulation for all others but nevertheless allowed a challenge from an individual applicant. In *International Fruit Company v Commission* **(41–44/70)**, a group of fruit importers were held entitled to challenge a Regulation where the identity of the natural or legal persons affected was already known and thus fixed and identifiable. In the present case, the Regulation under challenge was required specifically to take account of those who had already obtained export licences to export in 2019; hence, an argument for admissibility. In order though for the application to be admissible, the act must be both of direct and individual concern. In this answer, 'direct' will be considered first. Direct concern will be demonstrated if there is no intervening action by the Member State agencies or the Commission or any other discretionary action by either. In this problem there is not; therefore, it is of direct concern (see the *Alcan* case **(69/69)**).

Individual concern, on the other hand, has been very hard to demonstrate. In *Plaumann* v *Commission* **(25/62)**, a Decision was addressed to the German Government refusing permission to reduce duties on clementines. The test was whether the decision affects the applicant by virtue of the fact that he is a member of the abstractly defined class addressed by the rule, for example, because he is an importer of clementines, or affects him because of attributes peculiar to him which differentiate him from all other persons. Plaumann was held to be one of a class of importers and not therefore individually concerned. The CoJ confirmed in the Commission appeal case of *Jégo-Quéré* **(C-263/02)** that the test remains of individual concern. It therefore remains a question of an open or closed and fixed class. A much more likely exception to the rule that individuals cannot challenge Regulations, and also fitting within the closed group test, is because of the retroactive effect of the Regulation which imposes an export levy on exports, which at the time of export attracted a subsidy. The cases of *Bock* **(62/70)** and *Töpfer* **(106 and 107/63)** would be applicable here. The application is very likely to be admissible.

As a result of the fact that the Regulation specifically included those who have already obtain an export licence and that the legal rules have changed with retroactive effect, Hood is directly and individually concerned.[7] The company is in the group of those which have already exported sweet lupins in 2019, and the new Regulation also applies retroactively to exports already made.

The merits of the challenge

The merits or substance of the action can now be considered. The grounds of challenge are exhaustively[8] but widely[9] listed in **Art 263 TFEU**. Two which appear applicable in this case are an infringement of an essential procedural requirement, or an infringement of the Treaty or of any rule of law relating to its application.

In response to the first one, specific requirements are laid down by **Art 296 TFEU** that all EU secondary law must give reasons and refer to any proposals and opinions made in respect of the provisions. The CoJ has held that insufficient, vague, or inconsistent reasoning would constitute a breach of this ground. It was held in *Germany* v *Commission* **(Wine Tariff Quotas) (24/62)** that reasons must contain sufficient details of the facts and figures on which they are based. Although **Art 296 TFEU** requires the reasons for legislation and the opinions on which they are based to be stated, there is no express

[7] Having considered the admissibility and if satisfied, you can then consider the merits or grounds of the action to determine whether R Hood Ltd will be successful in its challenge.

[8] This means it cannot be added to.

[9] Which means it covers a lot of grounds in any case.

requirement to state the legal base. However, it was held in *France v Commission* **(C-325/91)** that there is a requirement to state the Treaty base, without which the measure is void.

In the present case there are no reasons stated, hence it will be held to be in breach of an essential procedural requirement.[10] The grounds then might include general principles of legitimate expectation to be able to export all of the sweet lupins without penalty and that there should be no retroactive law or double jeopardy of sanction. In addition, the removal of subsidies without prior notice can be argued to breach the same ground. The case of *Töpfer* **(112/77)** would be good authority for those latter points.

[10] It may be worthwhile suggesting that other, less certain grounds might be raised in respect of fundamental rights breaches amounting to a breach of a rule of law relating to the application of EU law.

Conclusion

The conclusion is that R Hood Ltd will be successful in the challenge to the second Regulation.

+ LOOKING FOR EXTRA MARKS?

■ If time, you may consider whether there are other grounds on which the Regulation could be challenged, particularly if the challenge using **Art 263 TFEU** proves unsuccessful. See the suggested additional sentences:

Alternative actions

Other challenges, which may be possible but not all necessary in view of the above conclusion, may include a damages action under **Art 340 TFEU** against the EU institutions, which is likely to be considered on the same substantive grounds. Furthermore, national proceedings including an **Art 267 TFEU** reference to ask the CoJ to rule on the validity of the EU act would be a possibility, providing there is a national element to the case, e.g. if the firm concerned were being fined or prosecuted by the national authorities in the national courts, the legality of their basis in EU law may be challenged, a point recently reconfirmed by the CoJ in *Rothley and others* v *EP (C-167/02)*. Such action, though, must not be an attempt to get round the strict two-month time limit (*TWD Textilwerke Deggendorf* v *Germany* **(C-188/92)**).

■ If there is time, advise that normally the Court considers 'individual' first and sometimes only.

■ Also if there is time, assure that the Regulation is a legislative one and not an administrative or delegated one which would be considered within condition iii of **Art 263 TFEU**.

Q QUESTION | 5

'The circumstances in which an individual can recover damages for loss suffered as a result of a legislative act of the Union institutions are unduly restrictive.'

Discuss.

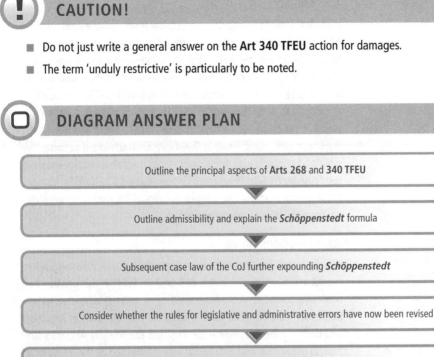

CAUTION!

- Do not just write a general answer on the **Art 340 TFEU** action for damages.
- The term 'unduly restrictive' is particularly to be noted.

DIAGRAM ANSWER PLAN

> Outline the principal aspects of **Arts 268** and **340 TFEU**

> Outline admissibility and explain the *Schöppenstedt* formula

> Subsequent case law of the CoJ further expounding *Schöppenstedt*

> Consider whether the rules for legislative and administrative errors have now been revised

> Outline how damage is established

> Provide conclusions on whether the action is restrictive

SUGGESTED ANSWER

[1] Outline in brief the action which is the subject of this question and answer.

The action for damages[1]

An action for damages against the EU Institutions under **Art 340(2) TFEU** consists of the following requirements which have been identified as necessary to establish liability:

(a) there must be a wrongful act or omission on the part of the EU which has breached a duty

(b) the applicant must have suffered damage

(c) there must be a causal link between the act or omission and the damage.

In contrast to the challenge to EU acts under **Art 263 TFEU** and the action to establish an omission to act under **Art 265 TFEU**, there are less restrictive *locus standi* requirements imposed by **Art 340(2) TFEU**. Instead, it would appear that any attempt to restrict the number of cases is made at the stage of the consideration of the merits or grounds of the case by the CoJ and not at the stage of admissibility.

Admissibility[2]

With **Art 340 TFEU** actions, admissibility is not really a problem. First of all there is a much more generous time limit than with **Arts 263 or 265 TFEU**. **Article 340 TFEU** has a five-year limitation period on actions which commences from the occurrence of the event causing the damage, as held in the *Schöppenstedt* case (5/71). Furthermore, in contrast to **Arts 263 and 265 TFEU**,[3] there is not a restrictive *locus standi* imposed by either **Arts 268 or 340(2) TFEU** and essentially, if an applicant can show that they have been damaged in some tangible and provable way, then *locus standi* is established; for example, see *Polyelectrolyte Producers Group* (Case T-376/04). So from the point of admissibility, the conclusion would be that it is not either unduly restrictive or indeed restrictive.

[3] It is useful to contrast with **Art 263 TFEU** in particular as it helps assess whether the damages action is unduly restrictive.

[4] Including this point also demonstrates that launching an action is not unduly restrictive.

An autonomous action[4]

Initially it was considered to be a dependent action following a successful action under either **Art 263 or 265 TFEU**. If this position had been maintained it would have even more severely restricted its use. However, in the *Lütticke* case (4/69), the CoJ rejected this argument and declared that 'the action for damages provided by **Arts 235 and 288(2) [now 268 and 340 TFEU]** was established by the Treaty as an independent form of action and whose object was to compensate a party for damage sustained and not to secure the annulment of an illegal measure'. This ruling was confirmed in the *Schöppenstedt* case (5/71). Therefore, little difficulty faces applicants in respect of admissibility; the problem lies in proving an act of the EU caused damage.

The basis of liability

The act or omission of the EU must be shown to be wrongful. In respect of actions claiming damage resulting from the wrongful adoption of legislative acts, stricter requirements have been imposed on the breach of the duty. This is because the Court has decided that in challenging such acts, which involve the EU in making choices in economic policies, far more stringent requirements are necessary, otherwise the functioning of the EU would be hindered and the EU could not operate as it needs to. Thus, the CoJ laid down a strict test in *Zuckerfabrik Schöppenstedt v Council* (5/71), which provides that the EU does not incur liability on account of a legislative measure which involves choices of economic policy unless a sufficiently flagrant violation (or also sometimes termed 'sufficiently serious breach') of a superior rule of law for the protection of the individual has occurred.[5] Note, however, that since the *Bergaderm* case (C-352/98P), the CoJ has provided that a single test should apply to both administrative and legislative acts, which is considered in the section on case law on the breach and damage. Other actions, which do not challenge the legislative acts

[5] This makes stark the strict requirements for actions involving the legislative acts of the EU.

themselves but only seek to show the wrongful act was a failure of the administration in the implementation of law, do not need to satisfy the formula under *Schöppenstedt* **(5/71)** and *Bergaderm* **(C-352/98 P)**, hence a higher standard is imposed when individuals seek to obtain damages as a result of loss suffered from legislative acts of the EU.

[6] Then you should consider whether an action for damages is unduly restrictive to individuals by case law examples.

Case law on the breach and damage[6]

It has proved extremely difficult to determine exactly how severe a breach or violation must be and how serious the resulting damage must be, as can be observed from a review of the case law of the Court of Justice. Therefore, it is not just unlawful conduct that will attract liability, but the degree of unlawfulness of the conduct which is important under

[7] Part of the comparison with *Art 263*.

the formula developed by the CoJ. It may be argued that the[7] reasoning for this is very similar to the strict requirements for *locus standi* for **Art 263 TFEU**, in that the high degree of discretion that the institutions need to carry out the economic tasks necessarily affect many persons.

The rules of law which are accepted as coming within the formulation include general principles of law. The principles of equality, non-discrimination, and legitimate expectation are often raised.

Thus, in the *CNTA* **case (74/74)**, the Commission was held liable to pay compensation for losses incurred as a result of a Regulation which abolished with immediate effect and without warning the application of compensatory amounts. It was held to be a serious breach of the principle of legitimate expectation. In the *Gritz* and *Quellmehl (Dumortier Frères)* **cases (64 et al/76)**, the ending of a subsidy was held to be a breach because it was retained on starch which was in direct competition, and hence discriminatory.

Secondly, the breach must be sufficiently serious. In *HNL* **v Council and Commission (83/76)** this was required to be 'manifest and grave'. This was interpreted later in *KSH* **v Council and Commission (143/77)** as conduct verging on the arbitrary. Factors which influence the CoJ in its determination of whether the breach is sufficiently serious are the effect of the measure and the nature of the breach.

The effect of a measure relates to its scope, the number of people affected, and the damage caused. For example, in *HNL* **(83/76)** there was little damage and it did not, in the view of the Court, exceed the bounds of economic risk, thus the action was not successful. The damage must be over and above the risks of loss or damage normally inherent in business but, in the *Amylum and Tunnel Refineries* and *KSH Isoglucose* **cases (116 & 124/77 and 143/77)**, even though the damage was severe and in the latter case, so extensive to have caused insolvency of the company, the actions were not successful. See the *Dumortier Frères* v *Council* **(Gritz and Quellmehl cases) (64 and 113/76)** and *Sofrimport* **(C-152/88)** in respect of the decision that the Court requires that only a small defined and closed group of applicants is affected. However, in the case of *Mulder* **(C-104/89 and**

37/90) the presence of a large group of claimants did not defeat a claim, although a serious breach still had to be demonstrated, and that there was no higher public interest of the Community (EU) involved.

The nature of the breach relates to its seriousness. In the *Isoglucose* **case (143/77)** the damage was extensive, causing the insolvency of one company, but the action was not successful because the breach of the law was not verging on the arbitrary, although in the later case of *Stahlwerke Peine-Salzgitter* **v** *Commission* **(C-220/91P)** the CoJ held that it was no longer necessary to show that the conduct was verging on the arbitrary. The applicants in the *Sofrimport* case were successful because of the complete failure of the Commission to take into account the interests of the applicants, despite prior knowledge. More recent cases, such as *My Travel Group plc* **(Case T-212/03)** or *Holcim* **(Case C-282/05P)**, do little to demonstrate that the standard has been relaxed. The 2011 article by Gutman has focused on how effective actions under Art 340 have been.

Proving damage[8]

Having established the existence of an act or omission attributable to the EU, damage to the applicant must be proved. *Polyelectrolyte Producers Group* **v** *Council and Commission* **(Case T-376/04)** was rejected as inadmissible by the CFI (now General Court) as the allegations of loss made were unsupported by any evidence of loss. Damage can be purely economic as in the *Kampfmeyer* **case (5, 7 and 13–24/66)**, involving a cancellation fee and loss of profits, but this must be specified and not speculative. It can be moral damage and anxiety (*Willame* **v** *Commission* **(110/63)**).

Finally, it must be shown that the act of the EU caused the damage. There must be a sufficiently direct connection between the act and the injury. The damages must be ascertainable (*Kampfmeyer* case **(5, 7 and 13–24/66)**). It cannot, however, be too remote, as held in the *Lütticke* case **(4/69)**. In *Dumortier Frères* **v** *Council (Gritz and Quellmehl)* **(64 and 113/76)** it was held that there was no need to make good every harmful consequence, especially where remote. Damage must be a sufficiently direct consequence of the unlawful conduct of the institution concerned. In *Compagnie Continentale France* **(169/73)** it was held that the causal link was only established if, in the case, the misleading information given would have caused an error in the mind of a reasonable person.

Conclusion

The conclusion is that **Art 340 TFEU** does allow wider and less restrictive access to commence an action. However, the action seeking damages as the result of the adoption of a wrongful legislative act nevertheless overall imposes equally severe restrictions in proving the merits of the case, the result of which is that applicants rarely succeed.

Q QUESTION | 6

A UK company, UK Foods, has invented a substance known as 'Isolactic', which can be used as a substitute for milk in the manufacture of butter, cheese, and ice cream. Isolactic is also significantly cheaper than milk. A few months after UK Foods has begun commercial production of Isolactic, with encouraging sales, the Council and EP, alarmed at the probable adverse consequences of Isolactic for EU milk producers, adopts a (fictitious) Regulation 15/2018 imposing a production levy on Isolactic producers. The effect of the levy, which is to be collected by the national authorities of the Member States on behalf of the Commission, is to make Isolactic significantly more expensive than milk.

UK Foods, which is one of only three firms in the EU making Isolactic, feels that the Regulation is discriminatory and that its effect has been to completely undermine sales and make production of Isolactic uneconomic, thus causing UK Foods to cease Isolactic production, without having recovered its research and development costs. Their losses are so great that the company expects to be forced into liquidation within three months unless something is done.

Advise UK Foods whether it could recover damages from the EU for any losses it has suffered.

❗ CAUTION

■ Numbers in a question are always something to be aware of. Note in this question 'one of three firms' is mentioned.

■ Do not confuse this action with *Francovich* state liability actions for damages against a Member State.

DIAGRAM ANSWER PLAN

Identify the issues	■ Identify the facts which give rise to legal issues: the banning of the production of Isolactic
Relevant law	■ Outline the relevant law: **Art 340 TFEU** action for damages
Apply the law	■ Application of the *Schöppenstedt* formula and *Bergaderm* case to the facts ■ Consider the substantive merits of the action
Conclude	■ Conclusion as to the likelihood of success

A

SUGGESTED ANSWER[1]

[1] This is a problem-type question which deals with the application of much of the discussion which arose in the answer to Question 5.

An action under **Art 340(2) TFEU** is an action to recover loss caused by the unlawful action or inaction of an EU institution or institutions which cause damage. This answer will determine whether an action should be undertaken by UK Foods to recover losses already incurred and whether it will be successful.

The action under **Art 340 TFEU** which might be contemplated for UK Foods concerns the adoption by the EU of a legislative act which is allegedly wrongful. Apart from admissibility, the problem raises the difficulty of demonstrating that damage resulting from the alleged breach is serious enough for the action to be successful.

[2] Material facts are those which may affect the outcome.

The material facts and issues[2] arising in this problem can be identified easily. UK Foods consider the Regulation which imposes a levy on their production is already and will be extremely damaging to them, and that it was unlawfully enacted on the grounds that it is discriminatory. As a consequence, they seek damages. Hence under EU law, they would turn to the action under **Art 340(2) TFEU**.

[3] Set out the law in the form of the main elements of **Art 340 TFEU**.

The Art 340 action[3]

First of all, it may be stated that for **Art 340(2) TFEU**, the *locus standi* requirements are much more relaxed and success is not so dependent on admissibility as with **Arts 263 and 265**. There is a much more generous five-year time limit in which to make an application.

From case law it has been established that for a successful claim under **Art 340(2) TFEU**, an applicant must demonstrate:

(a) a duty

(b) a breach of that duty by an action or inaction

(c) damage which is caused as a result of the act or omission.

[4] The question also involves a choice of court issue which should be considered.

Before the action may commence,[4] a further issue arises in this case regarding the choice of court. It is stated the levy is collected by national authorities. Hence, if there is an intervention by national authorities, the action should take place in the national courts with a reference to the CoJ if necessary (see the *Haegemann* (181/73) and *Kampfmeyer* (5, 7, 13–24/66) cases). However, it also depends on the discretion given to the Member States. If none is given and they merely act as agents for the EU then the action can also commence in the Court of Justice. In this problem, there is no mention of any further activity on the part of the state, nor discretion in how it collects the levy, so it is reasonably safe to assume that a direct action before the CoJ would be appropriate.[5]

[5] In case of doubt, you should recommend that it would be advisable to go to the national courts and ask for a reference rather than have the case dismissed by the Court of Justice.

Requirements of the action

In this case the applicants are seeking to challenge a legislative Act of the EU. It has been held in the *Schöppenstedt* case (5/71) that where actions concern legislative measures involving a choice of economic policy it is necessary to demonstrate in respect of the breach that it is a sufficiently serious breach of a superior rule of law for the protection of individuals. This then enhances the requirements to show a breach of a duty, the level of damage suffered, and that the breach must be a sufficiently serious one. According to the *Bergaderm* case (C-352/98P), the emphasis for the court is that the legislative act involved must confer an individual right rather than demonstrating a superior rule of law designed for the protection of individuals. Whilst the new formulation has been followed up in a number of cases the more complex approach in *Schöppenstedt* has not necessarily been abandoned. Hence, the consideration of the possible breach needs to be aware of both standards and can be divided into two parts, i.e. the breach of the rule of law for the protection of the individual and whether it was sufficiently serious.

[6] The rule breached includes breaches of general principles.

There are many cases[6] in which the CoJ has recognised general principles as superior rules of law (see the *HNL* (83/76), *Isoglucose* (103 and 145/77), *CNTA* (74/74), and *Sofrimport* (C-152/88) cases).

In the *Gritz and Quellmehl Dumortier Frères* cases (64 and 113/76), the ending of the subsidy was held to be a breach of the principle of non-discrimination because it was retained on starch, which was its direct competition. Non-discrimination is one importantly covered specifically by **Art 40(2) TFEU** and thus more likely to be regarded as a superior rule of law.

[7] Note this is not just a breach, but that it must be 'a sufficiently serious or flagrant a breach'.

Turning to the requirement that the breach be sufficiently serious,[7] this has been further defined as 'manifest and grave' in the *HNL* case, and as 'verging on the arbitrary' in the *Isoglucose* cases, although the later case of *Stahlwerke Peine-Salzgitter* v *Commission* (C-220/91P) suggests this latter requirement is not necessary. A breach of the rule on its own is not enough. In order to determine whether the breach was sufficiently serious a number of criteria must be considered and the nature and the effect of the breach must be examined. In the *Gritz* and *Quellmehl* cases the CoJ looked at the numbers affected, the extent of the loss suffered and the seriousness of the damage caused, i.e. is it far beyond the risks normally associated with business?

In the *HNL* case, which concerned the requirement to buy milk products rather than soya products, the increase in production costs was limited. The CoJ considered whether the company could pass on the increases with little loss of profit. If the company could not pass on the increases, then this suggests that the breach was serious, but if the company could pass on the increase then it is not sufficiently serious to succeed.

The damage must go beyond the risks normally associated with business. In the *Isoglucose* case (143/77), however, the damage was beyond normal, including causing the liquidation of some of the companies involved, but the breach was not flagrant and therefore not verging on the arbitrary.

The CoJ will look at the number of people affected, the degree of loss, and most importantly whether there is an EU interest involved. The *Sofrimport* case (C-152/88) involved the import of Chilean apples which were on the high seas when the Regulation took effect. It was held that this involved a closed group because no other could be similarly affected after the date of the Regulation. However, in the case of *Mulder* (C-104/89 and 37/90) the presence of a large group of claimants did not defeat a claim although a serious breach still had to be demonstrated and also that there was no higher public interest of the EU involved.

[8] Application of law to the facts of the problem.

In applying this to the above problem[8] it must first be determined whether there is an act which caused damage. The damage would be the losses incurred caused by the Regulation imposing the levy. However, since a Regulation involves a choice of economic policy, the action is subject to the *Schöppenstedt* (5/71) formula and it must be considered whether the superior rule of law has been breached, subject to the comments already made about the *Bergaderm* case.

The rule of law alleged to have been breached in the case of UK Foods is that of non-discrimination, which is contained both in **Art 40(2) TFEU** and clearly acknowledged in previous case law. This can be demonstrated by showing that equal or similar products have not been similarly affected. A factor in this consideration is whether the products are substitutable products. In the *Isoglucose* (143/77) and *Gritz* and *Quellmehl* cases (64 and 113/76) the alternative products of sugar and starch were held to be in competition or substitutable and therefore the rule was breached. However, in the *Walter Rau* case (261/81), where equality of treatment was pleaded for margarine and butter, it was held the products were not substitutable and so there was no breach of the superior rule.

[9] This is a summary of the position reached so far and not the final conclusion.

On balance[9] in the case of UK Foods there is a likely breach as the product is in direct competition and can be used as a substitute for milk.

The attention then turns to whether the breach was sufficiently serious. As noted, a number of criteria can be considered, including the nature and the effect of the breach, the numbers affected and whether it was a closed group of three, and the seriousness of the damage. On the basis of the *Isoglucose* case, where companies were driven out of business, it would not be sufficiently serious, but on the basis of the *Gritz* and *Quellmehl* cases (64 and 113/76) and the *Sofrimport* case (C-152/88), it was considered that the risk went beyond that normally inherent in business and in view of the small numbers involved, that it would be sufficiently serious. It is not, however, predictable with certainty. Whilst the group is not entirely fixed it is unlikely that others would join at this stage and the losses are enough to drive them out of business.

Conclusion

[10] The conclusion on the problem.

Thus[10] according to the information given in this case, it is likely but not certain that UK Foods will succeed with its action; however, the Council of Ministers does have a legitimate aim in preventing the over-production of milk due to the drop in sales and this may well weigh heavily in the decision of the CoJ.

LOOKING FOR EXTRA MARKS?

■ Suggest, although there are no facts to support it, that if it is within two months of the Regulation being published, the company could challenge the Regulation under Art 263. Equally though there are no facts to deny this. This would not replace the action for damages but support it.

■ Along these lines, even if it is not within two months, an action before the national courts might be accepted, in view of the fact that the Member States collect the levy, and followed by a reference to the CoJ.

Q | **QUESTION** | **7**

Define the circumstances in which the Court of Justice would refuse to accept a reference under the Art 267 TFEU preliminary ruling procedure, and outline the guidelines for courts of last instance and other national courts in determining whether a reference should be made to the CoJ on:

a   the interpretation of EU law

b   the validity of EU laws.

! | **CAUTION**

- Don't write an 'all I know about **Art 267 TFEU**' answer.
- Address the question itself, which will be made clear in the suggested answer and comments.
- Make sure you answer all parts: there are two parts with the second part further divided, so plan this answer carefully, and allow sufficient time to answer each part.

O | **DIAGRAM ANSWER PLAN**

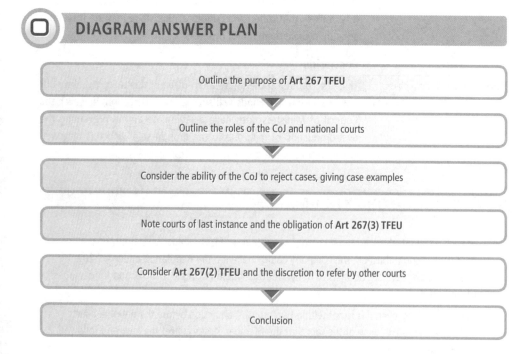

Outline the purpose of **Art 267 TFEU**

⬇

Outline the roles of the CoJ and national courts

⬇

Consider the ability of the CoJ to reject cases, giving case examples

⬇

Note courts of last instance and the obligation of **Art 267(3) TFEU**

⬇

Consider **Art 267(2) TFEU** and the discretion to refer by other courts

⬇

Conclusion

[1] This is a two-part question, clearly concentrating on the preliminary ruling procedure under **Art 267 TFEU** and with the second part itself divided into two parts.

[2] First, you should state the basic purpose of **Art 267 TFEU** and outline the procedure involved in national courts making references.

Outline of Art 267

The purpose of **Art 267 TFEU**[2] is to act as a bridge or a link between the EU and national legal systems. It is to ensure the uniform interpretation of EU law throughout the Member States and thus provide consistency in EU law. It provides the national courts with assistance in cases concerning EU law by obtaining rulings on the interpretation and validity of EU law.

Article 267 TFEU is a judicial device and not part of an appeal system, nor is it a remedy of the individual, therefore the decision to refer remains that of the Member State court.

The respective roles of the Court of Justice and national courts

Article 267 TFEU basically provides that where a question of interpretation of the Treaty or a question of the validity and interpretation of Acts of the institutions arises, any court or tribunal in a Member State may request the CoJ to give a ruling on it. The national court should determine the facts of cases and decide whether a question of EU law arises which it considers must be resolved in order to decide a case before it. The CoJ, for its part, should consider the reference and provide a ruling for the national court. When the ruling of the CoJ is received the national court must faithfully apply that ruling to the case. References should not be made until the facts have been determined.

[3] Secondly, you should discuss the Court of Justice's refusal to accept a reference, referring to established case law to assist your answer.

Refusals by the Court of Justice[3]

Initially, the CoJ stated that it was up to the Member States to decide whether a reference was necessary (see the case of *Da Costa* (28–30/62)). As the number of cases before the CoJ increased and a considerable backlog developed, the CoJ may well have been prompted to start considering whether all the references were entirely necessary. The Court has considered the validity of some of the references and has on occasion refused references which in its opinion are an abuse of the system. There may be genuine circumstances, particularly where EU law proves not to be relevant, where the CoJ is right to refuse the reference. Thus, in a limited number of cases the CoJ has decided that there are reasons not to accept and has refused a reference. It has decided that cases which do not involve a real dispute and that concern only a theoretical consideration which will not give an answer to a case before a court or tribunal will not be accepted. In *SPUC v Grogan* (C-159/90), the case had been terminated at the national level, therefore the CoJ held there was no question left to be resolved. In *Mattheus v Doego* (93/78) a contract's continuation was determinable by the entry of Spain, Portugal, and Greece into the Community (now EU). The CoJ held it had no jurisdiction as this was a matter to be determined by the Member States and the potential new states and refused jurisdiction.

The case of *Foglia v Novello* (104/79) concerned a contract for wine between a French buyer, Novello, and Italian supplier, Foglia. Clauses stipulated that the buyer and the carrier (Danzas) should not be responsible for French import duties which were contrary to Community (EU) law. These were charged on the French border and re-imbursed by Foglia. Foglia sought to recover from Novello who denied responsibility to pay them on the basis that they were illegally charged by the French authorities. The Italian judge made a reference to the CoJ asking whether the French tax was compatible with the Treaty. The CoJ rejected the reference on the grounds that there was no genuine dispute between the parties and that the action had simply been con-cocted to challenge French legislation. The CoJ considered this to be an abuse of the **Art 177 EEC (now 267 TFEU)** procedure. Not satisfied by this, the Italian judge made a further reference, *Foglia v Novello* **(No 2) (244/80)**, in which he specifically pointed out that the previous case marked a radical change in the attitude of the CoJ to a national court's decision to refer. He requested the CoJ to give guidelines on the respective powers and functions of the referring court. The CoJ held its role was not to give abstract or advisory opinions under **Art 177 EEC (now 267 TFEU)** but to contribute to actual decisions and that although discretion is given to the national courts, the limits of that discretion are determinable only by reference to Community (EU) law.

The CoJ has also held that facts and issues must be sufficiently clearly defined in *Telemarsicabruzzo SpA* **(Case C-320/90)**. A fur-ther case in which the Court has refused jurisdiction is *Meilicke v ADV/ORGA* **(C-83/91)**. The CoJ held that the questions raised in the reference concerned could not be answered by reference to the lim-ited information provided in the file: the Court would be exceeding its jurisdiction in answering what was really a hypothetical question. A refusal of jurisdiction also occurred in *TWD Textilwerke* **(C-188/92)**, in which a Commission decision addressed to Germany was not chal-lenged within the two-month time limit under **Art 230 EC (now 263 TFEU)** but instead via the national court and **Art 234 EC (now Art 267 TFEU)**. The ECJ held this to be an abuse of the procedure for not acting within the time limit, although the previous case of *Walter Rau* **(133/85)** and subsequent case of *Eurotunnel SA* **(C-408/95)** seem to suggest that this may be an acceptable way to proceed.

[4]Having outlined when and why the CoJ might refuse references, whilst not asked by the question, if there is time this would be a valuable addition to make and may gain extra marks.

Is the Court of Justice justified in refusing references?[4]

If the CoJ goes too far, it may be infringing the discretion of the Member States. It has been argued that the case of *Foglia v Novello* may have gone too far in that direction. The CoJ may understand-ably have not wished to become involved in a dispute which chal-lenged the law of another Member State and which arguably should have been pursued in the courts of the Member State or by the of-fended Member State under **Art 259 TFEU** or by the Commission under **Art 258 TFEU**. It should, however, be stressed that the CoJ has refused jurisdiction in only a small minority of cases referred to it. It is not therefore a major problem. The Court has, however, issued Recommendations to national courts, updated to 2012[5] (OJ 2012 C338/01), to help them to decide whether a reference should be made. These summarise the previous case law and will be considered further at the end of this answer.

[5] These are reproduced for your assistance in Foster, *EU Treaties and Legislation*, OUP, latest edition, which most Universities allow you to take into the examination.

Guidelines for national courts

Turning to the second part of the question,[6] guidelines for national courts are contained in **Art 267 TFEU**, in the pronouncements of the CoJ, and in the Recommendations to national courts published by the CoJ in 2012.

[6] This is now the second but multi-part of the question. It requires you to consider Guidelines: for a) last instance and b) other courts, on i) interpretation and ii) validity.

Courts of last instance

The obligation for courts of last instance to refer on points of interpretation[7] are covered by **Art 267(3) TFEU**. As they are courts from which there is no further judicial remedy they are obliged to refer, subject to the view of the CoJ in the *Da Costa* **(28–30/62)**, *Costa* v *ENEL* **(6/64)**, and *CILFIT* **(283/81)**, cases which essentially require there to be a materially identical question to be resolved before a national court of last instance can be relieved of the obligation to refer. The guidelines which the CoJ laid down in *CILFIT*, which would relieve the national court of the obligation to make a reference, suggest that national courts have a great deal more discretion than that given by **Art 267 TFEU**. The French principle of law *acte clair* is employed, so that national courts need not make a reference where the application of EU law is so clear that the outcome of the case is not in doubt. Although this point is now confirmed in the 2012 Recommendations to national courts, the CoJ also provided in *CILFIT* that before the obligation to refer was relieved, the national court should be sure that the outcome would be equally obvious to the courts in other Member States, taking into account language variations; something which in practice would be close to if not entirely impossible to achieve. Hence the view that only materially identical cases would not require a reference to be made.

[7] The order in which you tackle this is up to you as it allows for various combinations. This answer started with last instance courts on interpretation. You could start with last instance on validity or lower courts—all though are equally valid, some may just present more neatly than others.

Courts of last instance which require a ruling on validity[8] are also governed by **Art 267(3) TFEU** and the CoJ has confirmed that a declaration of validity must be referred; but equally, if a decision on validity has already been made on the same provision, this has a general effect which all courts may follow (see the *ICC* **case (66/80)**). The more recent cases of *Köbler* **(C-224/01)** and *Traghetti* **(C-173/03)** have re-emphasised the obligation of last instance courts to refer rather than rely on *acte clair*.

[8] This then, last instance on validity as the route chosen, but you could choose a different order.

Art 267 (2) TFEU and lower instance courts[9]

[9] And so on to the second main part of the second half of the question.

Lower national courts requiring interpretation have a discretion to refer but would also be able to apply previous judgments of the Court of Justice. Whilst it is not expressly stated, the application of the *Da Costa* principle would clearly be logical.

Finally, lower courts with questions of validity also have the discretion to refer or to allow an appeal to a higher court to decide the matter. They may not themselves rule on validity, and it was held in *Foto-Frost* **(314/85)** that they have an express obligation to refer where an answer to a question on validity is considered necessary to decide the case at hand. The 2012 Recommendations to national courts and the *Zuckerfabrik* **case (C-143/88 and C-92/89)**, however, provided an exception where an urgent matter required interim measures suspending the application of an EU measure whilst a preliminary ruling was sought. The Recommendations, which are not binding, also provide that the national courts should accompany questions with a clear statement of facts, reasons, and national law where relevant. Changes have been introduced to the Court's Rules of procedure whereby a reference dealing with a question already considered by the CoJ will be subject to a simplified procedure and certain subject **Art 267 TFEU** references may also be heard by the General Court **(Art 256 TFEU)**. If, however, the General Court considers that a question raises a point on EU law consistency, the case may be referred to the CoJ or, exceptionally, the CoJ may review a General Court decision but on more restrictive grounds than other appeals from the General Court to the CoJ.

Conclusion

In conclusion, the **Art 267 TFEU** cases and Recommendations to national courts published by the CoJ are there to ensure the overriding aim of the uniformity of EU law is upheld whilst at the same time maintaining respect for national courts. However, the latter may be tempered by the overriding objective such that, in limited circumstances, references may be refused.

LOOKING FOR EXTRA MARKS?

- Refer to discussions on this area of law. See for example: Anagnostaras, G, 'Preliminary Problems and Jurisdiction Uncertainties: The Admissibility of Questions Referred by Bodies Performing Quasi-judicial Functions' (2005) 30 EL Rev 878; Broberg, M, 'Acte Clair Revisited: Adapting the Acte Clair Criteria to the Demands of the Times' (2008) 45 CML Rev 1383; Broberg, M and Fenger, N, 'Preliminary References as a Right—But for Whom? The Extent to which Preliminary Reference Decisions Can Be Subject to Appeal' (2011) 36 EL Rev 276; Broberg, M and Fenger, N, 'Variations in Member States' Preliminary References to the Court of Justice: Are Structural Factors (Part of) the Explanation? (2013) 19 ELJ 488; Komarek, J, 'In the Court(s) We Trust? On the Need for Hierarchy and Differentiation in the Preliminary Ruling Procedure' (2007) 32 EL Rev 467.
- Further discussion of whether it is correct for the CoJ to refuse at all.
- Suggestions for reform of the system which might include setting up EU courts in the Member States, allowing national courts to decide themselves, making it a true appeal and not a reference system.

The Council and EP addressed a (fictitious) Directive to the Italian Government requiring it to ensure that paid holiday schemes and sickness schemes are equalised for male and female workers. The Italian Dentists Association, a professional body to which 90 per cent of Italian dentists belong, has, with the approval of the Government, constituted its own professional arbitration tribunal to settle disputes relating to pay and conditions of work. Decisions of the tribunal are legally binding and there is no appeal. Angelo, a trainee dentist, claims to have received unfair treatment by comparison with female trainees and brings a case before the tribunal.

The tribunal dismisses his claim to protection by the Directive on the grounds that he is not a worker but a trainee, despite the fact that the CoJ had held that the term 'worker' included trainees.

The tribunal panel do not want to make a reference under Art 267 TFEU, whereas Angelo insists that it must do so.

Consider whether the Tribunal is obliged to refer a question to the Court of Justice and whether Angelo has a right to have it referred.

CAUTION

- This question, like a number of problem questions, refers to a fictitious Directive, so deal with that, even though you may know an actual Directive exists. This is so the examiner can focus on particular points and not be distracted by other matters regulated by the real Directive.

- Be sure to consider that the CoJ has already decided on an important point in the question.

DIAGRAM ANSWER PLAN

Identify the issues	■ Identify the facts which give rise to legal issues
Relevant law	■ Outline the relevant law: the **Art 267** Preliminary Ruling Procedure
Apply the law	■ Define a Court or Tribunal for the purposes of **Art 267 TFEU** and consider the case law and guidelines of CoJ on 'Court or Tribunal' ■ Outline obligation of courts of last instance to refer under **Art 267(3) TFEU** ■ Consider the *Da Costa* and *CILFIT* cases and the circumstances which excuse the obligation to refer
Conclude	■ Conclusion

[1] The underlying question is whether this tribunal should or must make a reference to the CoJ under **Art 267 TFEU**.

[2] First of all you have to consider whether this is a court or tribunal for the purposes of **Art 267 TFEU**.

[3] Not all bodies have been so recognised.

Court of Tribunal for the purposes of Art 267?[2]

The ability of a national court or tribunal to make a reference to the CoJ depends on whether it is a court or tribunal recognised by the CoJ for the purposes of **Art 267 TFEU**. If it is, it has a right to refer a question.[3] A duty or obligation to refer arises when it is a court or tribunal of last instance and the obligation to refer has not been relieved under the criteria outlined by the CoJ in case law and guidelines.

The CoJ has accepted references from a varied number of bodies including administrative tribunals, arbitration panels, and insurance officers. The determination of what is an acceptable court or tribunal is a question for the CoJ and is not dependent on national concepts. Certain criteria have, however, now been established by which it may reasonably be determined whether a particular body may refer to the CoJ for guidance under **Art 267 TFEU**. For example, it was clear from *Van Gend en Loos* (26/62) that administrative tribunals were acceptable for the purposes of **Art 234 EC (now 267 TFEU)**. Whilst the majority of bodies which decide legal matters in the Member States pose no problem, it is the bodies which lie either partially or entirely outside the state legal system which raise the question of whether it is suitable for the CoJ to accept a reference from them. A few examples will highlight some of the considerations taken into account by the Court of Justice.

The *Vaassen* case (61/65) concerned a reference from the arbitration tribunal of a private mine employees' social security fund. The CoJ held that the panel qualified as a court or tribunal in the eyes of Community (EU) law because of the following criteria: it possessed its own power to nominate members and to approve rule changes, a power also in the hands of a government minister, and the panel was a permanent body operating under national law and rules of procedure.

Broekmeulen v *HRC* (246/80) concerned a reference made by the appeal committee of the Dutch medical profession's organisation. This was held by the CoJ to be acceptable because it was approved and had the assistance and considerable involvement of the Dutch public authorities, its decisions were arrived at after full legal procedure, the decisions affected the right to work under Community (EU) law, they were final, and there was no appeal to Dutch courts, despite the fact that a legal remedy was in private hands.

In the next two cases jurisdiction was refused. In the case of *Borker* (138/80), a reference from the Paris Bar Association Council on the right of a French lawyer to appear as of right before German courts was refused on the ground that there was no lawsuit in progress and the Council was not therefore acting as a Court or Tribunal called upon to give judgment in proceedings intended to lead to a decision of a judicial nature. In **Nordsee v Nordstern (102/81)** there was no involvement by national authorities in the case. Despite the fact there was a legally binding decision and there was no appeal, the CoJ held that because there was no involvement of national authorities in the process, there was not a sufficiently close link to a national organisation of legal remedies and thus the arbitrator could not come under **Art 234 EC (now 267 TFEU)**.

Thus,[4] it is not an essential factor whether the body is private or public or that there is no appeal from its decision. A strong indicator is the level of involvement by national authorities. However, the lack of an appeal may lead to instances where the national body itself has to interpret EU law without guidance if the CoJ is unwilling to accept jurisdiction, something which must be less desirable from a Union point of view. In **Dorsch (Case C-54/96)**, the CoJ provided guideline questions for national courts to pose. These are: whether the body is established by law, whether it is permanent, whether its procedure is *inter partes*, whether it applies rules of law, and whether it is independent. The CoJ also issued Recommendations to national courts updated to 2012.[5]

Is the tribunal in the question acceptable?[6]

It must therefore be decided on a balance of factors whether the arbitration tribunal in the above problem is one which is acceptable for the purposes of **Art 267 TFEU**. The factors in the present case are:

(a) the governmental approval

(b) the fact that 90 per cent of all potential members are included

(c) the legally binding decisions with no appeal.

The membership figure could be used as evidence to decide either way in that it would suggest that this is not the only way in which dentists can have disputes resolved. The other 10 per cent must presumably be able to avail themselves of the ordinary national courts. On the other hand, since this body clearly is involved with EU legislation, it would defeat the uniformity of EU law if it cannot refer and must decide matters of EU law itself. Individuals, such as Angelo, may thus be deprived of their true rights. This, in the end, may be the most important consideration and is certainly one the CoJ would consider.

Thus, it is probable that it is a tribunal for the purposes of **Art 267 TFEU**.[7]

Is there an obligation or discretion to refer?[8]

The next question is whether it is obliged to refer or whether it has a discretion to refer. It can be stated immediately that whatever the answer to that question, it is clear that Angelo has no right under **Art 267 TFEU** to a reference and that this matter comes within the discretion of the tribunal where they have a discretion. Case **6/64 Costa** is also a good authority for this point. As a tribunal against which there is not a judicial remedy under **Art 267(3) TFEU**, the tribunal is obliged to make a reference. This obligation will only be relieved if the question has already been decided and the case thus comes within the guidelines of the **Da Costa (28–30/62)** or the **CILFIT (283/81)** cases. The cases of **Köbler (C-224/01)** and **Traghetti (C-173/03)** have re-emphasised the obligation of last instant courts to refer. The tribunal is not obliged to refer where the provision in question has already been interpreted by the CoJ or the correct application is so obvious as to leave no scope for any reasonable doubt and therefore no question to be decided arises. The **Da Costa** case raised the same question as had previously been asked in the **Van Gend en Loos** case **(26/62)**. The CoJ referred to its previous judgment in **Van Gend en Loos** as the basis for deciding the issue and advised that such a situation might, if the national court wished, excuse the obligation to refer.

The **CILFIT (283/81)** judgment expanded the decision of **Da Costa (28–30/62)**. In **CILFIT** the Italian Supreme Court asked the CoJ directly in what circumstances it need not refer. The CoJ replied that in addition to the reason given in **Da Costa** a court might not refer if the correct application, but not interpretation, may be so obvious as to leave no scope for any reasonable doubt that the question raised will be solved. However, the CoJ qualified this by stating that the national court must be convinced that the matter is equally obvious to courts of other Member States, that it is sure language differences will not result in inconsistent decisions in Member States, and that EU law will be applied in light of the application of it as a whole with regard to the objectives of the Union.[9] The cases of **Köbler (C-224/01)** and **Traghetti (C-173/03)** have re-emphasised the obligation of last instant courts to refer rather than rely on *acte clair*.

[9] These criteria would be extremely difficult to fulfil if properly followed to the letter.

Application of law to the tribunal in the problem and conclusion

In the case of Angelo, the identical question has already been resolved by the CoJ which has given a ruling on the interpretation of the relevant provision, that a trainee is considered a worker under EU law and is thus subject to EU rules in respect of non-discrimination. Therefore, there would be no need to refer and the tribunal could simply apply the previous ruling of the Court of Justice. However, the national court retains its discretion to refer if it so wishes.

For references identical to previous questions decided by the CoJ the 2012 Recommendations to national courts provide in Point 12 that the reference be referred back to the national court.

The only problem left is that caused if the tribunal, despite its obligation to apply EU law, still followed its own decision in considering a trainee not to be a worker and not making a reference. In such circumstances it could not be prevented by the CoJ, although following case law such as *Francovich* **(C-6 and 9/90)**, *Factortame III* **(C-46 and 48/93)**, and *Köbler* **(C-224/01)**, the state may be held liable for damages providing the criteria for such a claim are satisfied.

Conclusion

The overall conclusions are that the Tribunal is probably one that can make references but need not as there is a previous decision of the CoJ on the matter, but that it retains a discretion to do so if it wishes. It should not decide for itself, though.

➕ LOOKING FOR EXTRA MARKS?

- Angelo may be able to take an action against the state for any loss sustained, but as this is not the main issue of this question, a brief consideration of this would demonstrate your wider knowledge of EU law procedural actions.
- If there is time, provide further supporting case law.

Ⓠ QUESTION 9

How and to what extent are the rights of individuals protected in the EU legal order?

❗ CAUTION

- This is a very open question and is inviting, in that you would seem to be able to write about anything in answering it, but you must be careful that you still answer the question.
- You should think carefully what is meant by the key words in the question: 'rights of individuals' and 'protected'.
- This is a general overview question on the range of actions which are available to individuals to protect their rights in EU law.

DIAGRAM ANSWER PLAN

> Generally introduce the EU legal regime and its impact on individuals

> Outline the range of individual protective procedural rights in EU law

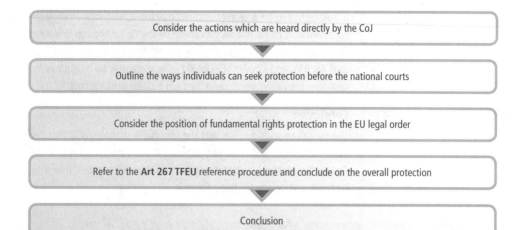

Consider the actions which are heard directly by the CoJ

Outline the ways individuals can seek protection before the national courts

Consider the position of fundamental rights protection in the EU legal order

Refer to the **Art 267 TFEU** reference procedure and conclude on the overall protection

Conclusion

SUGGESTED ANSWER[1]

[1] You should identify the range of legal activities encompassed by the EU, outlining the major areas of EU law included in the Treaty and secondary legislation which may affect individual rights.

[2] An underlying aspect of the question is that many EU laws directly affect individuals by both bestowing advantages on them but also imposing duties and sometimes infringing their rights.

[3] The vast scope of this law can be discovered from a review of the Treaties and EU legislation.

[4] Yet, the means by which individuals can protect their rights are less obvious.

Introduction

The EU now covers vast tracts of the economic and increasingly the social spheres of the Member States' national jurisdictions, such as the freedom of persons.[2] The Treaties and secondary law established under the Treaties thus straddle many areas of law and impose very many duties and rights, but not just on the Member States. Individuals in the EU are also subject to very many new laws which emerge from the Council and the EP and the Commission in Brussels. They have created a new source of law,[3] additional to the Member States' own laws, and not only created laws which impose duties and obligations but also established new rights and protections of individual rights.[4] Since the establishment of the EU, individuals in the Union have become subject to the legislative, executive, and judicial authority of the Union. Concerns have quite rightly been raised about the protections that individuals have in the face of this new legal source of authority, particularly as the democratic protection in the EU from the EP is not as strong at the EU level as most national parliaments and political answerability in the Member States.

Thus, it is necessary first to define how the EU affects the individual and then to outline the legal protections available. The term 'individuals' is taken to mean both natural and legal persons in the Union who are concerned in some way with the substantive and procedural law of the EU.

Essentially, three different aspects need to be considered: the substantive rights under the various chapters of the Treaty; the procedural rights, i.e. the various actions that can be pursued in the Union courts; and a set of general fundamental rights. The impact of the EU on individuals will be considered first of all.

The range of rights and ways in which EU affects individuals

Individuals are affected by a vast range of substantive laws enacted by the EU. Legislation enacted in any of the areas of EU law can affect the rights of individuals. Legislation can be enacted to regulate agricultural activities, to ensure or standardise product or trading rules, to ensure the free movement of goods, to ensure that competition in the EU is being maintained, or to provide for the free movement of persons, to give just a few examples of the range of areas covered by the EU. This legislation can either promote or infringe individual rights. Individuals may, as a result, consider their rights to have been infringed by the institutions of the Union in enacting these rules. Sometimes they can also be affected by the national implementation of EU law by Member States. Whilst for the most part these laws impose duties on the Member States, they can also give rise to corresponding rights of individuals; see as a classic example the *Van Gend en Loos* **case (26/62)** and the establishment of the doctrine of direct effects by the Court of Justice.

The ways to protect individual rights[5]

[5] You should now outline the procedures by which these rights can be protected in the EU legal order and where these rights can be protected, i.e. in which legal fora.

Thus, individuals may need to be protected against the acts of the Union institutions and the Member States or to challenge Member States where they have failed to implement EU law. Protections need to be considered in the actions both against the Union and the Member States.

The main forms of protection are provided by the EU Treaties which outline a number of actions that, in varying circumstances and subject to differing criteria, may aid an individual in the protection of rights. In addition the CoJ has also developed a number of remedies. These remedies are also generally considered in the 2011 article by Arnull. Actions against the EU which can be made under a number of Treaty provisions and other remedies are the following:[6]

[6] Introduce the list, then provide a brief outline of each. Perhaps, however, check the attitude of your lecturers to lists during the progress of your course.

- Action to Annul **Art 263 TFEU**
- Action for failure to Act **Art 265 TFEU**
- The indirect challenge **Art 277 TFEU**
- Action for damages **Art 340 TFEU**
- Direct effects
- Indirect effects
- State liability
- Incidental indirect effects
- *Mangold* general principles.

Treaty procedural rights[7]

[7] The difficulties experienced in pursuing these actions or, in terms of the question posed, the extent of the protection will be considered at the same time.

Article 263 TFEU allows a direct challenge against legislative acts of the institutions where they are unlawful and the infringement can be classified under one of the four grounds listed in the Article itself. This action, however, can only be used by individuals in limited circumstances. It can only be employed to challenge an act addressed to that person or which is of direct and individual concern to them, and against a regulatory act which is of direct concern to them and does not entail implementing measures. There is a time limit of two months in which actions can be brought following the fifteenth day after publication in the Official Journal.

Article 265 TFEU provides an action against the institutions of the EU for a failure to act but this can only be employed by the potential addressee of the legal act, or those, in view of more recent case law, who are in an analogous position as applicants under **Art 263 TFEU**, in that they are directly and individually concerned with a potential act. **Articles 263 and 265 TFEU** are regarded as particularly difficult actions in which individuals are unlikely to succeed. They seem more designed for use by the Member States and the institutions of the Union.

An indirect challenge to an EU Regulation can be made under **Art 277 TFEU** but this is only available providing a related matter of EU law is already being adjudicated in the CoJ and, again, is of limited use to individuals. Of more use, and more likely to be successful in assisting individuals, is an action for damages where loss has been suffered as a result of the action or act of the Union and its institutions, which can be made under **Art 340(2) TFEU**. However, where legislative acts are concerned, the damage must be the result of a sufficiently serious breach of a superior rule of law for the protection of an individual or, as appears to be developing, a sufficiently serious breach of a rule of law intended to confer rights on individuals, something which has been demonstrated in the case law of the CoJ to be extremely difficult to prove.

All of the above actions take place before the General Court or the Court of Justice.

Protection before the national courts for individuals

As far as the Member States and the national courts are concerned, individuals can defend their rights arising from EU law generally against the inconsistent legislation of the Member States in the national courts or where Member States have failed to implement EU law and seek to prosecute individuals for breaches of national law; see the *Van Gend en Loos* (26/62), *Ratti* (148/78), *von Colson* (14/83), *Francovich* (C-6 and 9/90), and *Factortame* (C-213/89 and 46/93) cases. The latter cases highlight the developments by which individuals can sue a Member State where he or she has suffered damage which was the result of the Member State's breach of EU law. Individuals can also be protected incidentally by EU legislation which has not been complied with by a Member State in an action involving another individual, as in the case of *CIA Security* v *Signalson* (C-194/94). They may also be able to count on the protection horizontally of general principles of EU law against other individuals, such as discrimination as in the *Mangold* case (C-144/04).

The Member States now are specifically required by a new **Art 19(1) TEU** to 'provide remedies sufficient to ensure effective legal protection in the fields covered by Union law'.[8]

Fundamental and human rights protection[9]

Individuals can also defend their rights against EU law provisions if these unlawfully affect individual rights by infringing fundamental rights of an individual. Fundamental rights for the protection of individuals can be brought into play in the course of any of the procedural actions to enforce individual rights in substantive areas of EU law. These have been recognised by the CoJ because they are contained in many of the Member States' constitutions, and the European Convention for the protection of Human and Fundamental Rights has been held by the CoJ to apply in the EU legal order. Further, **Art 6(1) and (3) of the Treaty on European Union** now obliges the EU to conform to it and to observe the **Charter of Fundamental Rights of the European Union** attached in a **Declaration to the Treaties** by the **2007 Lisbon Reform Treaty**, which will be binding if it comes into force, although with opt-outs for the internal application of the Charter in Poland, the Czech Republic, and the UK. The EU is also now set to officially accede to the Council of Europe and the ECHR under the power granted by **Art 6(2) TEU**.

The role of the Art 267 preliminary ruling procedure[10]

In support of all of these actions before the national courts, individuals may, if necessary, request that a reference to the CoJ be made using the preliminary ruling procedure of **Art 267 TFEU**. It is through this that leading principles of EU law have been developed by the CoJ which have greatly enhanced the protection of individual rights in the Union. One only has to consider the cases of *Van Gend en Loos* (26/62) or *Francovich* (C-6 and 9/90) to see how the CoJ has secured the rights of individuals.

Conclusion[11]

In conclusion, there is a considerable range of rights, although some of them are still criticised as being too restrictive, for example the **Art 263** *locus standi* requirement for individuals. The development of direct effects in actions before the national courts may be regarded as far more successful than the use of direct actions before the CoJ, and potentially more useful, in respect of Member States' breaches, is the action to claim damages from the Member State for loss under the *Francovich*-type actions. Accession to the Council of Europe and the ECHR may strengthen further individual rights against infringements by the EU institutions and legal order.

LOOKING FOR EXTRA MARKS?

If there is time, you could mention briefly the attempt by the AG to ease the *locus standi* restrictions in **Art 263 TFEU** actions to make challenges by individuals easier, but that this was not accepted by the CoJ in ***Unión de Pequeños Agricultores v Council*** **(C-50/00P)**, but this will only add very few marginal extra marks.

- The Fundamental rights section, see earlier, can also be regarded as additional.
- Also **Art 267** as mentioned in the annotations.

TAKING THINGS FURTHER

- Arnull, A, 'The Principle of Effective Judicial Protection in EU Law: An Unruly Horse?' (2011) 36 EL Rev 51.

  Good summary article on actions.

- Balthasar, S, 'Locus Standi Rules for Challenges to Regulatory Acts by Private Applicants: The New Article 263(4) TFEU' (2010) 35 EL Rev 542.

  Suggests that regulatory acts be taken to be non-legislative and generally therefore just implementing and delegated acts under Arts 290 & 291 TFEU, but suggests also this might include legislative regulations. However, the discussion is not definitive or convincing, and later case law actually refutes that. Balthasar had suggested that the Plaumann formula was likely to be history but this is obviously not the case!

- Gutman, K, 'The Evolution of the Action for Damages against the European Union and its Place in the System of Judicial Protection' (2011) 48 CML Rev 695.

  This article considers how effective actions for damages are.

- Kornezov, A, 'Locus Standi of Private Parties in Actions for Annulment: Has the Gap Been Closed?' (2014) 73 CLJ 27.

  Looks to see if the reforms have made things any easier.

- Wennerås, P, 'Sanctions Against Member States Under Article 260 TFEU: Alive, But Not Kicking' (2012) 49 CML Rev 145

  Article states that despite Lisbon changes Member States are still able to take a long time before complying and revised Art 260 change won't do much.

Online Resources
www.oup.com/uk/qanda/

Go online for extra essay and problem questions, a glossary of key terms, online versions of all the answer plans and audio commentary on how selected ones were put together, and a range of podcasts which include advice on exam and coursework technique and advice for other assessment methods.

The Free Movement of Goods

6

ARE YOU READY?

In order to attempt questions in this chapter, you must have covered all of these topics in both your work over the year and in revision:

- The basic provisions governing the free movement of goods which remained unchanged following the Treaty of Lisbon.
- The Court of Justice of the EU (CoJ) decisions and statements in the cases of **Cassis de Dijon (120/78)**, **Keck**, and **Mithouard (C-267 and 268/91)** and subsequent case law.
- Charges and measures having equivalent effect, the restrictions allowed under **Art 36 TFEU**, and the principles of law which have emerged from the case of **Cassis de Dijon** and subsequent cases.

KEY DEBATES

Debate: the continuing significance of the Keck case

Whilst this title includes the Common Customs Tariff in **Arts 31–32 TFEU**, questions are more likely to be concentrated on the elimination of customs duties and measures having equivalent effect, **Art 30 TFEU**, and the elimination of quantitative restriction and measures having equivalent effect under **Arts 34–36 TFEU**, and in particular what the significance of the CoJ judgment was in the case of **Keck**.

QUESTION | 1

'However wide the field of application of Article 34 TFEU may be, it nevertheless does not include obstacles to trade covered by other provisions of the Treaty. Thus, obstacles which are of a fiscal

⊙

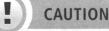

nature or have equivalent effect and are covered by Articles 28–30 and 110 TFEU do not fall within the prohibition of Article 34 TFEU.'

Discuss.

! CAUTION

■ Although apt to cause difficulties in any part of the course, the renumbering of the **EC Treaty** by the **Treaties of Amsterdam** and now **Lisbon** is even more problematic in this area, as very old Art 30 EEC is old Art 28 EC, and now **Art 34 TFEU**. Very old Art 36 EEC is old Art 30 EC but back again following **Lisbon** to **Art 36 TFEU**! Make sure you make it clear which Treaty you are referring to.

■ The caution on renumbering applies, of course, to all questions in this chapter.

■ This quotation is taken from the Court of Justice judgment in the case of *Ianelli and Volpi v Meroni* **(Case 74/76)**, but amended to take account of the renumbering of the Treaty. However, it is not necessary to know that, or even that it is a quotation from the Court of Justice, to be able to discuss the meaning of the quotation.

⭕ DIAGRAM ANSWER PLAN

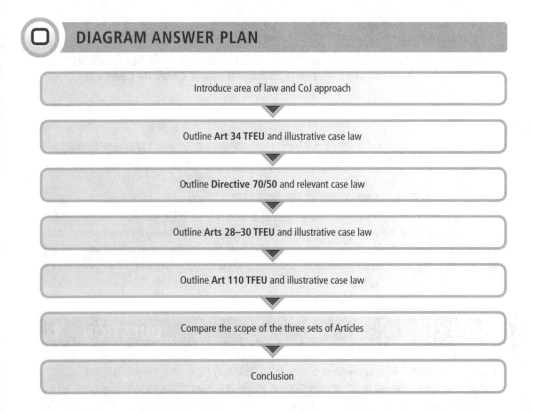

Introduce area of law and CoJ approach

⬇

Outline **Art 34 TFEU** and illustrative case law

⬇

Outline **Directive 70/50** and relevant case law

⬇

Outline **Arts 28–30 TFEU** and illustrative case law

⬇

Outline **Art 110 TFEU** and illustrative case law

⬇

Compare the scope of the three sets of Articles

⬇

Conclusion

[1]Determine whether **Arts 28–30** and **110 TFEU** apply only to charges or measures with an equivalent effect or to fiscal measures and whether **Art 34 TFEU** applies only to physical measures with no overlap.

[2]Start with a general view of the approach of the Court of Justice to this area of law.

[3]You will need to consider the scope of the application of **Art 34 TFEU** by considering the provision itself and by giving examples from the case law of the Court of Justice.

The free movement of goods, as one of the fundamental freedoms[2] or cornerstones of the internal market and the original Community and Union itself, has been carefully protected by the Court of Justice in its judgments. It interprets the main provisions, which provide the freedoms, very widely, but any exception allowed the Member States, very restrictively.

The scope of Art 34 TFEU[3]

Article 34 TFEU provides a general prohibition on quantitative restrictions and measures having equivalent effect. Its scope has been determined both by legislation and case law. In *Geddo* v *Ente Nationale Risi* **(2/73)**, the CoJ held that a prohibition on quantitative restrictions covers measures which amount to a total or partial restraint of imports, exports, or goods in transit. The most obvious examples of quantitative restrictions on imports and exports are complete bans or quotas restricting the import or export of a given product by amount or by value. These are clearly in contravention of **Art 34 TFEU** and prohibited. The cases of *Commission* v *France (Import of Lamb)* **(232/78)** and *Commission* v *UK (Import of Potatoes)* **(231/78)** are straightforward examples of unlawful import bans.

The concept of measures having equivalent effect was defined by **Directive 70/50, Art 2**, which provides 'measures having equivalent effect' to include those which 'make imports, or the disposal at any marketing stage of imported products, subject to a condition, other than a formality, which is required in respect of imported products only'. They also include any measures which subject imported products or their disposal to a condition which differs from that required for domestic products and which is more difficult to satisfy.

In *Procureur du Roi* v *Dassonville* **(8/74)** the term 'measures having equivalent effect' was held to include 'all trading rules enacted by a Member State which are capable of hindering, directly or indirectly, actually or potentially, intra-community trade'.

Basically, therefore, any measure which makes import or export unnecessarily difficult, and thus discriminates between the two, would clearly fall within the definition.

Article 34 TFEU has been held to apply widely to a number of indirect measures including:

(a) a government sponsored advertising campaign in *Commission* v *Ireland (Buy Irish Campaign)* **(249/81)**

(b) national marketing rules in the *Commission* v *Belgium (Packaging of Margarine)* **(314/82 and 189/83)**

(c) import bans on health grounds on food additives have been held to be in breach of **Art 34 TFEU** in two cases against Germany, *Commission* v *Germany (Beer Purity)* **(178/84)** and *Commission* v *Germany (Sausage Purity)* **(274/87)**

(d) in *R* v *Pharmaceutical Society of Great Britain* **(267/87)** the rule of the Pharmaceutical Society prohibiting dispensing pharmacists from substituting for the product named on a doctor's prescription any other with identical therapeutic effect except under certain exceptional conditions.

Moreover, the scope of **Art 34 TFEU** applies not just to measures which are directly discriminatory but also to measures affecting both imports and domestic goods, termed equally or indistinctly applicable measures. **Directive 70/50, Art 3** provides that measures which are equally applicable to domestic and imported goods will breach **Art 34 TFEU** where the restrictive effect on the free movement of goods exceeds the effects necessary for the trade rules, i.e. they would be disproportionate to the aim and would thus tend to protect domestic products at the expense of the imports. See e.g. cases concerned with health checks and spot checks, *Commission* v *UK (UHT Milk)* **(124/81)** and *Commission* v *France (Italian Table Wines)* **(42/82)**. Thus, the scope of **Art 34 TFEU** is extremely wide,[4] covering physical trade barriers, government assistance, and measures which are applicable to both imports and domestic products. The scope of **Arts 28–30 and 110 TFEU** will now be outlined to compare with **Art 34 TFEU**.[5]

[4] The first sentence of the question suggests that the scope of application of **Art 34 TFEU** does not extend to prohibiting obstacles which are covered by other Treaty Articles.

[5] The question proceeds in the second sentence to spell out which other Treaty Articles serve to cover the obstacles that lie outside the scope of **Art 34 TFEU**, which you should now outline.

The scope of Arts 28–30 TFEU

Articles 28–30 TFEU are aimed at the abolition of customs duties and charges having equivalent effect and at prohibiting the introduction of any such measures.

Article 28 TFEU states that the Union shall be based on a customs union, with a common customs tariff, involving the prohibition of all customs duties on imports and charges having equivalent effect.

Article 28 TFEU prohibits the introduction of new customs duties or charges having equivalent effect, and equally prohibits the increase of those which are already in existence. The prohibition applies both to imports and exports. A customs duty is usually clear to recognise but a charge having an equivalent effect is more difficult and has been the subject of a considerable body of case law. In *Commission* v *Luxembourg and Belgium (Gingerbread)* **(2 and 3/62)**, the Court of Justice held that:

a duty, whatever it is called, and whatever its mode of application, may be considered a charge having equivalent effect to a customs duty, provided that it meets the following three criteria:

(a) it must be imposed unilaterally at the time of importation or subsequently;

(b) it must be imposed specifically upon a product imported from a Member State to the exclusion of a similar national product; and

(c) it must result in an alteration of price and thus have the same effect as a customs duty on the free movement of products.

Furthermore, charges which are argued to be fees for services rendered have also been classified as contrary to **Art 30 TFEU** unless they meet specific criteria including that they have been sanctioned under either EU or international law. The **Treaty of Amsterdam** amended what is now **Art 30 TFEU** by adding a second sentence to make it expressly clear that the prohibition also applies to customs duties of a fiscal nature which are applied when goods cross the border.

Is it a duty, a charge, or a tax?

However, if a fee, imposed by a Member State on imported goods, is a measure of internal taxation, it cannot be a charge having equivalent effect, and cannot be caught by **Arts 28–30 TFEU**. It is instead governed by **Art 110 TFEU** on taxation but **Art 110 TFEU** is designed to prevent circumvention of the customs rules by the substitution of discriminatory internal taxes.

The scope of the tax provision in Art 110 TFEU

Article 110(1) TFEU prevents Member States from imposing on imports internal taxation of any kind in excess of that imposed directly or indirectly on similar domestic products. This prohibits discrimination in favour of the domestic products. **Article 110(2) TFEU** prohibits Member States from imposing on the products of other Member States any internal taxation of such a nature as to afford indirect protection to other products. This serves to cover products that may be different but are nevertheless in competition with the domestic products.

Taxation was defined in ***Commission v France (Re: Reprographic Machines)*** **(90/79)** as a general system of internal dues applied systematically to categories of product in accordance with objective criteria irrespective of the origin of the products. In ***Molkerei-Zentrale*** **(28/67)** the Court of Justice ruled that the words 'directly or indirectly' were to be construed broadly and embraced all taxation which was actually and specifically imposed on the domestic product at earlier stages of the manufacturing and marketing process.

The relationship between Arts 28–30 and 110 TFEU

Article 110 TFEU is therefore complementary to **Arts 28–30 TFEU** in that it is also concerned with outlawing fiscal measures which are discriminatory. **Article 28 TFEU** applies to charges which occur as goods pass a frontier and **Art 110 TFEU** should apply only internally within the importing state. **Articles 28 and 110 TFEU** were held to be mutually exclusive by the Court of Justice in the case of ***Deutschmann v Germany*** **(10/65)**.

[6] The question suggests the Treaty Articles create mutually exclusive categories, so you need to address this specific point.

The final part of this answer[6] addresses the issue of whether **Arts 28 and 110 TFEU** overlap in any way with **Art 34 TFEU**. The area of fees charged for inspection has emerged as the situation where all of the Articles under examination may come into play. The imposition of charges or alleged taxes may occur at the same time or following an inspection of goods. Thus a consideration of measures having equivalent effect may be undertaken, the result of which may be that the inspection proves to be a breach of **Art 34 TFEU** and not excused by **Art 36 TFEU**. If a fee for this is charged, it will still have to be considered either as a measure of taxation under **Art 110 TFEU** or under **Arts 28–30 TFEU** because it may not be acceptable as a tax (see *Dansk Denkavit* **(29/87)**). However, if it is the case that a Member State claims that a charge made on import inspection is a tax and there is not a fee levied at a similar stage internally of a counterpart domestic product, it may be held to be a charge having equivalent effect, as in the cases of *Commission* v *Belgium* **(314/82)** and *Commission* v *Denmark* **(C-47/88)**. The distinction, however, between the physical barrier of the inspection and the fee charged remains quite distinct. The Court of Justice has considered in the case of *Ianelli and Volpi* v *Meroni* **(74/74)** that **Arts 28–30 and 110 TFEU** do not overlap with **Art 34 TFEU**. It is possible that inspections may be lawful, but the fees for them may not; see e.g. the *Marimex* **case (29/72)**. Note though, as a matter of law and logic that if an inspection was held to be unlawful, it must follow that the fee levied for it must also be unlawful. Therefore, the conclusions to be drawn from observing the scope of the articles are that there is no overlap of **Arts 28–30 or 110** with **Art 34 TFEU**.

➕ LOOKING FOR EXTRA MARKS?

- More general information on the approach of the court with reference to case law as in the cases of *Van Gend* **(26/62)**, *Commission* v *Italy* (Art Treasures) **(7/68)** and *Commission* v *Belgium and Luxembourg* (Gingerbread) **(2 and 3/62)**.
- If time, inclusion of *Denkavit* **(29/87)** on the border or distinction between cases arising under **Arts 28–30** and **110 TFEU**.

ⓠ QUESTION | 2

Healthy-eat Ltd is a UK manufacturer of fruit-flavoured yoghurt and breakfast muesli. It has recently decided to try to export to the Continental European market. In order to ensure the products are in good condition when they reach the shops in the Member States, certain measures are taken by Healthy-eat Ltd in the marketing of three special Continental product lines. The first is 'frozen yoghurt' containing

⊙

only natural ingredients. The second is unfrozen yoghurt to which preservatives are added. The third is muesli in sealed cellophane bags. All the ingredients of the products are listed on the packaging.

Healthy-eat Ltd found that the products were particularly popular in Germany and for four months sales boomed until Germany imposed a ban, justified on 'public health grounds', on the importation of any dairy product containing preservatives. A new German consumer protection law forbids the application of the description yoghurt to all frozen yoghurts. Following this, consignments of yoghurt were turned back at the frontier.

Meanwhile, consignments of muesli were subject to long delays at the German ferry port whilst spot checks for health reasons were carried out. These involved opening three packets in every fifth case of muesli. Payment was required for the inspections and parking fees were imposed on the trucks whilst they were parked up waiting for the inspections to take place.

When Healthy-eat Ltd challenged the parking fees and charges for the health checks, they were told that they are the equivalent of an internal tax imposed on domestic food products to finance a system of factory inspection in the German food industry.

Advise Healthy-eat Ltd as to its rights under EU law.

CAUTION

- As with other long and involved problem questions, pacing your answer and getting a good balance in dealing with the issues is crucial.

- Additionally, as there are a number of issues a good structure to your answer also is vital.

DIAGRAM ANSWER PLAN

Identify the issues
- Identify the facts which give rise to legal issues: which are the yoghurts containing additives, frozen yoghurts, and the checks and payments for the muesli

Relevant law
- Outline the relevant law: free movement of goods major provisions (**Arts 28–30, 34–36 and 110 TFEU**)
- Outline **Directive 70/50** and the *Dassonville* and CoJ case law

Apply the law
- Consider in turn the various bans in the light of **Arts 34 and 36 TFEU** and *Cassis de Dijon*
- Address the spot checks and charges under **Arts 30, and 34** and, if taxation, **Art 110 TFEU**

Conclude
- With the aid of relevant cases, reach conclusions on all the issues

[1] This problem is concerned with the free movement of goods including aspects of charges having equivalent effect, measures having equivalent effect, and internal taxation measures.

Subject area of the problem and the principal legislative provisions[1]

The applicable legal regime is that of the free movement of goods contained in **Arts 28–30, 34–36 TFEU and 110 TFEU** concerned with taxation. Free movement of goods is one of the fundamental freedoms guaranteed by the **EU Treaties** and is a cornerstone or one of the foundations of the Union.[2] As a result, the Court of Justice has interpreted the legislative provisions widely and the exceptions allowed to the Member States have been interpreted restrictively. Furthermore, **Art 110 TFEU** may be applicable, because a claim has been made that the charges are equivalent to a domestic tax.

[2] A brief introduction to the area of law and the attitude of the Court of Justice would help to set the scene before answering the specific points in the question.

[3] The material facts to be considered are the yoghurts containing additives, frozen yoghurts, and the checks and payments for the muesli.

The facts of the problem[3]

The problems that have been identified are those concerned with the additives in yoghurts, the frozen yoghurts, and the checks and payments for the muesli.

[4] Determine whether the bans breach **Art 34 TFEU** or the measures introduced by the German government are justified under EU law by **Art 36 TFEU** or justified under the rule of reason.

The law applicable to the facts[4]

First of all, in relation to the yoghurt with preservatives, **Art 34 TFEU** prohibits all quantitative restrictions or measures having equivalent effect (MHEE). Measures which are in breach of **Art 34 TFEU** are those which meet formulae provided by the provisions of **Directive 70/50** or the Court of Justice in the *Dassonville* case **(8/74)** in that they impose measures to hinder imports. The imposed ban would appear to be the case here. However, **Art 36 TFEU** allows exceptions on public health grounds and this is what Germany pleads in respect of the ban on preservatives. There is considerable case law[5] now dealing with bans on health grounds to the effect that any measure must be reasonable and proportional to the aim; see *Commission v UK (UHT Milk)* **(124/81)** and *Commission v Germany (German Beer Purity Law)* **(178/84)**. In the latter case it was not contested that the prohibition on the marketing of beers containing additives fell within the definition of a measure having equivalent effect to a quantitative restriction in present **Art 34 TFEU** but the German Government argued instead that it was justified, under present **Art 36 TFEU**, on public health grounds. The Court of Justice held that the use of a given additive—which was permitted in another Member State, was tested and found safe by international scientific research, in particular the work of the World Health Organization, and was present in the eating habits in the country of importation—did not constitute a danger to public health. Certain of the additives used in beers from other Member

[5] Careful selection then of cases is vital, and do not include lists of cases for the same point when one will do.

States were permitted in Germany in the manufacture of almost all drinks other than beer. Therefore, there must be a real danger to human health, the alleged harmful effects must be proved, and the additives must be banned in all products. It is thus unlikely therefore that this ban will be acceptable, unless it meets those strict requirements laid down by the Court of Justice.

The second problem concerns the ban on the grounds that the term 'yoghurt' cannot be used to describe frozen yoghurt. If not excused or justified, this will also be a breach of **Art 34 TFEU**. This time, however, the justification for the prohibition is not made on the basis of **Art 36 TFEU** but based on the new consumer protection law. As the rules appear to apply to both imports and domestic products and consumer protection lies outside the list of derogations in **Art 36 TFEU** the case law of the Court of Justice, notably thè case of *Cassis de Dijon* **(120/78)**, must be considered. The Court held that Member States are allowed to impose restrictive mandatory rules provided they apply to both imports and domestic products and providing certain criteria were met. This rule has become known as the rule of reason. The criteria are that the measure must not be covered by an EU system of rules, it must be proportionate, and it must not be an arbitrary restriction or a disguised discrimination.

Thus, the question that must be asked is whether the measure applies to national and imported frozen products equally and whether a more appropriate measure could protect the consumer. The *German Beer Purity Law* case, *Commission* v *Germany* **(178/84)**, and the *Italian Pasta Purity Law* case, *Drei Glocken GmnH* v *USL -Centro-sud* **(407/85)**, would be applicable here. It was held that protection would be equally, if not better, served by appropriate labelling together with an indication of the sell-by date, to guarantee consumer information. Hence, unless the measures meet the above, they will not be acceptable. There is a case concerned with deep-frozen yoghurt in which the insistence of the French authorities that it be given a different description from yoghurt was held to be capable of infringing **Art 34 TFEU**; see *Smanor* **(298/87)**.[6]

[6] This is an actual case dealing with frozen yoghurts but you would not be required to know this or indeed to know it in order to answer the question effectively.

The aspects concerned with the muesli involve a consideration of both measures and charges having equivalent effect. Are these 'spot checks' for health reasons prohibited under **Art 34 TFEU** or permitted under **Art 36 TFEU**? Provided they are only random spot checks and they take place with the same frequency as checks on the equivalent domestic product, they will be acceptable. They must not be an arbitrary discrimination or a disguised restriction on trade. They are also subject to the principle of proportionality; see *Commission* v *France (Italian Table Wines)* **(42/82)** and *Commission* v *UK (UHT Milk)* **(124/81)**. The checks in this case appear disproportionate and discriminatory because they are systematic and excessive.

The charges for the checks are argued to be an equivalent tax and it must first be considered whether they are. If not an acceptable tax, it then needs to be considered whether they are then an acceptable or unacceptable charge prohibited by **Arts 28–30 TFEU**.

[7] Furthermore, it must be considered whether the charges are in fact non-discriminatory taxation or charges contrary to the Treaty.

Consideration of the internal tax argument[7]

Article 110 TFEU allows internal taxes to be imposed on imports as long as it is the equivalent of an internal tax and is not discriminatory in its application. In **Denkavit v France (132/78)**, it was held that the tax to which an imported product is subject must be imposed at the same rate on the same product, must be imposed at the same marketing stage, and the chargeable event giving rise to the duty must be the same for both products. The chargeable event here is different because, if a tax, it would be on distribution, whereas the domestic product would be taxed pre-production, and thus would not come within the provisions of **Art 110 TFEU**.

If not a tax, is it a charge?

It must now be considered whether the fee imposed is an unlawful charge. **Commission v Italy (Statistical Levy) (24/68)** defined a charge having equivalent effect to include 'any pecuniary charge, however small and whatever its designation and mode of application, which is imposed unilaterally on domestic or foreign goods by virtue of the fact that they cross a frontier', and which is not a customs duty in the strict sense. The Court held that 'such a charge is a charge having equivalent effect even if it is not imposed for the benefit of the Member State concerned, even if it is not discriminatory or protective in effect and even if the product on which it is imposed is not in competition with any domestic product'.

Under certain conditions charges may be acceptable. If they are health checks with a legal basis in EU law, they may be charged for; see **Commission v Germany (Health Inspections) (18/87)**. They cannot be regarded as charges having effect equivalent to customs duties if: the fees do not exceed the cost of the actual inspections in respect of which they are charged; the inspections in question are mandatory and uniform for all the products in question in the EU; the inspections are provided for by EU law in the interests of the EU; and the inspections promote the free movement of goods. It would seem unlikely that EU law would be the basis of these inspections, particularly as the inspections appear to be breaching **Art 34 TFEU**, and therefore the charges in this case do not meet the criteria and thus would appear to breach **Art 28 TFEU**.

The parking fees will also be held to be charges having equivalent effect to customs duties, prohibited by **Art 28 TFEU**; see two cases concerned with customs warehouses, **Commission v Belgium (314/82)** and the **Marimex case (29/72)**.

Conclusion

In conclusion, none of the products could be restricted lawfully under EU law.

LOOKING FOR EXTRA MARKS?

■ If there is time, a longer look at the *German Beer Purity Law* case, *Commission* v *Germany* (**178/84**) would be beneficial.

■ Also if there is time, expand the conclusion to go through each of the issues and conclusions point by point.

QUESTION | 3

How, why, and with what success did the Court of Justice 'clarify' the scope of application of **Art 34 TFEU** in *Keck and Mithouard* (**267 and 8/91**) and subsequent cases?

CAUTION

■ This is another question which might seem to invite you to write an 'all I know about Art 34 TFEU' answer. It is required but that is just one part of a more complex question and answer.

■ This question very much concerns the *Cassis de Dijon* case. It is not explicit but the clarification provided by *Keck* was to the ruling in *Cassis*.

DIAGRAM ANSWER PLAN

Define **Art 34 TFEU** and its expanding scope of application through *Cassis de Dijon*

▼

Outline the reasons why the *Keck* judgment was considered necessary

▼

Consider what *Keck* was supposed to achieve

▼

Consider subsequent cases to see if it had the desired effect

▼

Summarise the present state of the law after these developments

[1] This question concerns the case law development of one of the central elements of the free movement of goods regime provided by the TFEU.

Free movement of goods and Art 34 TFEU[1]

The free movement of goods has been declared to be one of the fundamental policies of the Common Market and hence the EU. As a result, the Court of Justice adopted a liberal interpretation of the freedoms to allow goods to circulate freely in the EU and at the same time adopted a restrictive approach to measures enacted by the Member State which impinge on these freedoms. Article 34 TFEU prohibits quantitative restrictions and all measures having the equivalent effect.[2] This prohibition has been progressively interpreted by the Court of Justice, most notably through the case of *Procureur du Roi* v *Dassonville* (8/74), to include essentially any measure which makes import or export unnecessarily difficult and which discriminates between domestic products and imported products.

[2] Start with an introduction to the free movement of goods and a definition of **Art 34 TFEU** then run through the development of the confusion over its scope and application.

However, **Art 34 TFEU** prohibits not only national rules that overtly discriminate against imported products; subject to the possibility of justification under **Art 36 TFEU**, it may also be used to challenge national rules which on their face make no distinction between domestic and imported goods and are termed equally or indistinctly applicable.[3]

[3] Look at the case law development after *Cassis de Dijon* (120/78) and consider the judgment in *Keck and Mithouard* (C-267 and 268/91), and subsequent cases.

The *Cassis de Dijon* case **(120/78)** took *Dassonville* further by showing that these indistinctly applicable rules could also breach **Art 34 TFEU** by their dual burden effect. This is where the imported product has to comply with two sets of product requirements in order to be marketed lawfully in the state of import—those operated by the state of origin and those of the state of importation, placing an additional burden on the import, e.g. the *Rau Margarine* case **(261/81)** requirement that margarine be marketed in a different shape container in the host state from the home state such that a separate production line would have to be set up for the Belgium market.

[4] Any answer to this question must start with a consideration of the *Cassis* case as it is pivotal not only to this answer but the whole area of law and the development of **Article 34 TFEU**.

The *Cassis de Dijon* case[4]

The case of *Cassis de Dijon* had started to cause the CoJ problems because it was seized on both by Member States to justify restrictions and by traders to attack virtually any nationally imposed restriction on trade practices or commercial freedom, particularly to get round national laws which were not just aimed directly at imports and which actually were serving another genuine purpose not connected with trying to restrict free movement of goods. Hence, **Art 34 TFEU** slowly extended through court action to cover so-called 'Equal Burden' measures which are neither directly nor indirectly discriminatory and where the same requirement applies to both without adding an additional burden on the imports.

[5] These cases demonstrate that perhaps the ruling from *Cassis* was being taken too far and being applied to matters which were not really intended to be prohibited by **Art 34 TFEU**.

See, as good examples of these, rules relating to Sunday trading in the UK:[5] *Torfaen BC* v *B & Q plc* (**Cases 145/88, [1989] ECR 3851, [1990] 3 CMLR 455**) and *B & Q Ltd* v *Shrewsbury BC* (**[1990] 3 CMLR 535**), and protecting the film industry in France: *Cinéthèque* (**60–61/84**).

The CoJ recognised that traders were using Community (now EU) law to challenge laws which were not aimed at restricting imports but in fact restricted the sales of all goods without regard to origin, e.g. the Sunday trading laws in the UK, many of which were enacted in Victorian times for then understandable reasons far from any consideration of the EU and free movement of goods.

[6] The *Keck* case was regarded as a correcting case to stop the abuses of **Art 34 TFEU** by traders seizing on any national rule and arguing that it prevented imports and was thus a breach of **Art 34 TFEU**.

The *Keck* case re-alignment[6]

When presented with a suitable occasion, the CoJ was able to reconsider the case development in this area.[7] In **Cases C–267 & 268/91** *Keck and Mithouard*, the French prohibition of goods sold at a loss was argued to be a restriction of sales and thus imports and thus like the earlier Sunday trading and videos cases, contrary to **Art 34 TFEU**. The rule, though, affected all goods. Hence the CoJ singled out selling or marketing arrangements as not coming within the concept outlined in *Dassonville* or **Art 34 TFEU** and held that, providing national rules do not impede access to markets but merely regulate them without discrimination, either direct or indirect, they will be acceptable, i.e. such rules therefore fall outside the scope of **Art [34]** of the Treaty. However, there were problems with the *Keck* judgment and instead of clarifying the law as was hoped, it raised more questions than provided answers, including what was actually overruled and what are 'selling arrangements'?

[7] This is the 'why' part of the question. The 'how' simply relates to outlining the judgment in *Keck* itself.

[8] This concept then becomes central to the development post-*Keck*.

The meaning of selling arrangements[8]

Selling arrangements are broadly defined as rules relating to the market circumstances in which the goods are sold. They are measures dealing with where, when, how, and by whom goods may be sold, e.g. **Cases C-401 and 402/92,** *Tankstation't Heustke*[9] accepting Dutch laws concerning the times and places at which petrol could be sold. There may be all sorts of good reasons behind this: making safety paramount, ensuring petrol supplies in country or remote areas by restricting sales outlets—i.e. guaranteeing a wider catchment area and thus sales. see *Commission* v *Greece* (**C-391/92**) in which the Greek prohibition of the sale of any processed milk for babies other than in pharmacies was accepted.

[9] This case and a number of other cases are certainly examples of selling arrangements but do they really clarify what was meant by it—which leads us up to the answering the final part of the question.

There appeared, however, cases which showed that some selling arrangements hindered market access or acted in a manner which favoured domestic or disadvantaged imports such as rules on marketing, advertising, and sales promotion which can be problematic.

These difficulties have led slowly to the development of a test of market access discrimination.

Market access and differential impact[10]

Selling arrangements are not automatically outside, but it is a rebuttable presumption and the question posed is whether the national selling arrangement prevents access to the market or impedes access any more than it impedes the access of domestic products.

See **Cases C-34–36/95** *Konsumenten–ombudsmannen* v *De Agostini* in which TV advertising directed at children under 12 was prohibited; however, other ads were allowed. The measure was considered to be a selling arrangement which applied without discrimination, thus equal burden. However, it was held that would seem to have a greater impact on products from other Member States because of the difficulties faced in trying to get access to the market, advertising being the only effective form of promotion. If the national court found that the impact of the prohibition was different it would therefore breach **Art 34 TFEU** unless justified by **Art 36 TFEU** or the mandatory requirements under *Cassis*.

In the subsequent **Case C-405/98** *Gourmet International*, a ban on alcohol advertising was challenged under the same argument that it had a greater impact on imported products trying to gain access to the Swedish market because, without advertising, consumers would only be familiar with domestic products. Thus it was held that the measure would be caught by **Art 28 EC Treaty (now 34 TFEU)** if it prevents access to the market by products from another state, or impedes access any more than it impedes access of domestic products.

In the *Heimdienst* case **(C-254/98)**, a non-discriminatory Austrian law which applied to all operators trading in the national territory (Austrian and other EU) required goods sold on the doorstep to come from a locally established premises. It was held to be a selling arrangement but one which impeded access to the market of the Member State of importation for products from other Member States more than it impeded access for domestic products.

This has been termed a test of differential impact, i.e. affecting imports more than domestic products. Thus cases involving situations which, although classified as certain selling arrangements, have a different burden on imported goods, albeit that some domestic goods might also be affected, breach **Art 34 TFEU** and to be saved, must be justified. The 'Market Access' development was considered in the 2010 article by Snell.[11]

So, the first assumptions after *Keck* were that all selling arrangements fell outside **Art 34 TFEU**. There followed a correction to bring back into **Art 34 TFEU** any selling arrangements which were in fact discriminatory in either law or fact which, whilst not actually preventing imports, hindered or restricted them in some way and which would therefore be caught by **Art 34 TFEU** unless justified under *Cassis* such as the advertising cases. It means though that each case must be carefully assessed on its own facts for how, if at all, the market for the imported goods is disturbed by the national rule.

The clarification in *Keck*, it seems, has led instead to further uncertainties in this complex and developing area of law.[12]

✚ LOOKING FOR EXTRA MARKS?

- Not strictly necessary, but it would show you are up to date with developments and if time would be to add this following section before the final conclusion, which would remain the same:

Finally, or finally thus far in the post-*Keck* case law, are cases of a further development dealing with so called 'residual rules' which concern the use of products. These have added yet another gloss on the free movement rules. They concern restrictions on the use of products, which have nevertheless been lawfully produced and marketed and which are known as 'residual rules'. Typical of these cases is *Commission* v *Italy* (Trailers) (C-110/05), in which a ban on mopeds towing trailers was held to have a significant impact on the marketing of such trailers and thus import of trailers and was therefore in breach of **Art 34 TFEU**. However, in this case the road safety argument could justify the measure especially as there was no EU common rule on this activity. In *Aklagaren* v *Mickelsson and Roos* (C-142/05), the Swedish ban on the use of jet-skis, was held to be a MHEE but justified on the grounds of the protection of health and life and environmental protection. However, as the ban was a general one and not confined to waterways where jet-ski use constituted a threat to humans, it was held to be disproportionate. Hence at the end of these developments post-*Keck*, any measures which either hinder access to the market via a differential (discriminatory) impact or residual rules which impact on market access without discrimination may also breach Art 34 TFEU, but equally may be justified. These cases were considered by Spaventa in a 2009 article.

Ⓠ QUESTION | 4

The Government of Spain has been concerned about the use of e-cigarettes and has introduced a ban on the use of them in all government and public buildings. Their use in non-public buildings has not been included in the ban as this would require a public statute for which there is no parliamentary time. Instead it has issued Guidelines which advise the owners and occupiers of all buildings open to the public to decide whether to introduce their own ban. As a consequence the overall use of e-cigarettes has been significantly reduced. Their import, sale, and marketing are all permissible and have not been affected; 95 per cent of e-cigarettes are imported and only 5 per cent are manufactured in Spain.

The largest importer of e-cigarettes in Spain, Nico Teen (NT), has complained to the government ministry responsible for the ban and asked for an explanation for the measures. The minister has cited health grounds and that their unrestricted use may cause confusion amongst consumers. There is presently no EU ban on their use, although it has been discussed in the EP and considered by the Commission.

Nico Teen considers that the ban infringes the free movement of goods and asks your advice before deciding what action it may take.

CAUTION

- This problem question focuses on the more recent series of cases concerned with use of product bans or restrictions, hence you must be confident that these have been covered adequately in your EU law course.

- It is also quite cryptic in that it states your advice is sought before deciding what action the company may take, which invites you to advise them on the possible actions they might be able to take. Not to answer this part would miss valuable marks.

DIAGRAM ANSWER PLAN

Identify the issues	■ Identify the facts which give rise to legal issues, which is essentially the ban on the use of e-cigarettes in public buildings
Relevant law	■ Introduce area of law and attitude of the CoJ to prohibitions and exceptions ■ **Arts 34, 36 TFEU, Directive 70/50,** and the ***Dassonville*** case
Apply the law	■ Consider issues against the case law of **Arts 34 and 36 TFEU** and ***Cassis de Dijon*** ■ Consider the post-***Cassis*** and ***Keck*** case law
Conclude	■ With the aid of relevant cases, reach conclusions on all the issues

A   SUGGESTED ANSWER

[1] You are asked to comment on the ban on the use of e-cigarettes which may come under EU law provisions on the free movement of goods.

[2] Briefly outline the free movement of goods and that the Court of Justice, if it considered these bans, would interpret the provisions with the aims of the Union in mind, and any restrictions allowed the Member States, restrictively.

Introduction[1]

The free movement of goods has been declared to be one of the fundamental policies of the original Common Market and hence now the Union.[2] As a result, the Court of Justice has adopted a liberal interpretation of the freedoms to allow goods to circulate freely in the Union and at the same time adopted a restrictive approach to measures enacted by the Member States which impinge on these freedoms.

[3] Hence, you should identify the material facts, and outline the applicable law to discuss the issues that arise and the likely outcome of the case.

[4] Analysis of the facts is crucial here. The material facts are the ones which may alter the outcome of the case and here it is material that the ban is not discriminatory and not total. See answer for the details.

[5] The principal and initial provision to consider is **Art 34 TFEU** which prohibits quantitative restrictions on imports.

[6] **Art 36 TFEU** which allows the Member States to restrict imports for specific reasons and these include the protection on health grounds of humans and animals.

[7] You should therefore consider whether the bans might come within **Art 34 TFEU**.

The facts[3] and issues

There is one major issue to be decided in this answer and some consequences which flow from this. This is the ban on the use of e-cigarettes in public buildings.[4] The ban is not on imports and it is not total so the issue is whether this amounts to a measure having equivalent effect of an import ban under **Art 34 TFEU**. If it does, it has then further to be considered if there are grounds by which the measure may be justified under **Art 36 TFEU**, which provides a number of grounds by which a Member State can lawfully hinder imports including the protection of life and health of humans and animals or be excused under reasons recognised by the Court of Justice in case law.

The law[5]

Article 34 is the starting point for this answer but **Art 36 TFEU**[6] and the case law of the Court of Justice, notably *Dassonville* and *Cassis de Dijon*, are also crucial to the answer.

The reasoning and application

The ban on the use of e-cigarettes is not a prohibition on imports so it is not certain it comes within the terms of **Art 34 TFEU**;[7] however, both **Directive 70/50** and the case of *Dassonville* (8/74) have made it clear that the scope of matters that may be caught by **Art 34 TFEU** is very wide. This issue comes within a set of rules which relate to the use of products and are known as 'residual rules'. These are rules which are indistinctly applicable; are not product requirements or selling arrangements; do appear to hinder access to markets but not in a discriminatory way; but may nevertheless still, potentially if not actually, hinder imports. In our case the ban affects both imports and domestically produced e-cigarettes. Such bans will therefore breach **Art 34 TFEU** unless justified either by **Art 36 TFEU** or the rule of reason from *Cassis de Dijon*. See *Commission v Portugal* (C-265/06), which involved Portugal banning the fixing of tinted film on vehicle windows. It applied to both imports and domestic products so was indistinctly applicable. The Court of Justice found that the impact of the ban on potential purchasers would probably reduce imports. **Directive 70/50, Art 3**, provides that bans which apply both to imports and domestic products may also infringe **Art 34 TFEU**. The products would have a smaller and less attractive market. It was therefore considered a measure having equivalent effect (MHEE) and thus in breach of **Art 34** but could be justified.

It does not matter that the ban on use is partial as from the facts it has had a significant impact in reducing the use of e-cigarettes and, as most of them are imported, this would probably actually rather than just potentially affect imports.

[8] Then you should determine whether the reasons given by Spain will be held to be justified under **Art 36 TFEU** or under any other justification.

[9] Not all the grounds stated by the Spanish Government are mentioned in **Art 36 TFEU**, only the health grounds.

Can the ban be justified though on the grounds cited by the Spanish minister?[8] The measures can be argued to be justified on the grounds that it is protecting the health and life of humans[9] and animals included in **Art 36 TFEU**. However, the second sentence of **Art 36 TFEU** does not allow a health ban to be an arbitrary discrimination or a disguised restriction. To rely on this, it must be proved by those relying on the ban that a threat to life and health exists. This case is therefore similar to the bans of products on health grounds, most notably in the purity cases; see *Commission v Germany (Beer and Sausage Purity)* **(178/84 and 274/87)** which made it clear that where health was cited as a ground, there must be clear scientific evidence to support it. In our case, none is cited, so we must conclude that on that aspect the Member State fails. The measure must also be proportionate. It is not, though, a complete ban and one might argue that if e-cigarettes are a genuine threat to health, nothing less than a complete ban would be the correct measure to take.

The ban appears not to conform with the second sentence of **Art 36 TFEU** and appears to be a breach of **Art 34 TFEU**.

[10] The protection against the confusion of consumers is not contained in **Art 36 TFEU** and the case of *Cassis de Dijon* **(120/78)** must therefore be considered.

Such bans can, however, also be justified on other grounds,[10] in the case stated to be consumer protection, which is not covered by **Art 36 TFEU**, but may nevertheless be excused if it meets criteria established by the Court of Justice in case law. The case of *Cassis de Dijon* **(120/78)** and subsequent case law have added to the grounds by which the Member States may lawfully restrict the free movement of goods. The measure taken must, however, apply on an equal footing with domestic products. In the case of *Cassis de Dijon*, the Court of Justice stated that, in the absence of harmonising EU rules, obstacles to the free movement of goods may be allowed as far as these provisions are justified by an objective of public interest taking precedence over the free movement of goods. Mandatory requirements of the Member State could be imposed to relate in particular to:

- the effectiveness of fiscal supervision
- the protection of public health
- the fairness of commercial transactions
- the defence of the consumer.

However, the measures are subjected to further requirements:

- they must be justified and proportional, i.e. necessary to achieve results and not arbitrary
- there is no EU system of rules
- there must be neither an arbitrary discrimination nor a disguised restriction on trade.

Thus, if measures which are adopted by a Member State satisfy either the provisions of **Art 36 TFEU** or the requirements laid down in the case of *Cassis de Dijon* for mandatory requirements, the Member State will be able, lawfully, to hinder the free movement of goods. It must therefore be established that the interest cited by the Member State as the ground for the ban on use comes within the reasons acceptable to the Court of Justice. The ground stated was recognised by the CoJ as an interest which comes within the scope of the ruling in the *Cassis de Dijon* case (120/78) and the principle of the rule of reason but the measure is not mandatory and thus may not be acceptable to the CoJ.

It must, though, be established whether it satisfies the criteria established by the CoJ in the *Cassis de Dijon* case:

- It must apply to both imports and domestic products
- There must not be in force an applicable EU system
- The measure must not be a disguised restriction on trade or an arbitrary discrimination
- It must meet the requirements of proportionality.

In the limited case law on this, *Commission v Italy* (Trailers) (C-110/05), involving a ban on mopeds towing trailers, was held to have a significant impact on the marketing of such trailers and thus import of trailers and was therefore in breach of **Art 34 TFEU**. However, a road-safety argument was held to be able to justify the measure especially as there was no EU common rule on this activity. In *Aklagaren v Mickelsson and Roos* (C-142/05), the Swedish ban on the use of jet-skis, was held to be a MHEE but justified on the grounds of the protection of health and life and environmental protection. However, as the ban was a general one and not confined to waterways where jet-ski use constituted a threat to humans, it was held to be disproportionate. These cases were considered by Spaventa in a 2009 article.[11]

[11] Cited in the following sections and the 'Taking Things Further' Section at the end of the Chapter.

From the facts of the present case, it is not a mandatory requirement but it does apply to both imports and domestic products and it is stated that there is not an EU regime on the matter, therefore it is to be concluded that these aspects are satisfied. It does not appear to be an arbitrary discrimination but it might not meet the requirement of proportionality, thus it appears that the ban is acting as a disguised restriction on imports and thus contrary to **Art 34 TFEU**.

Conclusion

The overall conclusion is rather mixed. On the face of it, the ban would appear to infringe **Art 34 TFEU** and not be excused by either **Art 36 TFEU** or the rule of reason from *Cassis de Dijon*. A comparison with real cigarettes and various bans on their use in public does not help because there is clear scientific evidence that they are seriously damaging to health. There is no similar body of scientific evidence for or against e-cigarettes. Thus Nico Teen would be best advised to encourage the Commission to consider the ban and possibly take action against Spain. It may also be possible, if it has suffered losses as a result, to take the Spanish Government before the national courts to see if it might obtain damages under the *Francovich* state liability principle.

LOOKING FOR EXTRA MARKS?

■ As this is a yet and still developing area of law and thus a bit uncertain, access to academic articles would help, such as Wenneras, P and Boe Moen, K, 'Selling Arrangements, Keeping *Keck*' (2010) 35 EL Rev 387 or Spaventa, E. 'Leaving Keck Behind? The Free Movement of Goods after the Rulings in Commission v Italy and Micklesson and Roos' (2009) 34 EL Rev 914. These confirm essentially that the law is still in flux, so if you are unable to reach firm conclusions, this is not your fault, it is where we presently are.

TAKING THINGS FURTHER

■ Barnard, C, *The Substantive Law of the EU: The Four Freedoms*, 4th edn (Oxford: Oxford University Press, 2013), chs 2-4.
These chapters provide a very good overview on the whole area of the free movement of goods.

■ Jansson, M and Kalimo, H, '*De Minimis* Meets "Market Access": Transformation in the Substance-and the Syntax-of EU Free Movement Law?' (2014) 51 CML Rev 523.
This article considers recent developments in this difficult area of law.

■ Snell, J, 'The Notion of Market Access: A Concept or Slogan?' (2010) 47 CML Rev 437.
Considers the development of the 'market access' group of cases.

■ Spaventa, E, 'Leaving Keck Behind? The Free Movement of Goods after the Rulings in Commission v Italy and Micklesson and Roos' (2009) 34 EL Rev 914.
Looks at the development of the 'use of' cases.

■ Wenneras, P and Boe Moen, K, 'Selling Arrangements, Keeping *Keck*' (2010) 35 EL Rev 387.
This article considers recent developments in this difficult area of law.

■ Wilsher, D, 'Does *Keck* Discrimination Make Any Sense? An Assessment of the Non-discrimination Principle within the European Single Market' (2008) 33 EL Rev 3.
As identified in the 'Are you Ready' Feature, the **Cassis de Dijon** *case, and the development of the rule of reason from that case, continues to cause difficulties.*

Online Resources   www.oup.com/uk/qanda/

Go online for extra essay and problem questions, a glossary of key terms, online versions of all the answer plans and audio commentary on how selected ones were put together, and a range of podcasts which include advice on exam and coursework technique and advice for other assessment methods.

The Free Movement of Persons

7

ARE YOU READY?

In order to attempt questions in this chapter, you must have covered all of these topics in both your work over the year and in revision:

- The free movement of workers, the freedom of establishment, and freedom to provide services; all of which are dealt with within the **Treaty (Arts 45–62)** and Union Citizenship **(Arts 20–25 TFEU)**.

- Citizenship is the new big area of law so I have included questions on this and, as will be seen in the answers, highlight the leading cases including the *Sala* and *Grzelczyk* cases **(C-85/96 and C-184/99)**, *Metock* **(C-127/08)**, *Zambrano* **(C-34/09)**, *O, S & L* **(C-356-7/11)**, *Avello* **(C-148/02)**, *Chen* **(C-200/02)**.

- Questions may concentrate on any one of the topics above or might involve a combination of any two or all of them.

KEY DEBATES

Debate: the shift of emphasis from the rights of the economic active workers and self-employed, to citizenship.

More recently the case law of the CoJ has focused on the rights which result from the very fact of being an EU citizen without the need for economic activity on the part of the rights' holder. This is becoming a much more integral part of this topic because much of the case law now does not focus on whether a person is a worker or self-employed but on citizenship and what that means. Indeed, the main provision of secondary legislation in this area, **Directive 2004/38**, is known as the Citizenship Directive, even though it applies and provides rights also for the economically active.

The Court of Justice of the EU (CoJ) has interpreted the provisions of **Arts 45–62 TFEU** and the secondary legislation in a more liberal manner than would be dictated by a purely functional view of the Treaty based on its economic motives.

Discuss.

CAUTION

- The secondary legislation in this area of law has been overhauled and the most important acts are **Directive 2004/38**, on the right of citizens of the Union and their family members to move and reside freely within the territory of the Member States, and **Regulation 492/2011**. These have replaced and repealed most of the previous secondary legislation in this area. Case law, though, will often still refer to the now repealed acts.

- This is a very wide question and covers the topics of the free movement of workers, the freedom of establishment, and the freedom to provide services. You must therefore plan carefully to make sure you are covering relevant material.

DIAGRAM ANSWER PLAN

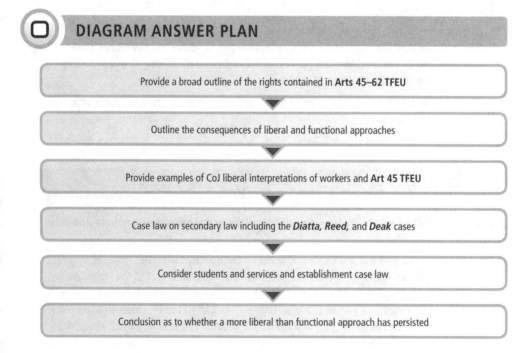

Provide a broad outline of the rights contained in **Arts 45–62 TFEU**

⬇

Outline the consequences of liberal and functional approaches

⬇

Provide examples of CoJ liberal interpretations of workers and **Art 45 TFEU**

⬇

Case law on secondary law including the *Diatta*, *Reed*, and *Deak* cases

⬇

Consider students and services and establishment case law

⬇

Conclusion as to whether a more liberal than functional approach has persisted

[1] The answer could be structured in two ways. The first would be to consider the functional economic view and then give examples of the Court's liberal interpretations. Alternatively, give the examples first from case law of the liberal interpretations and compare these with how a purely functional view would look.

[2] Start though with reviewing the Treaty Articles covered by the question.

[3] The range of legislation noted in the question is very wide. It would be too time-consuming to go through every provision, so you have to take an overall view.

[4] Discuss the view that the Court of Justice has been liberal in its interpretation of the provisions and the fact that this leads to quite different consequences from the CoJ taking a purely functional view of the economic motives of the Treaty.

[5] The functional view appears to be restricted to considering Treaty Articles and secondary provisions and it would seem best to take an overview of the Treaty objectives and then select examples from the provisions.

[6] The liberal interpretation could be demonstrated by an overview and then by explaining selective examples.

The scope of Arts 45–62 TFEU[1]

Articles 45–62 TFEU cover the areas of the free movement of workers, freedom of establishment, and the freedom to provide services.[2] The free movement of persons has been described as one of the fundamental foundations of the Union but the reason it may be so described is not obvious. Two main grounds might be given. One is that it is fundamental because the area assists the economic goals of the Union in establishing an internal market in which all factors of production can freely circulate. Alternatively, the view might be taken that the aims for these areas of EU law are to improve the opportunities and working conditions of the individuals in the work forces of the Member States. A third alternative is that it is a combination of both the above.

Essentially, the Treaty Articles in the question[3] provide that workers and the self-employed can take up employment opportunities in the other Member States without discrimination on the grounds of nationality. Furthermore, they should enjoy the same rights and benefits granted in such circumstances to nationals but certain restrictions may be made in respect of employment in the public service. These basic rights can be viewed, then, in two ways.[4]

The functional view[5]

A purely functional view might be that the economic motives are paramount and therefore it is only the economies of the EU and the Member State that are important. The granting of individual rights is incidental and just a way of ensuring that the commodity of labour can be imported and exported to suit the demands of European capital, and so that it can take advantage of the free market and can compete equally in attracting and securing labour. The personal rights given to workers are then secondary to the prime objectives in setting up the internal market and ensuring that business in the Member States are operating under the same rules. Under this view, it would be expected that the rights would be subject to the minimum interpretation possible to give effect to the rights granted. For example, there would be no right to be in other Member States whilst unemployed and looking for work; the Member States would have complete freedom to discriminate in the public service, or rights would not be extended to members of the family or to students.

The liberal view[6]

The contrasting view is that of the liberal interpretation. The CoJ clearly interprets all parts of the Treaty in a distinct style using the so-called teleological approach. This means that specific measures are interpreted in the light of the objectives and goals of the Union and are not just subject to a literal interpretation of the words.

It is clear that in respect of the free movement of persons the CoJ has gone far beyond a literal or functional interpretation of the provisions and has, in its judgment, sought to give the widest possible scope to the rights provided. The following are examples and are not exhaustive.

Examples of generous interpretations[7]

[7] There are very many cases you can choose from as examples. It may be that in your course or module other cases have been highlighted which you could cite instead.

Article 45 TFEU and the secondary legislation have been held to provide the status of worker to those who are not employed in the host state and have entered for the express reason to search for work; see the *Antonnisson* (C-292/89) and *Lebon* (316/85) cases. The term 'worker' for the purposes of EU law also applies to those in part-time work and those who have worked only a few hours per week or were paid also in kind. See e.g. the cases of *Kempf v Staatssecretaris van Justitie* (139/85), *Lawrie-Blum v Land Baden-Würtemberg* (66/85), and *Steymann v Staatssecretaris van Justitie* (196/87). The cases of *Trojani* (C-456/02) and *Ninni-Orasche* (C-413/01) confirm the liberal view of the CoJ in respect of who can constitute a worker under the Treaty.

The general prohibition of discrimination contained in **Art 45** was considered in the *Alluè and Coonan v University of Venice* case **(33/88)** concerning two non-national language teachers employed by the University of Venice. It was held that discrimination in circumstances where the rule was being applied to both nationals and other EU citizens would still be present but affected the non-nationals indirectly; i.e. indirect discrimination is covered by **Art 45 TFEU**.

The exception, allowed to the Member States under the public service provision in **Art 45(4) TFEU**, has been restricted in two ways. First, once a worker is employed in the public service, there can be no discrimination in respect of the conditions of work and employment. Furthermore, entry is not restricted to levels of the public service which do not exercise power conferred by public law and safeguard the interests of the state. See the cases of *Sotgui v Deutsche Bundespost* **(152/73)** and *Commission v Belgium* **(149/79)**. Such restrictions on the Member States' ability are not to be perceived from a functional view of the provision.

When we turn to the secondary legislation, even more surprising interpretations can be cited as examples. Whilst it may be possible to perceive that a non-EU national spouse has the right to stay in a Member State after separation from the EU worker, as in *Diatta* **(267/83)**, it is unlikely that one would realise from the legislation that the rights to the same treatment in social matters would include the right to the companionship of a cohabitee; see *Netherlands v Reed* **(59/85)**. The case law on **Art 7(2) of Regulation 1612/68**, now replaced by **Regulation 492/2011**, has certainly demonstrated the very liberal interpretation that can be achieved by the CoJ. These include the right of members of the worker's family, regardless of nationality, to join the worker but also to claim various types of social security benefit to financially help them stay in the host state. See e.g. *Fiorini aka Christini* v *SNCF* (32/75) and *ONE* v *Deak* (94/84).

The Court has even accorded the status of worker, although not necessarily all of the benefits, to work-seekers in cases including *Lebon* (316/85), *Antonissen* (C-292/89), and *Collins* (C-138/02).

Finally, by way of example, is the extension of the term 'worker' to apply in specific circumstances to students, an interpretation which is not obvious from a reading of the appropriate provisions and took place even before the Directives granting rights of residence were passed by the Council in 1990 and before the citizenship rights of entry and residence were incorporated in the Treaties in 1993. See the cases of *Lair* v *Universität Hannover* (39/86) and *Bernini* v *Netherlands Ministry of Education and Science* (C-3/90).

[8] As the question is not restricted to workers, you should also include cases involving the self-employed and the provision and reception of services.

Furthermore, in respect of establishment and services,[8] the CoJ ruled that **Arts 49 and 56 TFEU** were capable of giving rise to direct effects, an interpretation which could not be expressly derived from the Articles. The fact that the CoJ did not see the need for completing legislation is a liberal interpretation; see the cases of *Reyners* (2/74) and *Van Binsbergen* (33/74).

With regard to the free movement of services, there was originally nothing in the Treaty to suggest its application to education or the receivers of services; but this has been achieved in a number of cases. For example, *Luisi* v *Ministero del Tesauro* (286/82) concerned a prosecution under Italian currency regulations for taking money out to pay for tourist and medical provisions abroad. These were held by the CoJ to be payments for services and thus coming under the provisions of the **EEC Treaty**, payments being a fundamental freedom of the Community (now **Arts 56 and 57 TFEU and 18 TFEU**). *Gravier* v *City of Liège* (293/83) concerned the decision that the fee charged to foreign students for vocational training courses but not to nationals was contrary to EU law. It is to be noted that **Directive 2004/38** has consolidated both most of the previous secondary legislation in these areas and the case law developments of the CoJ which built upon the statutory rights.

Conclusion

It can be seen from the above cases that there are good examples demonstrating that the CoJ has interpreted Articles and secondary legislation in a far more liberal manner than a functional view would dictate. Adding to this view now is the interpretation that the CoJ has been giving to the citizenship provisions (**Arts 20 and 21 TFEU**) in the cases of *Sala* (C-85/96) and *Grzelczyk* (C-184/99), and today many more cases which have extended Union citizens' rights into the areas of social and welfare law of the Member States.

(+) **LOOKING FOR EXTRA MARKS?**

■ You could mention that citizenship rights and case law are blurring the above boundaries and have provided very extensive rights, not dependent on an economic activity, and serve as further examples of the liberal interpretation of the CoJ, although citizenship is outlined in **Arts 20–25 TFEU** and not **Arts 45–62 TFEU,** which were the focus of this question. Hence, then, any inclusions must be only in addition to a full answer to the question.

■ Citing cases to back up the above would be good and the following are just three from many that could be chosen: *María Martínez Sala* (C-85/96), *Grzelczyk* (C-184/99), *Chen* (C-200/02).

(Q) | **QUESTION** | 2 |

Lister, a UK citizen, has moved to Denmark to take up employment in the Virtual Reality Computer Company (VRCC) as a technician. He is accompanied by his girlfriend Kristine, also a UK national, who is an expectant mother of twins. The claims she has made for unemployment benefit and maternity payments have been rejected by the authorities in Skive, the town where they have settled. The grounds given are that she is not a national and has not been resident for the required one year. Her claim that she is dependent on Lister is also rejected as she is not married to him and the authorities have now issued a deportation order against her.

Another UK national, Rimmer, has also obtained work as a technician in VRCC. Once settled, he is joined by his distant cousin, Cat, who is not a Union national. Cat attempts to claim unemployment benefit but is refused. The authorities, now aware of his presence, have issued him with a deportation order which only states that he has no right to remain in Denmark. On a visit to Rimmer's home, a quantity of drugs brought in by Cat was discovered. As a result, Rimmer is also issued with a deportation order, stating that the presence of persons in the possession of drugs is considered to be contrary to public policy.

Advise the parties as to their rights under EU law.

(!) **CAUTION**

■ The secondary legislation in this area of law has been overhauled and the most important acts are **Directive 2004/38**, on the right of citizens of the Union and their family members to move and reside freely within the territory of the Member States, and **Regulation 492/2011**. These have replaced and repealed most of the previous secondary legislation in this area. Case law, though, will often still refer to the now repealed acts.

■ Do not spend an inordinate amount of time proving that Lister or Rimmer are workers, as it is the rights of the others that are more problematic. You should, of course, state that they are workers but only briefly as this point is not contentious.

■ Avoid also entering into a discussion about how criminal law and procedure would regard the discovery of drugs in the home of Rimmer. Stick to the EU law issues at hand.

DIAGRAM ANSWER PLAN

Identify the issues	■ Identify the substantive and procedural facts which give rise to legal issues
Relevant law	Outline the area of law, CoJ approach, and **Art 45 TFEU**
Apply the law	■ Consider the procedural issues according to legislation and case law ■ Consider each substantive issue according to legislation and case law ■ The position of a worker's family and non-EU nationals must be considered ■ The substantive law on deportation must finally be considered
Conclude	■ Concluding summary

SUGGESTED ANSWER¹

¹This problem question on the free movement of persons concentrates to a large extent on the rights of persons connected to and dependent on the worker.

The free movement of workers is provided for in **Arts 45–48 TFEU**,² secondary EU law, and the case law of the Court of Justice. In this area of law, the CoJ has taken a line which has sought to promote and protect the freedoms available to individual workers and to restrict, where possible, the reasons by which the Member States can restrict those freedoms.

²Start with a general introduction to the area of law and the attitude of the CoJ to the rights provided and restriction allowed the Member States.

The facts³

The issues arising in this question are the deportation orders issued against Kristine, Cat, and Rimmer; the right of Kristine to remain and claim benefits; the right of Cat to remain and claim benefits; and the reasons given for deportation of Kristine, Cat, and Rimmer.

³If you used the plan matrix, you can simply extract the factual issues from that.

Deportation procedural rights⁴

⁴The rights of Rimmer and Cat facing deportation should be considered before moving on to consider the substantive rights at issue in the problem as this is of immediate concern to them.

Union citizens in such circumstances and members of the family who are given rights under other EU legislation are provided with rights not to be deported immediately, but to be allowed to stay for at least a month by **Art 30 of Directive 2004/38**. Whether they can stay longer depends on the facts of the case; e.g. whether they can stay to argue the substantive grounds of the deportation decision through the courts, which may take longer (see **Art 9 of Directive of**

2004/38 and the cases of *Adoui* and *Cornaille* (**115 and 116/81**) and *Pecastaing* (**98/79**)). However, they cannot be subject to immediate deportation. The grounds for deportation can be discussed later now that the immediate threat of deportation has been diverted.

Kristine's right to remain[5]

[5] You have to consider the rights of Kristine, the girlfriend of Lister, to stay and claim benefits.

The first substantive[6] consideration is that of the right of Kristine to stay in Denmark and claim unemployment and maternity benefits. It should first be noted that, as it is stated in the question that Lister has taken up employment and is a Union national, it can safely be concluded that he is a worker for the purposes of EU law. This point is more important for Kristine.

[6] This quite simply means the actual rights and not the procedural ones just considered.

First, however, it must be determined whether Kristine has any EU law rights under the free movement of persons.[7]

[7] This is because Kristine may have rights of her own and not just rights dependent of the status of Lister.

Kristine could be looking for work and would benefit from limited rights provided under **Art 45(3)(b) TFEU**, confirmed in the case of *Antonnisson* (**C-292/89**), that Union nationals have the right to enter a host state and stay for a limited period providing they are actively seeking work and there is a genuine chance of being engaged. Given the facts of the case it is unlikely that this conclusion could be reached; however, if she could prove these requirements, she should be given the right to stay for six months at least.

A second and probably stronger possibility exists under **Directive 2004/38, Arts 6 and 7**. Whilst **Art 6** provides that Union citizens have a right of residence for up to three months without condition, **Art 7** extends this beyond three months but subject to the EU citizen being covered by adequate sickness insurance, which Lister could provide, but also that they do not become a burden on the state. The facts do not reveal how long they have been in the host state but the claims she is making would seem to undermine the rights to claim the protection under **Art 7** of this Directive and it appears unlikely that it is applicable in her favour. However, case law has now determined that a person can be a reasonable burden (*Grzelczyk* (**C-184/99**)), which is ultimately up to the national court to decide, and that the resources of others is acceptable (*Commission v Belgium* (**C-408/03**)), which would seem to strengthen Kristine's case to stay.

The EU free movement of workers provisions not only give rights for the worker but also rights for the worker's family. **Directive 2004/38** provides the details of those who can claim rights by virtue of their relationship to the worker. The spouse and other members of the family are defined in **Arts 2 and 3**. The Directive extends the rights available to the worker to the spouse and descendants and ascendants regardless of nationality. The descendants can be any nationality and include those under 21 and adult children over 21 where they are dependent on the worker. **Directive 2004/38** includes non-married partners and this issue was also considered previously by the CoJ in the case of *Netherlands v Reed* (59/85). Reed applied for a residence permit in Holland claiming her right to remain was based on her cohabitation with a UK national working in the Netherlands. The Dutch Government refused to recognise this. The CoJ was aware that provisions of national laws regarding cohabitees' legal rights could be quite varied. It was unable to overcome the clear intention of **Art 10 of Regulation 1612/68** (now repealed) which referred to a relationship based on marriage. The Court referred instead to the 'social advantages' guaranteed under **Art 7(2)** of the Regulation (now same **Art in 492/2011**) as being capable of including the companionship of a cohabitee which could contribute to integration in the host country. Under the **2004/38 Directive, Art 3**, where such stable and registered partnership relationships amongst nationals were accorded the legal advantages under national law, these could not be denied to nationals of other Member States without being discriminatory and thus breaching **Arts 12 and 39** of the **EC Treaty (now 18 and 45 TFEU)** in addition to the Directive. **Directive 2004/38** will strengthen these rights by providing that partners, where officially recognised by the host state law, shall be equated with spouses in the host state (**Art 2**) and have the same rights to work, education, and social assistance.

Kristine's right to claim benefits

Therefore, as a cohabitee, or as a partner, Kristine would obtain residence rights to stay but can she claim benefits? There are a number of cases from the CoJ which have confirmed that a number of benefits may be claimed by members of the family. See, in respect of unemployment benefit, the case of *ONE v Deak* (94/84). Furthermore, it has been held that **Art 7(2)** also applies to maternity and childbirth allowances without discrimination; see *Commission v Luxembourg* (C-111/91). Her rights therefore depend on how a national cohabitee would be treated because, if possessing the right to stay, the general prohibition of discrimination under **Art 18 TFEU** would ensure that she should be treated the same. Provided that unemployment benefit and maternity rights were granted to the cohabitees of national workers, it is at least arguable that they would be extended to other Union cohabitees, but a certain result is unclear at this time and a reference to the CoJ would be advisable. The same considerations would seem to apply even under the **2004/38 Directive**.

[8]Likewise you must consider all of Cat's possible rights to stay and claim benefits.

Cat's right to stay[8]

A consideration of the legal position of Cat also involves a discussion of the rights provided in respect to non-immediate members of a worker's family. He is not a Union national and therefore cannot acquire his own right to stay. **Directive 2004/38, Art 3(2)** also provides that other family members, who are dependent on the Union citizen with primary right of residence, are to be afforded entry and residence rights but a reference would be advisable to the CoJ to confirm this.

A further argument, which is admittedly slim, to find a right for him to stay is that as cohabitee of Rimmer. Quite whether the CoJ would entertain this and whether the facts would allow this conclusion to be drawn are speculative and would certainly need a reference to the CoJ under **Art 267 TFEU**. This situation is covered by **Art 2(2)** of the **2004/38 Directive** as a registered partnership regarded as the equivalent of marriage in the host state. This can be examined by the host state and a reference may still be required to confirm if this is the correct interpretation of the Directive. Therefore, at present, there is no clear and direct obligation to allow Cat to remain, let alone to claim benefits. In the case of *Lebon* (316/85), a dependent who had the right to stay to find work could be classed as a worker for this purpose but not to be able to claim benefits. Other members of the family have, however, been able to claim benefits when their right to stay was established; see *Deak* (94/84).

[9] Although you have already covered deportation rights, those were the procedural rights; you must now consider whether Cat can actually be deported lawfully. The same will be asked of Lister in the next section.

Cat's deportation[9]

In this case, as the Member State is not obliged to let him stay, it is possibly the case that the possession of drugs would be sufficient excuse for the Member State to deport him, although the Member State has not given the reasons for the deportation, which they are required to do under **Art 30 of Directive 2004/38**. The Directive will only apply if Cat has a right to stay in the first place; if not, then deportation cannot be prevented. The deportation for drugs may well depend on the nature of the drugs involved. On balance, his rights to avoid deportation and stay are very weak.

Rimmer's deportation

The right to deport Rimmer would be subject to other considerations. **Article 27(2) of Directive 2004/38** provides that measures adopted on public policy or security must be based on personal conduct. In this case it appears not to be the personal conduct of Rimmer but that of Cat which have prompted the Member State to order deportation. Thus, as no other reasons are apparent, Denmark would not be justified under EU law in deporting Rimmer.

✚ LOOKING FOR EXTRA MARKS?

- If there is time, provide an overall summary chart of the various conclusions reached on each part of the answer.
- Also if there is time, further procedural rights might be included regarding the way in which the deportation is advised, rights to attend court and present your evidence, and the right to remain in the host country whilst doing so.

QUESTION | 3

Discuss the extent to which free movement of persons and citizenship in the EU legal order now allows EU citizens and their families to reside and obtain equal rights in any Member State of the EU.

! CAUTION

- The secondary legislation in this area of law has been overhauled and the most important acts are **Directive 2004/38**, on the right of citizens of the Union and their family members to move and reside freely within the territory of the Member States, and **Regulation 492/2011**. These have replaced and repealed most of the previous secondary legislation in this area. Case law, though, will often still refer to the now repealed acts.

- This is quite an open question, which allows you to effectively choose the areas of citizenship you write about which brings with it the danger of choosing too many and writing a long rambling answer, so be careful in your choice of material.

O DIAGRAM ANSWER PLAN

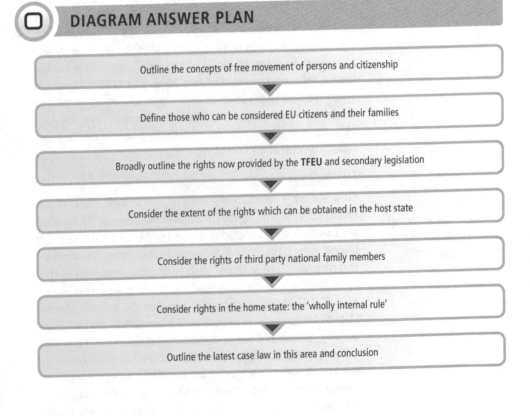

Outline the concepts of free movement of persons and citizenship

Define those who can be considered EU citizens and their families

Broadly outline the rights now provided by the **TFEU** and secondary legislation

Consider the extent of the rights which can be obtained in the host state

Consider the rights of third party national family members

Consider rights in the home state: the 'wholly internal rule'

Outline the latest case law in this area and conclusion

[1] This question asks for a discussion of a consideration of the economically active person, and any EU citizen and members of the family, who can be from outside the EU.

Outline of the legal regime for the free movement of persons and citizenship[1]

From the start, the EC (now EU) provided for the free movement of persons for workers and those wishing to establish or provide services in another Member State. These rights were granted in favour of the economically active and, with later secondary legislation such as **Regulation 1612/68 (now replaced by Regulation 492/2011)**, rights were also granted to members of that person's family. The legislation also envisaged that those seeking work could also obtain limited rights and this was confirmed by the CoJ in cases such as *Lebon* and *Antonisson* **(316/85 and C-292/99)**. Rights of entry and residence were extended to the non-economically active first by three general Directives in 1990 and then by the **Treaty of European Union** signed at Maastricht, through the introduction of the citizenship provisions to the **EC Treaty (Arts 17–22 (now 20–25 TFEU))**. Essentially, the rights provided are that the economically active worker or self-employed person who does nothing to offend the public policy or security of the host state has the right not only to reside and stay in the host state but also to bring with him or her other members of the family and to receive employment, social, and tax benefits on an equal basis as nationals of the host state. Members of the family also have extensive rights, whereas a person not economically active has general rights now provided by **Arts 20 and 21 TFEU** to move and reside in a host state subject to any existing restrictions on the free movement of persons in the EU legal order. This means that they must be adequately insured and do not become a burden on the social security systems of the host Member State.

[2] Consider the extent of the rights provided under EU law and whether these rights also apply in the home state and whether all rights can be enjoyed on a par with nationals in a host state.

EU citizenship[2]

EU citizenship is defined by reference to each Member State's definition of citizenship as agreed by the Member States in **Declaration No 2** on Nationality attached to the original **TEU**, although no longer present in the Declarations listed by the **Lisbon Treaty**. This provided that nationality shall be settled solely by reference to the national law of the Member State concerned and was upheld in the case of *Manjit Kaur* **(C-192/99)**, in which the CoJ held that it is for each Member State to lay down the conditions for the acquisition and loss of nationality. The case of *Chen* **(C-200/02)** further upholds this position.

Family members are not restricted to citizenship of the Union and may include persons from any country as many cases have previously demonstrated, e.g. *ONE* v *Deak* **(C-94/84)**, where the Hungarian (then not a Member State) son was also able to obtain social security benefits.

[3] It therefore requires a knowledge of Treaty and secondary law and the range of case decisions which has considerably extended EU law and far exceeds any legislative changes to the free movement of persons.

[4] Provide an outline of the cases in which the CoJ has stepped back from the previous very generous interpretation of citizens' rights.

[5] Noted in the 'Taking things Further' section at the end of the chapter.

[6] Consider whether in the home state of the EU citizen they can rely on EU law rights or whether the wholly internal rule still continues to apply which does not involve any cross-border element and thus falls entirely within national law.

Recent cases by the CoJ have provided a generous interpretation of the rights provided now.[3] For example, in the *Sala* and *Grzelczyk* cases **(C-85/96 and C-184/99)**, the CoJ held that citizenship required the Union citizen to be treated equally even where claiming non-contributory benefits providing they were not an unreasonable burden on the host state. In the light of these cases, it was considered that this would mean now that once lawfully resident in a host state, citizenship would require that all rights could be enjoyed on an equal basis with nationals, i.e. there would be complete equality before the law. However, in *Collins* **(C-132/02)**, and confirmed in *Ioannidis* **(C-258/04)**,[4] the CoJ has stepped back from confirming this position by following the AG in some of the recent cases in requiring that the EU citizen has some greater degree of connection or genuine link to the state than mere lawful residence to be able to claim all benefits on the same basis as nationals. This position is further confirmed in the cases of *Morgan and Bucher* **(C-11–12/06)**, *Förster v IB-Groep* **(C-158/07)**, and *Vatsouras and Koupatantze v ARGE Nürnberg* **(C-22 and 23/08)**. However, as held in *D'Hoop* **(C-224/98)**, any conditions on lawful residence in a host state which are argued to apply to EU citizens must be applied in a proportionate and non-discriminatory way. The development and extension of citizenship rights have been explored in the 2011 and 2012 articles by Hinarejos.[5]

Do EU citizens have EU law rights in any Member State?[6]

The early law on this demonstrates how a wholly internal rule appears to give rise to reverse discrimination because nationals are denied rights which EU nationals from another Member State can uphold. In the cases *Morson and Jhanjan v Netherlands* **(35 and 36/82)**, the applicants, both Surinamese nationals, claimed the right to stay in Holland with their Dutch national son and daughter working there. It was held by the CoJ that there was no application of Community (now EU) law to the wholly internal situation where national workers had not worked in any other Member State. However, because there was no movement from one Member State to another, Community (now EU) law did not apply and movement from a third country does not qualify.

More recent case law has weakened this position slightly. EU citizens who have moved across one of the Union internal borders and who have either provided or received services in the host state are able to take advantage of all EU law rights in both the host state and the home state when they return. For example, in *Surinder Singh* **(C-370/90)**, an Indian spouse of a British national was able to use EU law to derive a right of residence in the UK on the basis that the spouse had previously exercised the right of free movement by providing services in another Member State but then re-established herself in the UK. Further, in *Carpenter* (C-60/00), the CoJ held that even where there was no movement of the third country national spouse, she had the right to remain in the UK because the husband had provided services in another EU Member State. However, the situation has not yet arisen that all EU law rights can be enjoyed in the home state, unless some form of cross-border economic activity triggers those EU law rights. It is at the moment unclear just how minimum the activity needs to be; e.g. would supplying or ordering cross-border internet services allow an EU citizen to have a spouse from a third country join them and live in their home state? Only a preliminary ruling reference to the CoJ will adequately clear this up.

[7] Try to provide a balanced view of the developments thus far which have extended rights but have put a limit on that extension, as outlined in the case law in the answer.

Summary[7]

It is clear from the recent case law that EU law is now much more generous than was previously considered to be the case. This has also been backed up by a Directive which consolidates the previous legislation and case law and provides new rights. **Directive 2004/38** has, for example, extended the concept of family to that of the partner's family, where the partnership would be recognised in the host state as equivalent to marriage and will establish a right of permanent residence after five years for both EU citizens and third-country family members. However, the complete equality suggested by the question has not yet been established in EU law and a Member State may impose a time condition on getting all rights and benefits on an equal basis with nationals.

+ LOOKING FOR EXTRA MARKS?

- As this was such an open question there is considerable room for you to add material in the areas of the right to educational services, carer rights, further welfare rights, family rights.

- Additional cases could include: *Metock* (C-127/08), *Zambrano* (C-34/09), *O, S & L* (C-356-7/11), *Avello* (C-148/02), and *Chen* (C-200/02) according to how much time and space you have.

Q   QUESTION | 4

Roger is a Belgian national made involuntarily unemployed in Belgium who decides to spend some time in the UK using his redundancy money. He is questioned on entry to the UK about his intentions, financial state, and insurance and is allowed entry. He rents a large room in a guest house, where he is joined by his sister Auriana from Belgium and his cousin Benedicta from Turkey. He wants to stay long term in the UK but after 12 weeks his money was running out. He therefore applied for social security benefit and housing benefit to enable them to move out of the guest room into a house of their own. Both of these applications are refused.

Auriana is 16 and is physically and mentally disabled. She has applied for a place at a special needs school in the town. Roger applies for a non-contributory educational allowance for her which is refused by the local education authority.

Benedicta is 25 years old, has not worked at all previously and has applied for social benefit as a member of Roger's family. This is refused by the local authorities.

All three appeal against the decisions of the authorities on the grounds that they are being discriminated against in comparison with nationals. The local authorities wish to deport them as contrary to public policy because they have become a burden on the state.

Advise the parties of their rights under EU law.

Would your answer be any different if Roger claimed he was entitled to stay because of the services he had regularly received in the UK as a result of his extensive daily use of telephone sex lines?

! CAUTION

- The secondary legislation in this area of law has been overhauled and the most important acts are **Directive 2004/38**, on the right of citizens of the Union and their family members to move and reside freely within the territory of the Member States, and **Regulation 492/2011**. These have replaced and repealed most of the previous secondary legislation in this area. Case law, though, will often still refer to the now repealed acts.

- The structure of your answer is very important in identifying and dealing with the various issues arising from the scenario. To help, I have provided a matrix or blueprint which separates and highlights these.

DIAGRAM ANSWER PLAN

Identify the issues	▪ Identify the facts which give rise to legal issues
Relevant law	▪ Outline the relevant law and the rights of citizens in the **TFEU** and secondary legislation
Apply the law	▪ Outline the right of A and B to enter and remain and Roger's right to enter and remain ▪ Consider all three rights to various claims made
Conclude	▪ Conclusion

[1] This is a problem question which requires you to explore some of the issues discussed in essay form in Question 3.

[2] As usual, a brief general introduction sets the scene for the rest of the answer.

Introduction to citizens' rights[2]

This question is concerned with the rights of EU citizens under the citizen provisions of the **TFEU**. Whilst the Treaty provision is rather limited and was not expanded significantly for a number of years, these rights have now been supplemented by secondary legislation, in particular **Directive 2004/38** and by expansive interpretations of the CoJ. Certainly the free movement of workers was strongly upheld as one of the fundamental freedoms and rights with the EU legal order, but the status of citizenship was less clear until recent case law confirmed it as conferring directly effective residence rights on EU citizens.

The factual issues arising

The facts of this problem are that Roger, a Belgian national, enters the UK and is questioned about his intentions and financial state and is allowed entry. He is not working, nor seeking work, but is renting a house. After 12 weeks, he applies for social security and housing benefit but both are refused.

[3] The dependency of these two family members, one close and one who is not an immediate member of the family, needs to be discussed.

[4] We are dealing with citizens who on the facts clearly have no basis to claim rights as workers or as self-employed.

Roger's 16-year-old sister Auriana, also a Belgian national, joins him as does his Turkish cousin, Benedicta.[3] Auriana wants to go to a special needs school because of her disabilities and receive a grant to do so but the grant is refused.[4] Benedicta, who is 25, is not working and applies for social benefit, which is refused. All three face deportation on the ground given by the authorities of being a burden on the state.

The applicable law

The relevant law includes the citizenship **Arts 20–21 TFEU, Directive 2004/38**, and **Regulation 492/2011** (which strictly applies to workers only but has been extended by the CoJ to other categories), and the relevant case law of the CoJ.

[5] The first matter to address in respect of all three is the possible deportation.

Deportation threat[5]

Article 30(3) of Directive 2004/38 provides that even in the event of a deportation order being issued, all three will have a minimum of one month before they can be required to leave the host state. This protection, by virtue of **Art 27**, also applies to Benedicta, the Turkish national. Furthermore, case law—especially the French prostitutes cases, *Adoui* and *Cornaille* (**115 and 116/81**) and *Pecastaing* (**98/79**)—will allow them to argue that they should stay longer. In any event, **Directive 2004/38, Art 31**, requires that they must be allowed to present their case in person. Hence, having secured their temporary right to stay, the national court will have to decide whether they are a sufficiently serious threat along the guidelines of **Arts 27 and 28 of Directive 2004/38**. Whilst that is very unlikely, their right to resist deportation will ultimately depend on whether they have, in fact, any lawful basis to remain, which will be considered next.

Right of Auriana and Benedicta to enter and remain[6]

[6] You need to decide the legal basis and the extent to which they can enter and remain in lawful residence in the host state, and claims for various social rights and whether such claims can lawfully be refused by the host state authorities.

Auriana (A) and Benedicta (B)'s rights appear to very much depend on Roger and it is unlikely that they possess their own rights to stay. B is a non-EU national who on her own has no right under EU persons law to enter and remain on her own. The **TFEU** and **Directive 2004/38** do not expressly take into account the position of persons under 18, and whilst entry under **Art 6** of the Directive may be allowed, the degree of disability of A is most likely to be the determining factor for the national authorities. In view of the fact that there is no case law governing this, if it becomes a question in the national court, a reference under **Art 267 TFEU** would appear to be needed.

Thus, if Roger has no right to stay, it is probable that they also must go. The status of Roger must be determined.

Roger's right to enter and remain

Roger is an EU citizen, as defined by **Art 20 TFEU**. He is thus clearly allowed to enter and reside under **Arts 20–21 TFEU**. **Article 21 TFEU** refers obliquely to other rights in secondary law which then further determine his right to stay. **Article 5** of the Directive provides the basic right of entry and **Art 6** provides, without further formality, a right of residence for at least three months, which has not quite expired. Arguably, until it does so he has an absolute right to stay, but which will not last long, although he does now appear to be out of funds and thus presumably dependent on the state. Again, without clear guidance from the case law, a reference to the CoJ may be necessary.

When the three months expire, his right to remain longer is determined under **Arts 7** and **14 of Directive 2004/38** provided he continues to satisfy the criteria of **Art 7**. He is neither a worker nor self-employed and there are no facts to support the conclusion that he is seeking work and can thus avail himself of **Art 7(3)**, so none of these categories provide the right to remain.

He could stay if he were self-sufficient, as in the *Chen* case **(C-200/02)**, which he was but is arguably no longer. He is, though, lawfully resident in the UK and from the facts not yet a burden on the authorities although he has now made social benefits claims. Whilst remaining lawfully in the UK, he has the right not to be discriminated against as held in the *Sala* and *Grzelczyk* cases **(C-85/96 and C-184/99)**. But he must not be a burden according to **Art 7** of the Directive, although this has been interpreted in *Grzelczyk* as not being an unreasonable burden. It is up to Member State authorities to take a final view on this and the recent cases of *Morgan and Bucher*

(C-11–12/06) and *Förster v IB-Groep (C-158/07)* suggest that the Member States do still retain a discretionary right to refuse benefits to those not establishing a sufficiently close connection or degree of integration in the host state. Roger would appear not to possess that. However, whilst Roger is still for the moment lawfully resident in the UK until his money runs out, we have to consider the right of his relations. The development and extension of citizenship rights have been explored in the 2011 and 2012 articles by Hinarejos.[7]

[7] Noted in the 'Taking things Further' section at the end of the chapter.

A and B are not ascendant nor descendant members of the family within **Art 2** of the Directive but more likely under **Art 3(2)** as other family members and those whose health requires care by Roger. So yes, there is an arguable right to enter and remain under **Arts 2, 3, 5, and 6** of the Directive for up to three months.

Realising their claims[8]

[8] Furthermore, the question of whether the host state can actually deport them must also be addressed.

A seeks to attend a special needs school, a claim which could be made under **Art 10 of Regulation 492/2011**; strictly that does not apply to non-workers but it might receive a sympathetic interpretation by the CoJ. The various claims for social benefits they have made look less likely to be upheld in view of the later case law of *Collins, Bidar,* and *Ioannidis* (**C-138/02, C-209/03, and C-258/04**) and more recently the cases of *Morgan and Bucher* (**C-11–12/06**), *Förster v IB-Groep* (**C-158/07**), and *Vatsouras and Koupatantze v ARGE Nürnberg* (**C-22 and 23/08**), which suggest that a close connection or link to the state is required. There appears to be no such link and therefore it would appear that none of them have any right to the benefits. Finally, Roger is not a worker, so **Art 7(2)** of the Regulation would also not apply.

There is a really outside argument that A has the right to have a carer under the *Baumbast* and *Chen* cases (**C-413/99 and C-200/02**) but as she is not self-sufficient, this is very unlikely.

The conclusion under the present state of the law is that if they are deemed to be a burden on the state which is unreasonable, as they are likely to be found when their claims for benefits are denied, then it would appear that the host state would be justified in deporting them. A reference to the CoJ would certainly clarify this.

[9] Consider the alternative scenario, which will require you to discuss whether the new facts affect your conclusions as to whether Roger and his family may remain lawfully in the UK and whether in addition they may be successful in making their claims for social benefits.

The last part of the question asks,[9] would the answer be different if Roger had used sex lines as services received? No, not if the argument that the situation is wholly internal is employed, as with *Morson and Jhanjan v Netherlands* (**Cases 35 and 36/82**). Counter to this would be that fact that Roger has moved from Belgium to the UK (see the *Garcia Avello* and *D'Hoop* cases (**C-148/02 and C-224/98**)). Equally, it might be argued that the renting of premises constitutes receiving services and, whilst a repealed **Directive 64/221** expressly mentioned receiving services, **Directive 2004/38** does not. Indeed, the motive for moving or receiving services may not be important as in *Chen* (C-200/02) but, in view of the degree of uncertainty at this stage, an **Art 267 TFEU** reference would be advised.

Summary

The facts of this case are at the edge of case law, hence the uncertainty about the outcome of this case and the fact that at various stages a reference to the CoJ has been advised. It may be that cases will soon resolve some of these issues.

LOOKING FOR EXTRA MARKS?

- You could make some comments that the claiming of benefits is a very sensitive area of law and that the CoJ may now be aware of that as reflected in some of the latest judgments, which are not as generous in terms of recognising rights as the previous ones.

- You could then back up the general discussion with reference to the latest cases, which include: *Dano v Jobseeker Leipzig* (C-333/13) and *Alopka* and *Moudoulou* (C-86/12).

TAKING THINGS FURTHER

- Costello, C, 'Metock: Free Movement and "Normal Family Life" in the Union' (2009) 46 CML Rev 587.
  This article considers the support of family life shown in the cases of the CoJ.

- Hinarejos, A, 'Extending Citizenship and the Scope of EU Law' (2011) CLJ 310.
  Although a little dated this provides a good overview of the various developments in this important area of the free movement of persons in the EU.

- Hinarejos, A, 'Citizenship of the EU: Clarifying "Genuine Enjoyment of the Substance" of Citizenship Rights' (2012) CLJ 279.
  A further article on the meaning of citizenship in EU law.

- Kocharov, A, 'What Intra-Community Mobility for Third-Country Workers?' (2008) 33 (6) EL Rev 913.
  Looks at the rights of third-country nationals in the EU.

- Newdick, C, 'Citizenship, Free Movement and Healthcare: Cementing Individual Rights by Corroding Social Solidarity' (2006) 43 CML Rev 1645.
  Looks at the particular problem of welfare tourism.

Online Resources

www.oup.com/uk/qanda/

Go online for extra essay and problem questions, a glossary of key terms, online versions of all the answer plans and audio commentary on how selected ones were put together, and a range of podcasts which include advice on exam and coursework technique and advice for other assessment methods.

8 Competition and Merger Law

ARE YOU READY?

In order to attempt questions in this chapter, you must have covered all of these topics in both your work over the year and in revision:

- The procedural aspects of competition law, but which may not be covered in any significant way in all courses including competition law.

- The basic concepts and the main requirements of **Arts 101 and 102 TFEU**, which is the main focus of this chapter.

- The **2007 Lisbon Treaty**, although it made little substantive change to the competition law provisions.

- Depending on the coverage in your course, you should be aware of the **Competition Regulation 1/2003** and the **Mergers Regulation 139/2004**.

KEY DEBATES

Debate: the place of competition law within the Treaty and EU generally

As one of the original policy areas of the EU from its first establishment, competition is now a well-established and largely settled area of law; its place in the EU is still however subject to discussion.

QUESTION 1

Why is competition law policy an integral and necessary part of the EU?

! CAUTION

- This is a question which allows you considerable freedom in how you answer, but does require you essentially still to address the question of why competition law was included, when the central element of the original EEC was the common or single market consisting of the various freedoms.

◻ DIAGRAM ANSWER PLAN

Outline the main and competition objectives of the EU as contained in the **Preamble and Arts 2 and 3 TEU.**

▼

Outline the Treaty Articles in support of competition law policy

▼

Outline the specific competition law objectives and rules (**Arts 101–102 TFEU**)

▼

Role of the Commission in competition law enforcement

▼

Consider the relationship with other EU objectives

▼

Provide details on leading cases on the competition law policy

A ▶ SUGGESTED ANSWER

[1] This first question is one which concerns an overview of the topic and its place in the EU legal order.

The EU as originally established was aimed at the establishment of a common market and the progressive approximation of the economic policies of the Member States.[1] The **Preamble to the EU Treaty** generally sets out these basic objectives.

[2] To answer this you must consider the main objectives of the EU which are outlined in the Preamble to the EU Treaty.

The main objectives of the EU[2]

The general aims include the creation of the Common Market, which was to be achieved by abolishing obstacles to the freedom of movement of all the factors of production, namely goods, workers, and providers of services and capital. The Treaty also provided for the abolition of customs duties between the Member States and the application of a common customs tariff to imports from third countries. There were to be common policies in the spheres of agriculture and transport, and a system ensuring that competition in the Common Market is not distorted by the activities of cartels or market monopolists.

The main objectives of EU competition policy[3]

[3] This should be followed in turn by a consideration of the main objectives of competition policy itself.

EU competition policy was based both on the extensive American experience of the concentration of power in the market place in too few hands and also, to some extent, on the post-Second World War German legislative experience with large undertakings and cartels. Attitudes were also influenced by the desire to protect emerging and expanding industries and companies and to encourage the rebirth of European industry after the devastation of the Second World War. Thus, one of the fundamental positions of the competition law to be established was that there should be no barriers against the entry to the market of new companies and industries. The broad policy objective of competition law, therefore, which was formulated by the European Economic Community, was to maintain and encourage competition for the benefit of the Community (now Union) and its citizens.

Competition law was therefore constructed to ensure the maintenance of the Common Market. One of the aims of the internal market is to establish and maintain European-wide competition to stimulate the entire economy of the Community (now Union) for both the domestic and world markets and thus assist European capital in competing in the world market. Competition law is designed to help achieve a single market and the integration of the Union, to encourage economic activity amongst small- and medium-size enterprises, and to maximise efficiency by allowing the free flow of goods and resources. At the same time it must be ensured that companies do not become too successful, to be able to eliminate competition, thereby starting to dominate a market, or to cooperate in such a way with other companies as to act as one unit to the detriment of consumers and smaller firms in the Union. Competition law may also be regarded therefore as necessary to prevent these undesirable developments from being realised. In order to retain fair competition, more so in a capitalist free market, some form of intervention on the part of the state is required. Action is concentrated on the larger players in the market rather than the small and medium business enterprises.

The **Preamble to the old EC Treaty** stated that the 'removal of existing obstacles calls for concerted action in order to guarantee steady expansion, balanced trade and fair competition'. Whilst these aims are not so prominent in the **EU Treaties** as revised by the **Lisbon Treaty, Art 3(3) TEU** refers to a highly competitive social market economy and **Art 3(d) TFEU** provides an exclusive competence to the Union with the 'establishing of the competition rules necessary for the functioning of the internal market'.

[4] It is useful to supply some brief details of the general Treaty Articles which act in support of the overall objectives of the EU and its competition law.

General Treaty Articles in support of competition policy[4]

Article 10 EC (now 4(3) TEU) has also been pleaded as a general principle of law supporting the argument that competition law also applies in respect of the Member States and not just undertakings so that they are prohibited from encouraging or requiring acts or conduct by companies which may distort competition in the Union. **Article 12 EC (now 18 TFEU)** too has featured in cases on competition law to ensure equal access to markets and the distribution of goods and services without discrimination.

[5] Then it is suggested you provide a brief overview to the main provisions of competition law and the secondary legislation in order to explain how it is to be pursued in the EU legal order.

The broad aims are then expanded in three sets of rules:[5] one relating to the activities of legal persons—that is, the business undertakings, which now includes rules on concentrations and mergers; one relating to anti-dumping measures; and, finally, one relating to the activities of the Member States, principally state aid. The rules concerned with private undertakings are further subdivided into: **Article 101 TFEU** for agreements between cartels involving more than one entity; **Article 102 TFEU**, concerned with dominant positions, dealing predominantly with one entity but also applicable to one or more undertakings; and the rules applicable to concentrations and mergers. The specific EU competition rules are generally designed to intervene to prevent agreements which fix prices or conditions or the supply of products, to prohibit agreements which carve up territories, to prevent abuses of market power which have the effect of removing real competition, and to control mergers which would also remove competition.

[6] Additionally, outlining the role played by the Commission in EU competition law helps provide a complete answer.

The role of the Commission[6]

The Commission is given the task under **Art 105 TFEU** and **Regulation 1/2003** of ensuring that competition in the EU is not distorted by companies setting up their own rules and obstacles to trade, thereby replacing the national rules and obstacles which the EU is trying to abolish by application of the free movement of goods provisions.

[7] You should consider its relations with other policies of the Union and the reasons why it is considered to be a necessary policy in the Union.

The relationship with other rules and policies[7]

These rules seek to prevent the creation of artificial barriers to trade on the national boundaries. Competition law is therefore inextricably linked to other Union policy areas, especially to the free movement of goods, because it would prove impossible to have one without ensuring having the other. To have prevented the Member States on the one hand from restricting the movement of goods just to allow private companies to do it by their agreements and practices would defeat the objectives of the first policy, and, vice versa, to prevent companies from artificially dividing the markets, but to allow the Member States to do so, would undermine a competition policy. A further argument for having an effective competition policy is that some multinational companies are in a better position to divide the market than some Member States, because they have the same or greater turnover than the gross national product (GNP) of some of the EU Member States and so need to be subject to international control.

Judicial consideration of the policy[8]

The application of the rules by the Commission and the interpretation of the rules by the Court of Justice have not been done in isolation by looking at the provisions alone, but in the light of the objectives of competition policy. The rules are also applied in the light of the general objectives of the Treaty. In *Commercial Solvents* v *Commission* **(6 and 7/73)**, the CoJ held:

The prohibitions in **Arts 85 and 86 (now 101 and 102 TFEU)** must be interpreted and applied in the light of **Art 3(f) EEC Treaty (now 3(d) TFEU)**, which provides that the activities of the Community shall include the institution of a system ensuring that competition is not distorted, and **Art 2 EEC Treaty**, which gives the Community the task of promoting throughout the Community harmonious development of economic activities.

The case of *Metro* v *Commission* **(26/76)** is also a good example, whereby the Commission, in pursuit of a goal, was forced to rely on **Art 2 EC** to justify particular decisions reached. The agreements in question were deemed to satisfy competition rules because they helped to maintain employment. This latter case serves as an example of where the Commission, in carrying out its tasks in relation to competition law, is also required to balance this policy with other policies such as regional development or concern for unemployment and which may cause it to modify its position on the behaviour of companies. The Court of First Instance of the European Communities (CFI) (now the General Court) is now the primary EU court concerned with competition cases; it has also stressed the importance of the competition policy to the Union political and constitutional order in *Courage* v *Crehan* **(C-453/99)**.

The general economic climate also influences the Commission, particularly in respect of merger policy, in that in times of poor economic growth, the Commission may treat mergers as being more acceptable because of the efficiency gains to be achieved and the greater ability the emerging company will have in the world market. General developments in competition law were dealt with in the article by Slot.[9]

Competition law policy cannot, therefore, be pursued alone and it is to be concluded that competition law is an inextricable part of the EU and its policies.

(+) **LOOKING FOR EXTRA MARKS?**

■ If there is time, provide details on further leading cases to illustrate competition law in practice: *BRT* v *SABAM* (127/73), *Consten & Grundig* v *Commission* (58/64), *STM* (56/65), and *United Brands* (27/76).

■ Outline the changing enforcement regime and maturing of the system through national enforcement agencies under **Regulation 1/2003**.

■ Discuss EU involvement in merger control and **Regulation 139/04**.

(Q) **QUESTION** | 2

Branches of two non-EU Member State companies, the Red Dwarf Mining Corporation (RDMC) and Green Giant Mining (GGM), have moved into the EU to exploit the remaining European deposits of tin. In informal meetings of the management of the two companies, which took place before their move into the EU, they decided on a strategy to work the European market to their advantage. They have restricted supplies to customers in and outside the EU to drive up prices and thus profits for their parent companies. So far RDMC have secured 42 per cent of the market and GGM have secured 23 per cent.

Complaints have been made by competitors and customers to the Commission, which is investigating. The companies claim the investigations cannot apply to either companies or agreements from outside the EU.

a. **Advise RDMC and GGM.**

b. **Would your answer be any different if RDMC and GGM formally merge prior to any action being taken?**

(!) **CAUTION**

■ You are not supplied with any real facts to come to definitive conclusions on the second part of the question, thus all you can do validly in answering this question is to generally describe the EU concern and involvement in mergers.

DIAGRAM ANSWER PLAN

Identify the issues	■ Identify the facts which give rise to legal issues and outline competition policy
Relevant law	■ Outline the general scope of **Arts 101 and 102 TFEU**
Apply the law	■ Consider, with reference to case law, if **Arts 101 or 102 TFEU** have been breached. ■ Consider the position of companies outside the EU ■ The effect of merger must be discussed and the possible application of the Mergers Regulation to joint dominance
Conclude	■ Summary

A — SUGGESTED ANSWER

[1] This problem question will involve you in a general consideration of the application of the principal provisions of both **Arts 101 and 102 TFEU** and consideration of mergers.

Competition law is one of the fundamental policies of the Union and is generally mentioned in **Arts 3 of both the TEU and TFEU**.[1] **Article 3(d) TFEU** refers to the 'establishing of the competition rules necessary for the functioning of the internal market'.

The facts[2]

[2] Outline the pertinent facts.

The relevant facts in this case are that the branches of two non-EU Member State companies are pursuing a strategy agreed on outside the EU, which involves the restriction of supply to customers to drive up prices and profits. As a result, it would seem that both companies have secured a sizeable share of the EU market.

The applicable law[3]

[3] You should briefly outline the scope of **Arts 101 and 102 TFEU**.

The two principal provisions to combat anti-competitive behaviour are **Arts 101 and 102 TFEU**.

Article 101(1) TFEU prohibits agreements between undertakings, decisions by associations of undertakings, and concerted practices which may affect trade between the Member States and which have as their object or effect the prevention, restriction, or distortion of competition within the internal market. **Article 101(2) TFEU** provides that any agreements or decisions prohibited pursuant to this Article shall be automatically void.

Article 102 TFEU applies where individual organisations have a near monopoly position or share an oligopolistic market with a small number of other companies and take unfair advantage of this position to the detriment of the market, other companies, and the end consumers. **Article 102 TFEU** provides that the abuse by one or more undertakings of a dominant market position within the internal market or in a substantial part of which affects trade between Member States is prohibited.

[4] You need to determine whether the case concerns an agreement between the parties contrary to EU competition law, or whether it concerns the abuse of a dominant position by the parties.

Next it is necessary to determine whether the factual circumstances amount to a breach of either **Art 101 or 102 TFEU**.[4]

The possible breach of Art 101 TFEU[5]

[5] Apply **Art 101** with the assistance of case law to the facts.

In order for **Art 101 TFEU** to be breached, it must be shown that there is a form of agreement or concerted practice which may have affected trade between Member States. No actual agreement is necessary to breach **Art 101 TFEU** and a concerted practice will suffice. In *ICI* v *Commission (Dyestuffs)* (48/69) general and uniform increases were witnessed from a small number of leading producers. The Court of Justice defined a concerted practice as a form of coordination between enterprises that had not yet reached the point of a true contract relationship but which had in practice substituted cooperation for the risks of competition. See also the *Sugar Cartel* case (*Suiker Unie* v *Commission* (40–48/73)) in which the firms responsible for the alleged breach said there was no plan. The CoJ held there did not have to be one. In the *Polypropylene* cases (T-7/89, T-9/89, and T-11/89), the CFI (now the General Court) held that expressions of intention, even if not in writing, of particular conduct could constitute an agreement of concerted practice. Countering these cases is the *Wood Pulp* case (C-89, 104, and 125–129/85). The CoJ held that parallel conduct could not be regarded as proof of a concerted practice unless that was the only plausible explanation for the conduct. In the present case, providing there is some indication that an agreed practice is being pursued, it is likely that a concerted practice between undertakings will be established. In **C-199/92P** *Hüls AG* v *Commission*, the CoJ held that, to be a concerted practice, there is no need to demonstrate either conduct in the market or restricted competition, merely a requirement to demonstrate that there was participation.

Next, the agreement must be one which has the object or effect of restriction of competition which may affect trade between Member States. **Article 101(1) TFEU** focuses on particular practices which would offend competition law. Amongst these are those listed under **Art 101(1)(b) and (c) TFEU**, which limit markets or supply. In the present case the agreement is clearly one which has this object. In fact, even a potential impact will do; see the *Consten* and *Grundig* cases

(56 and 58/64). To infringe **Art 101 TFEU**, the practice complained of must be capable of affecting trade between Member States. The cases of **Consten** and **Grundig** and the **Cement Association (8/72)** are examples of the requirements for this. It has to be probable in law or fact that the agreement may have an influence, direct or indirect, actual or potential, on the pattern of trade between Member States. If there is an impact on the pattern of trade, then there is an effect on trade. The restrictions on supply and the consequent price increases would clearly fall into this category; therefore a breach of **Art 101(1) TFEU** is probable. A set of Guidelines issued by the Commission in 2004 (OJ 2004 C101/81) summarises the case law of the CoJ on effect on trade between Member States.

[6]Apply **Art 102** with the assistance of case law to the facts.

Article 102 TFEU[6]

Article 102 TFEU may also be breached if there is an abuse of a dominant position by a single undertaking in the EU. Dominance must be established both in terms of the product and geographic market.

The product market

The product must be a unique product which is not interchangeable. It must be assumed that there is no substitute for the raw metal tin. Is there dominance? We are only told that RDMC has 42 per cent and GGM has 23 per cent of the market in the Community. In **United Brands (27/76)**, the share of 45 per cent was considered sufficient but the next competitor had only 16 per cent, a greater difference than here with 42 per cent and 23 per cent. In the **Hoffman La Roche case (86/76)** the CoJ rejected the Commission finding that 43 per cent constituted dominance but instead referred only to a very large market share as being necessary. Thus, considering each company individually, it would be arguable whether RDMC or GGM alone would be dominant. Whilst there is no definitive word from either the Commission or the Court on this point, the Mergers Regulation states that concentrations whose market share does not exceed 25 per cent would not be considered to impede competition. However, **Art 102 TFEU** may apply to one or more companies and the combined share would be 67 per cent, which in a joint action would be a position of dominance. Difficulties in interpreting the requirements of **Art 102** may be resolved by consulting the Commission notice on it: Guidance on its enforcement priorities in applying Article 82 EC Treaty (now **102 TFEU**) to abusive exclusionary conduct by dominant undertakings (OJ C45/7).

According to the CoJ in **Compagnie Maritime Belge Transports (C-395 and 396P/96)**, an agreement within the meaning of **Art 85(1) (now 101 TFEU)** may result in undertakings being so linked that they become and act as a collective entity as far as their competitors and customers are concerned and as such a collective dominant position can arise, which can then be abused in the manner noted here.

The geographic market

The geographic market is also satisfied as it is the whole of the EU; see the *United Brands* **(27/76)** and *Tetra Pak* **(T-51/89)** cases.

Abuse

It then has to be shown that there is an abuse of dominant position. Limiting production is one of the grounds listed in **Art 102 TFEU,** as was refusal to supply in the *United Brands* case; therefore an abuse can be shown in the present case.

Effect on trade between Member States

Finally, trade between Member States must be affected. In the *Commercial Solvents* v *Commission* case **(6 and 7/73)** it was held that conduct which has the effect of altering the competitive structure within the Common Market will satisfy the requirement of effect on trade between the Member States. This would be the case with RDMC and GGM. Thus a breach of **Art 102 TFEU** is also likely to be established.

A significant objection of the two firms is that the companies and the agreements are from outside the EU and they would argue that they cannot be touched by the EU competition law rules. However, the position in the EU is that the competition rules apply to all undertakings whose operations or agreements affect trade between Member States and have as their object or effect a restraint on competition in the Union. The *ICI Dyestuffs* case **(48–57/69)** considered that the unity of conduct in the market between the parent and the subsidiary was the decisive factor in the case. The *Wood Pulp* case **(C-89, 104, and 125–129/85)** is also instructive. In this case the pricing agreements took place outside the EU but the implementation took place within the EU; therefore, if the agreements led to anti-competitive consequences through the activities of branches, they would infringe **Art 101 TFEU.**

[7] Consider the fact that the companies' head offices are based outside the EU and whether this will affect the ability of the Commission to investigate and prosecute a breach of EU law.

The fact that the breaches are committed in the Union[7] puts the companies within the territorial jurisdiction of the Treaty and thus the Commission and the General Court, even where the parent companies have no direct physical involvement and the agreements were outside of the EU (*ICI Dyestuffs* case).

If the undertakings merged?[8]

[8] You are required to address the alternative situation in which the companies merge.

In the alternative, it is necessary to consider the effect a merger would have. If the merger takes place outside the EU, as is assumed to be the case here, it may still be a concentration with a Union dimension as far as the **Mergers Regulation 139/04** is concerned; see the Decision of the Commission in *Matsushita/MCA* **(IV/M37). Article 1** states that it applies where there is a worldwide turnover of more than €5,000 million and an aggregate EU-wide turnover of each of at least two of the undertakings of more than €250 million. An EU dimension may nevertheless pertain, if:

(a) the combined aggregate worldwide turnover of all the undertakings is more than €2,500 million;

(b) in each of at least three Member States, the combined aggregate turnover of all the undertakings is more than €100 million;

(c) in each of at least three Member States, the aggregate turnover of each of at least two of the undertakings concerned is more than €25 million;

(d) the aggregate EU-wide turnover of each of at least two of the undertakings concerned is more than €100 million.

[9] As was outlined in the caution, without being supplied with the facts, you can only generalise.

This information is not provided in the problem,[9] but if the turnover does not reach these thresholds then the merger is not one of an EU dimension. If they do exceed the thresholds the companies are required under **Art 4(1)** to inform the Commission. Failure to do so will render them liable to a fine under **Art 14**. The Commission will determine under **Art 2** whether the concentration is compatible with the common market with a view to declaring it compatible or suspending it. This may be difficult to enforce outside the EU but an extraterritorial merger was blocked in the *GE/Honeywell* decision (M2220). However, recourse to **Art 102 TFEU** may still be necessary to combat the anti-competitive behaviour.

[10] Consider whether the **Mergers Regulation** applies to the situation of joint dominance of a market by the activities of more than one company (or whether this this should be caught by **Art 102 TFEU**).

Joint dominance short of merger[10]

A formal merger agreement might not be required to be subject to the **Mergers Regulation** and even independent firms may be subject to it. In joined cases *France v Commission* (C-68/94) and *Société Commerciale des Potasses et de l'Azote (SCPA) v Commission* (C-30/95), the CoJ determined that the **Mergers Regulation** applies also to collective dominance although, as noted, collective dominance short of merger may be caught under **Art 102 TFEU**. A reference to the CoJ would be required, however, to be certain about this.

➕ LOOKING FOR EXTRA MARKS?

■ If time, present a complete summary of the findings at the end of the answer: that there was a concerted practice which had the object or effect of affecting trade and was thus in breach of **Art 101 TFEU**; that, although there was not an individual breach of **Art 102 TFEU**, collective dominance and thus a breach was likely; and finally that the **Merger Regulation** may be applicable to the possible merger.

Q | QUESTION 3

Widgets Ltd (W) is a UK manufacturer of the widgets which are fitted into beer cans to ensure that the drink has a frothy head. It holds 40 per cent of the EU market. There are three other European manufacturers of this product, the largest of which is Krimskrams GmbH (K) in Germany, which holds 30 per cent of the EU market. The rest of the EU market, valued at more than €1,000 million p.a., is made up by two other EU companies with less than 10 per cent of the market between them and imports from the USA, Japan, Korea, and China.

W and K are the only manufacturers of the machines which produce the widgets.

Press reports have noted that, following the twice-yearly Convention of European Widget Manufacturers (CEWM), prices of the UK- and German-built widgets rise, followed shortly by the prices of other manufacturers. The companies stated, in a recent statement, that there was never any form of agreement between them in respect of pricing policy. However, W and K have now decided to merge to consolidate their position in the European and world market for widgets. They have also refused to supply spares for the machines to the non-EU manufacturers.

In the light of the developments, the Commission has commenced an investigation into the actions of the companies to determine whether any breach of EU law has been committed.

Advise the Commission as to the likelihood that the Court of Justice will uphold their claim:

a. **that the companies have breached either Art 101 or 102 TFEU;**

b. **that the companies have breached the Mergers Regulation.**

! | CAUTION

- This is a general question which concentrates on the main principles of each of the areas covered rather than going into precise details of any provision in particular, hence your answer should reflect this approach.

- Whilst the question has been split into two parts, this does not mean that you should spend 50 per cent of the time on each. If this was intended or required by the examiner, it would normally be made clear that each part carries 50 per cent of the marks. There is considerably more law and more to write about for Part (a) in this question but you have to decide the appropriate balance.

DIAGRAM ANSWER PLAN

Identify the issues	■ Identify the facts which give rise to legal issues and provide a broad outline of competition policy and law
Relevant law	■ Outline the relevant law: outline the general scope of **Arts 101 and 10 TFEU** and the **Mergers Regulation**
Apply the law	■ Consider with reference to case law, if **Arts 101 or 102 TFEU** have been breached ■ The lawfulness of the merger must be assessed ■ Possible joint dominance must also be considered
Conclude	■ Summary

A **SUGGESTED ANSWER**

[1] This is a general problem question on competition law covering aspects of **Arts 101 and 102 TFEU** (ex 81 and 82 EC) and the **Mergers Regulation**.

[2] It is always good to introduce generally the area of law and what it seeks to achieve.

General introduction[1]

Competition law in general is designed to ensure there is healthy competition in the EU which will benefit not only the EU market but also consumers.[2] The EU competition law policy seeks to achieve this by outlawing any behaviour which is contrary to this credo. Competition law in the EU therefore attacks concerted action which is anti-competitive and individual actions which abuse market strengths to the detriment of competition. The EU has also enacted legislation to combat anti-competitive mergers which have a European dimension.

[3] As with other problem-type questions, the factual issues to be tackled need to be identified.

Factual issues[3]

The issues to be considered in the answer are: the price rises which occur after the meeting of CEWM, the decision to merge, and the refusal to supply spares for the machines.

[4] This question asks you to consider whether the companies have breached either **Arts 101 or 102 TFEU** or the **Mergers Regulation 139/04**.

The law to be applied[4]

The law applicable to this answer is as follows. **Article 101(1) TFEU** prohibits agreements between undertakings, decisions by associations of undertakings, and concerted practices which may affect trade between the Member States, and which have as their object or effect the prevention, restriction, or distortion of competition within the internal market. **Article 101(2) TFEU** provides that any agreements or decisions prohibited pursuant to this Article shall be automatically void.

Article 102 TFEU provides that the abuse by one or more undertakings of a dominant market position within the internal market or in a substantial part of it, which affects trade between Member States, is prohibited.

The **Mergers Regulation 139/04** establishes a division between large mergers with a European dimension, over which the Commission will exercise supervision, and smaller mergers which will fall under the jurisdiction of national authorities.

Now to turn to each of the provisions in turn.[5]

Possible breach of Art 101 TFEU

First of all, the possible breach of **Art 101 TFEU** will be considered. In order for it to be breached it must be shown that there is an agreement which may have affected trade between Member States.

Whilst the companies have declared that there was no formal agreement between them, it has been demonstrated that no actual agreement is necessary to breach **Art 101 TFEU** and the Article allows for a concerted practice to suffice. In the case of *ICI v Commission* **(Dyestuffs) (48/69)** general and uniform increases were witnessed from a small number of leading producers. The Court of Justice defined a concerted practice as 'a form of coordination between enterprises, that had not yet reached the point of true contract relationship but which had in practice substituted cooperation for the risks of competition'.

In a particular instance there would be a need to show the similarity of rate and timing of increases and whilst not having to prove the existence of agreements; there is still a requirement to establish that some form of contract existed.

In our case it is the meeting of CEWM that should establish this. See also the *Sugar Cartel* case (*Suiker Unie v Commission*) **(40–48/73)** in which the firms responsible for the alleged breach said there was no plan. The CoJ held there did not have to be one. The *Wood Pulp* cases **(C-89, 104, and 125–129/85)** would, however, increase the burden on the Commission to demonstrate that in this case, there were no other plausible explanations for the parallel price increase other than by agreement of concerted action. The *Hüls* case **(C-199/92P)** makes it clear that it is not necessary to show conduct or impact on the market, but it is the taking part that counts.

Object or effect

Thus, if it is considered that a concerted practice is in existence it must be shown that the object or effect of it was to restrict competition. A potential impact will be sufficient for the requirements of the Article;

[5]Thus you can concentrate on whether the main requirements of these elements of EU law have been infringed by the actions of the parties.

see *Consten* and *Grundig* **(56 and 58/64)**. Price-fixing, which was the object of the present activity, clearly offends as it is an example provided by **Art 101(1)(a) TFEU**; therefore this aspect is established in the present case.

To some extent the same question of an impact on trade is applied to determine whether there has been an effect on trade between Member States. The cases of *Consten* and *Grundig* **(56 and 58/64)** and the *Cement Association* **(8/72)** are examples of the simple requirements for this to be met. If there is an impact on the pattern of trade then there is an effect on trade. Clearly price increases will impact on the pattern of trade between Member States.

Breach of Art 102 TFEU (establishing dominance)

Article 102 TFEU will be breached if there is an abuse of a dominant position in the EU. Dominance must be established both in terms of the product and geographic market. The Commission has published a Notice on the Definition of the Relevant Market (OJ 1997 C372/5) which provides a summary of the case law and Commission methodology and hence guidelines for determining the relevant markets. The first product market is widgets for beer tins. The product market of spares for the widget machines will be considered here. In the *United Brands* case **(27/76)**, it was held it must be a unique product which is not interchangeable. In the absence of any evidence to the contrary, this is the position in the present case. It then has to be considered whether there is dominance. We are informed that the two companies, Widgets and Krimskrams, have 40 per cent and 30 per cent respectively of the market in the EU. Taken individually, the market share of 40 per cent held by Widgets might not, in view of the case of *United Brands*, be enough on its own to constitute dominance, especially where the next competitor has 30 per cent. If this is uncertain, then it is even more unlikely that the 30 per cent held by Krimskrams would be enough to constitute market dominance.

[6] The possibility of joint dominance must also be entertained.

Joint dominance of widgets market[6]

However, **Art 102 TFEU** also covers the situation of one or more undertakings which together occupy a dominant position. If the two parties were subject to a joint decision of the Commission, the resultant market share of the two companies of 70 per cent would most probably be held to be a position of dominance. In fact, according to the CoJ case of *Compagnie Maritime Belge Transports* **(C-395 and 396P/96)** an agreement within the meaning of **Art 85(1) EEC (now 101 TFEU)** may result in undertakings being so linked that they become and act as a collective entity as far as their competitors and customers are concerned and as such a collective dominant position can arise under **Art 102 TFEU (ex 86 EEC)**, which can then be abused.

The supply of spares for the machines is also a separate market in which, in the case at hand, the 100 per cent share of the market by the two companies will establish complete dominance; see the *Hugin* **case (22/78)**. It may however be argued that, in respect of the machines, the refusal to supply only has effects outside the EU, but in the *Commercial Solvents* **case (6 and 7/73)**, where the supply was outside the EU market, the CoJ held that this fact did not remove its jurisdiction as the effect would still be prominent in the EU market. See also the *Wood Pulp* **case (C-89, 104, and 125–129/85)** in this respect.

The geographic market is also satisfied as it is the whole of the EU; see the *United Brands* and *Tetra Pak* **(T-51/89)** cases.

The abuse

The abuse which offends the EU regime is the price-fixing in respect of the widgets and the refusal to supply in respect of the spares, specifically noted in **Art 102(a) and (b) TFEU**.

The *Continental Can* **case (6/72)** also suggested that a further form of abuse could be the merger itself but this point can now be addressed under the **Mergers Regulation 139/04**.

The merger[7]

[7] The next topic for consideration is the lawfulness of the merger.

After merger the companies have 70 per cent of a market for widgets estimated at over €1,000 million and 100 per cent of the machines and spares supply market.

Article 1 of the **Mergers Regulation** states it applies where there is a worldwide turnover of more than €5,000 million and an aggregate EU-wide turnover of each of at least two of the undertakings of more than €250 million. **Article 1(3)** provides that an EU dimension may nevertheless pertain, if:

(a) the combined aggregate worldwide turnover of all the undertakings is more than €2,500 million;

(b) in each of at least three Member States, the combined aggregate turnover of all the undertakings is more than €100 million;

(c) in each of at least three Member States, the aggregate turnover of each of at least two of the undertakings concerned is more than €25 million;

(d) the aggregate EU-wide turnover of each of at least two of the undertakings concerned is more than €100 million.

Whilst we know the share of the EU market we do not know of their share of the world market. If they do exceed the limits of **Art 1**, **Regulation 139/04** requires them to inform the Commission. By failing to inform the Commission (**Art 4(1)**) they can be fined (**Art 14**).

The Commission will determine under **Art 2** whether the concentration is compatible with the internal market. The facts do not reveal whether this merger has taken place. If it has, the Commission may investigate with a view to declaring it compatible or suspending it. If not, the abuse of a collective dominance on the part of the two companies may still breach the Mergers Regulation according to the CoJ in the cases of *France v Commission* (C-68/94) and *Société Commerciale des Potasses et de l' Azote (SCPA) v Commission* (C-30/95) or **Art 102 TFEU** according to *Compagnie Maritime Belge Transports* (C-395 and 396P/96); however, an application to the General Court would be necessary to determine this. Collective dominance has been further considered in the *Airtours* case (T-342/99) in which it was held that three conditions must be shown by the Commission. There needs to be market transparency, the tacit coordination must have been maintained over a period of time in pursuit of the common policy, and that common policy must be safe from market disturbance. In this problem question, there is insufficient information to assess whether these conditions have been satisfied.[8]

[8]There may not be a clear, definitive answer you can provide, in which case try to present, first of all, both sides or possible solutions but then suggest that a reference under **Art 267 TFEU** may be needed for the CoJ to decide the matter.

LOOKING FOR EXTRA MARKS?

- You could mention that a review of merger policy has been taking place with a commission paper being published in 2014 COM (2014) 449 final, but which recommended only limited changes.

QUESTION 4

'Even though **Art 81 [now 101 TFEU]** is meant to cover concerted actions as opposed to abusive conduct covered by **Art 82 [now 102 TFEU]**, both provisions need to be interpreted in conjunction with each other.' (Van Bael and Bellis)

Discuss.

CAUTION

- As with other slightly cryptic essay-type questions, it would be easy to lapse into writing all you know about the two Treaty provisions rather than addressing the question specifically.

- The question is suggesting that, rather than treating the two provisions as mutually exclusive and thus never to be considered as overlapping or covering the same ground, in fact there are circumstances when both provisions may need to be taken into account when considering certain factual circumstances.

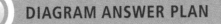

DIAGRAM ANSWER PLAN

Outline the broad principles of competition policy and law

▼

Outline the scope of **Arts 101 and 102 TFEU**

▼

Discuss the relationship and any overlap of the two Articles

▼

Consider the case law of the CoJ which addresses this issue

▼

Conclusion

A SUGGESTED ANSWER

[1]This question requires you to consider the relationship of **Arts 101 and 102 TFEU** to each other.

[2]Start with a general outline of the area of law and overall policy.

Competition law policy[1]

EU competition law is one of the fundamental policies[2] of the EU and is generally mentioned in **Art 3 of both the TEU and the TFEU**. Its aims are to prevent anti-competitive behaviour which will distort the competitive balance of the EU market. EU competition rules are generally designed to intervene to prevent agreements which fix prices or conditions or the supply of products, to prohibit agreements which carve up territories, and to prevent abuses of market power which have the effect of removing real competition, and to control mergers which would also remove competition.

Whilst these aims are not so prominent in the **EU Treaties** as revised by the **Lisbon Treaty**, **Art 3(3) TEU** refers to a highly competitive social market economy and **Art 3(d) TFEU** provides an exclusive competence to the Union, the 'establishing of the competition rules necessary for the functioning of the internal market'.

[3]You should then outline the basic legislative regime under the Treaty and then briefly outline the specific area covered by **Arts 101 and 102 TFEU**.

[4]Then you should address the quotation and consider whether the provisions do need to be interpreted in conjunction with each other or whether they can be regarded as mutually exclusive.

Articles 101 and 102 TFEU[3]

Two main provisions have been enacted to tackle two different situations. **Article 101 TFEU** deals with anti-competitive practices arising as a result of agreements or concerted actions of two or more undertakings and **Art 102 TFEU** concerns the abuse of a position of dominance by one or more undertakings.[4]

Article 101(1) TFEU deals with restrictive practices. It sets out the prohibitions and details of the consequences of the failure to observe the prohibition and provides a framework by which exemptions from the prohibitions can be obtained.

Article 101(1) TFEU prohibits agreements between undertakings, decisions by associations of undertakings, and concerted practices which may affect trade between the Member States, and which have as their object or effect the prevention, restriction, or distortion of competition within the internal market.

Article 101(2) TFEU provides that any agreements or decisions prohibited pursuant to this Article shall be automatically void, although there are ways in which an agreement may be held to be acceptable. The terms of an agreement may be acceptable as being consistent with one of the exemptions provided by the **Vertical Restraints Regulation 330/2010**.

Article 102 TFEU applies where individual organisations have a near-monopoly position or share an oligopolistic market with a small number of other companies, and who take unfair advantage of this position to the detriment of the market, other companies, and the end consumers. **Article 102 TFEU** provides that the abuse by one or more undertakings of a dominant market position within the internal market, or in a substantial part of it, which affects trade between Member States, is prohibited. The requirements are therefore a dominant position, abuse of it, and the effect between Member States.

[5] Consider further the scope of the two articles using case law to support your comments.

The scope of Articles 101 and 102[5]

At first sight, therefore, there seems to be at least a different focus of the two Articles, with **Art 101 TFEU** aimed at two or more undertakings in collusion and **Art 102 TFEU** aimed at just a single entity. However, it can be observed in the case of *Ford v Commission* (25 and 26/84) that the unilateral action of one undertaking may still fall foul of **Art 101 TFEU**, whereas **Art 102 TFEU** expressly provides that it also applies to the activities of one or more undertakings.

The relationship of **Arts 101 and 102 TFEU** is highlighted in a case concerned with the difficulties in dealing with the realities of complex commercial cross holdings. In *BAT v Commission* (142 and 156/84), the Court of Justice had to determine whether the Commission decision was correct that the acquisition of a minority holding in a competing company was not an infringement of **Arts 81 and 82 EC (now 101 and 102 TFEU)**. Two applicant and competitive companies had objected to the decision. The companies, whose activities were the subject of complaint, had remained independent after their agreement to establish cross holdings, so **Art 81 EC (now 101 TFEU)** was considered first. The Commission's decision that no anti-competitive object or effect had been established was upheld by the Court. Furthermore, no control by a particular company had been proved, and so there was no case under **Art 82 EC (now 102 TFEU)** either. However, the CoJ did consider that, although an acquisition of a share of another company or cross holdings might not restrict competition, it may lead to conduct restricting or distorting competition. Thus, it becomes necessary to consider the application of both Articles in such complex situations.

Concentrations/Mergers[6]

[6] The issue of concentration or mergers is the area which highlighted the potential overlap of the two provisions or where both provisions might be considered as applicable to the factual issue.

Originally the Commission was of the view that **Art 81 EC (now 101 TFEU)** would not apply to concentrations or otherwise termed: mergers. Thus, if competition was restricted or distorted by a concentration of companies, **Art 82 EC (now 102 TFEU)** was the appropriate measure with which to tackle it. This policy was pursued by the Commission in the case of *Continental Can* (6/72)[7] when the Commission tried to remedy an abuse of a dominant position which had been achieved by takeovers and substantial holdings in European companies by an American company. It was the first attempt at merger control in this way by the Commission. It was not successful, mainly because the Commission failed to establish the relevant markets, rather than failing to show abuses by the concentration. The view of the Court of Justice in the case was, however, instructive in respect of the relationship of **Arts 81 and 82 EC (now 1010 and 102 TFEU)** and the restrictive approach to the problem adopted by the Commission. The Court of Justice considered that, by refusing to consider the use of **Art 81 EC (now 102 TFEU)** as well, the Commission had handicapped itself.

[7] The *Continental Can* case is the case which prompted a rethink on the part of the Commission about the application of the provisions.

The Court of Justice held that:

> Articles 85 and 86 EC [now 101 and 102 TFEU] seek to achieve the same aim on different levels, viz. the maintenance of effective competition within the Common Market. The restraint of competition which is prohibited if it is the result of behaviour falling under **Article 85 EC [now 101 TFEU]**, cannot be permissible by the fact that such behaviour succeeds under the influence of a dominant undertaking and results in the merger of the undertakings concerned. In the absence of explicit provisions one cannot assume that the Treaty, which prohibits in **Article 85 EC [now 101 TFEU]** certain decisions of ordinary associations of undertakings restricting competition without eliminating it, permits in **Art 86 EC [now 102 TFEU]** that undertakings after merging into an organic unit, should reach such a dominant position that any serious chance of competition is practically rendered impossible. Such diverse legal treatment would make a breach in the entire competition law which could jeopardise the proper functioning of the Common Market.

Thus, firms could avoid **Art 101 TFEU** by establishing close connections but ones which did not constitute full merger and thus be caught by **Art 102 TFEU**. This would allow them to escape the applications of both and to partition the market, and thus defeat the aims of the EU competition policy. In support of the discussion on mergers is the 2013 article on European merger control by Moeschel.[8]

[8] Cited in the 'Taking Things Further' section at the end of the chapter.

In any case **Arts 101 and 102 TFEU** cannot be interpreted in such a way that they contradict each other, because they serve to achieve the same aim. So, depending on the circumstance, it would be wise to consider the possibility of the application of both **Arts 101 and 102 TFEU**. Following the *Continental Can* case, it was realised that a new approach was required to tackle the problems of concentrations and, after some delay, the first **Mergers Regulation (4064/89)** was enacted. This has been considered by the CoJ as applicable to situations of collective dominance rather than **Art 102 TFEU**. See the cases of *France* v *Commission* (C-68/94) and *Société Commerciale des Potasses et de l'Azote (SCPA)* v *Commission* (C-30/95). Therefore, under certain circumstances it might also be necessary to consider the application of the **Mergers Regulation (now 139/04)** as well. Case law also demonstrates a link between the two main competition law Articles in that the CoJ has held that an agreement within the meaning of **Art 101(1) TFEU** between legally separate undertakings may nevertheless result in undertakings being so linked that they become and act as a collective entity as far as their competitors and customers are concerned. As such, then, it can lead to a position of collective dominance which is then capable of being abused, contrary to **Art 102**. See *Compagnie Maritime Belge Transports* (C-395 and 396P/96). It is the conclusion, therefore, that some activities clearly need to be considered in the light of both **Arts 101 and 102 TFEU** and the **Mergers Regulation**.

➕ LOOKING FOR EXTRA MARKS?

- You could mention that a review of merger policy has been taking place with a commission paper being published in 2014 COM (2014) 449 final, but this only recommended limited changes and is still the latest statement on any possible future changes.

↗ TAKING THINGS FURTHER

- Eilmansberger, T, 'How to Distinguish Good from Bad Competition under Article 82: In Search of Clearer and More Coherent Standards for Anti-Competitive Abuses' (2005) 42 CML Rev 49.
  Focuses on what constitutes abuse in what is now Art 102 TFEU cases.
- Lianos, I, 'Collusion in Vertical Relations under Art 81 EC' (2008) 45 CML Rev 1027.
  Highlights what constitutes collusion for the purposes of what is now Art 101 TFEU.
- Moeschel, W, 'European Merger Control' (2013) 34 ECLR 283.
- Slot, P J, 'A View from the Mountain: 40 Years of Developments in EC Competition Law' (2004) 41 CML Rev 443.

■ Witt, A, 'From Airtours to Ryanair: Is the More Economic Approach to EU Merger Law Really about More Economics?' (2012) 49 CML Rev 217.

A closer look at merger policy in action in the EU.

Online Resources
www.oup.com/uk/qanda/

Go online for extra essay and problem questions, a glossary of key terms, online versions of all the answer plans and audio commentary on how selected ones were put together, and a range of podcasts which include advice on exam and coursework technique and advice for other assessment methods.

9 Sex Discrimination and Equality Law

ARE YOU READY?

In order to attempt questions in this chapter, you must have covered all of these topics in both your work over the year and in revision:

- The leading cases in this area which are also those on general principles of EU law; see e.g. the cases of *Marshall* (152/84) and *von Colson* (14/83), amongst others.

- The origin of only a very narrow Treaty provision in **Art 119 EEC (now Art 157 TFEU)** for sex discrimination law in the EU.

- The secondary legislation, which includes the consolidating **Directive (2006/54)** on gender discrimination replaced **Directives 75/117, 76/207, 86/378,** and **97/80** and which was introduced later to back up the limited treaty provision and the extensive case law now in this area of law. The leading case law includes the *Defrenne* litigation **(80/70, 43/75, and 149/77)**, the *Marshall* case **(152/84)**, the *Jenkins v Kingsgate* **(96/80)** and *Bilka-Kaufhaus* cases **(170/84)**, *Marschall* **(C-409/95)**, *Barber* **(C-262/88)**, and *P v S and Cornwall County Council* **(C-13/94)**.

- The fact that the Union has made further legislative moves into the area of social policy and equality rights on a broader front, hence more extensive further equal rights legislation has appeared under **Art 19 TFEU** and **Directives 2000/43, 2000/78 and 2004/113**.

KEY DEBATES

Debate: the development of a general principle of equality in the EU legal order

The **2007 Lisbon Treaty** has reaffirmed the recognition of equality rights in the European Union by the inclusion of equality and non-discrimination provisions in the **Charter of Fundamental Rights** which is attached to the Treaties via a declaration with legally binding status, excepting the

◁

opt-outs for the Czech Republic, Poland, and the UK. A new **Art 10** was introduced into the **TFEU** which provides that the Union in its policies shall aim to combat discrimination, including sex and sexual orientation. No specific substantive changes have been introduced though by the Treaty but the case law of the Court of Justice (CoJ) has substantially prepared the ground for the establishment of a general principle of equality or non-discrimination in the EU.

Q QUESTION | 1

How can the appearance of gender equality rights in the EU Treaties be explained, when the Union seems to be a vehicle for economic integration rather than a champion for women's rights?

! CAUTION

- Although the consolidating **Directive (2006/54)** on gender discrimination replaced **Directives 75/117, 76/207, 86/378, and 97/80**, much of the existing case law was decided under the previous Directives, so you need to be aware of both old and new Directives, and Articles' numbers and how they equate.

▢ DIAGRAM ANSWER PLAN

Outline the original aims and objectives of the European Community (now EU)

▼

Consider reasons for the inclusion of a narrow band of social rights

▼

Consider the development and extension of equal pay and treatment rights

▼

Outline the enactment of a series of equality Directives

▼

Review the judicial developments in equality law (*Defrenne* litigation and others)

▼

Outline the further policy direction of the EU

▼

Summary

[1] This is a general question aimed to address the reason for the inclusion of Articles concerned mainly with the prohibition of discrimination on the grounds of sex within the EU Treaties.

[2] The first part requires you to consider the original aims of the Community (now Union).

[3] Then, the reason for the inclusion of social rights and, in particular, rights concerned with gender equality, which requires you to consider the development of the Community and Union and those rights.

[4] Address the provision of rights in the Treaty, the suggestion that the Union is essentially an economic Union, and the limited place that social concern had or has in its development.

Introduction[1]

The area of sex discrimination law in EU law is a later developer than the other areas of law because of the original, less extensive provision for it in the Treaty, the delays by the Union and the Commission in introducing secondary legislation, and the delays by the Member States in implementing the principles of equal pay from **Art 119 EEC (now 157 TFEU)** and equal pay and equal treatment from the secondary legislation.[2] **Article 119 EEC** was the sole original Treaty provision for the EU concerned with sex discrimination.

Motives for the inclusion of equality rights[3]

Given that the EEC was, originally, of limited scope, it was clear that the main aim of the Community was the harmonisation of specific aspects of the Member States' economies and principally, the creation of the common or single market. Social policy was not regarded as greatly assisting this result. However, it is also suggested that the original reason for including **Art 119 in the EEC Treaty (now Art 157 TFEU)** when drafted was not for reasons of social justice, but out of economic considerations.[4] The Article was allegedly included more for the French, whose legislation purported to provide for equality between male and female workers. It was feared that French industry would be at a disadvantage if equal pay were not a principle enforced in the other Member States. Thus, the aim was to ensure similar economic conditions applied in all the Member States. A consideration which supports this view is the fact that **Art 119 EEC** originally applied only to equal pay and not to all discrimination on the grounds of sex, although the CoJ has since then considerably expanded its scope. There has since a considerable amount of secondary legislation and more general anti-discrimination Articles in the Treaties. The range is now much more extensive and includes **Arts 2 and 3 TEU, Art 8 TFEU,** new **Art 10 TFEU, Art 19 TFEU** (general power to prohibit discrimination across a range of issues), and **Art 153 TFEU** (equality of men and women in the work environment). Furthermore, the EU has enacted **Directives 2000/43 and 2000/78** dealing with other forms of discrimination. The objective to achieve an economic equality between Member States is acknowledged by the CoJ in the second **Defrenne case (43/75)**. The CoJ declared that **Art 119 EEC** also forms part of the social objectives of the Community (EU) and emphasised that the Community (EU) was not merely an economic union. The CoJ considered that it was at the same time intended, by common action, to ensure social progress and to seek the constant improvement of the living and working conditions of their peoples, as could be observed in the Preamble to the Treaty. It concluded that the double aim, which is at once economic and social, shows that the principle of equal pay forms part of the foundations of the Community (EU). This has been followed up in the case of *Deutsche Telekom* v *Vick* (C-324 and 325/96) in which the CoJ pronounced that the social aims of **Art 119 EEC** prevail over those of the economic aims.

Therefore, whilst the initial concern may have been for economic reasons and originally the economic goals of the Community (EU) were undoubtedly paramount, present aims are arguably more genuinely concerned with social rights and rights of equality, as demonstrated by developments, including the Directives on equal treatment and the body of EU law now. This developing concern was prompted by a desire by the Member States in the European Summit meetings in 1972–3 to demonstrate that the EU was also concerned about social needs and equal rights and the view adopted by the original Member States was that it was necessary to get their act together before the new Member States joined in 1973.

The adoption of equality Directives[5]

[5] Then you should consider what the position is now, following the legislative, judicial, and policy developments in the area.

Consequently, the Commission was encouraged to produce a Social Action Programme, from which the following Directives arose: **Council Directive 75/117, the Equal Pay Directive 1975; Council Directive 76/207, the Equal Treatment Directive**; and **Directive 79/7, the Social Security Directive**. Much later came **Directive 86/378** on equal treatment in occupational pensions, **Directive 86/613** concerning equal treatment of the self-employed, and **Directive 92/85** on pregnancy and maternity rights. To these can now be added the **Parental Leave Directive (96/34)**, the **Burden of Proof in Sex Discrimination Cases Directive (97/80)**, and the **Part-time Workers Directive (97/81)**. More recently, **Directives 75/117, 76/207, 86/378,** and **97/80** have been repealed and recast in **Directive 2006/54** but without substantive amendment. The more recent secondary legislation includes **Directive 2004/113** on equality in the access to and the supply of goods and services, **Directive 2010/41** on equal treatment between self-employed men and women, and **Directive 2010/18** on parental leave.

Judicial developments[6]

[6] The eventual provision of rights is best discussed in the light of the CoJ case law.

However, EU law often seemed unsuitable for the provision of individual rights and was criticised because of its formality, limited accessibility, and distance from those who needed the effective application and enforcement of the provisions, i.e. women at work. The effect was, at first, that very little knowledge of EU equal rights law was disseminated beyond the small number of people in direct contact with these laws except where given substantial media publicity after the event, as in the leading cases such as the *Marshall* case (152/84), the *Pickstone* v *Freemans* case ([1988] 3 CMLR 221), the *Drake* case (150/85), and the *Webb* v *EMO* case (C-32/93). EU law has, however, provided a considerable source of legislative impetus for women's rights in employment in the Member States.

EU law provisions have been dependent largely on individual enforcement for their effectiveness where either governments have failed to take appropriate measures to implement them or enforce them if implemented, or the European Commission has not taken enforcement actions against the recalcitrant governments. It has largely been on the individual level only that these rights have been successfully established as positive rights for women. Notable successes such include the *Defrenne* litigation **(80/70, 43/75, and 149/77)** involving a Belgian air stewardess whose action gave the Court of Justice the opportunity to interpret **Art 119 EEC** to include indirect and more subtle forms of discrimination. Another prime example of individual action required to force change is the *Marshall* case. These cases appear to have created more interest in the enforcement and the development of women's rights than the efforts of many national groups, although the backing of national agencies to promote equal rights has been fundamental in promoting women's rights, particularly in Belgium and the UK.

[7]Highlight that many of the judgments of the CoJ have been very generous in support of equality rights and give examples.

The liberal interpretation of the Court of Justice[7]

An important factor is that the EU legal provisions can be and have been subject to very liberal interpretations by the Court of Justice, far beyond a literal reading of the Articles; see e.g. the wide interpretation of **Art 157 TFEU (ex 119 EEC and 141 EC)**, including the concept of pay in the *Garland* case (12/81), and the concept of indirect discrimination in the *Jenkins* v *Kingsgate* (96/80) and *Bilka-Kaufhaus* cases (170/84). The Equal Treatment Directives have also been interpreted generously in cases such as *Marschall* **(C-409/95)** and *Barber* **(C-262/88)**. The Court has even advanced the cause of equal rights through procedural means so that an effective remedy should be given by the Member States in cases where rights have been breached; see the *von Colson* case (14/83) and the *Johnston* v *RUC* case (222/84). In *Richards* (C-423/04) equal treatment rights were held to apply to secure equal right to pension access for a transgendered woman. More recently the *Mangold* case (C-144/04) provides that non-discrimination as a general principle is one that can be enforced horizontally between individuals.

Although sex discrimination rights, of course, apply equally to men and women, they have been regarded as more beneficial, for the most part, for women, who were generally more discriminated against. However, the body of case law involving claims by men is increasing.

Equality rights in the EU were considerably strengthened by changes introduced by the **Treaty of Amsterdam**.[8] The Treaty introduced in **Art 2 EC** 'equality between men and women' and added in **Art 3 EC**: 'In all the activities referred to in this Article, the Community shall aim to eliminate inequalities, and to promote equality, between men and women.' These are now to be found in **Arts 2 and 3 TEU** and **Art 8 TFEU**. Furthermore, a new power was introduced in **Art 13 EC (now 19 TFEU)** that the Council, acting unanimously, and in consultation with the EP, may take appropriate action to combat discrimination based on sex or sexual orientation, amongst others. **Directive 2000/78** provides a framework to prohibit direct or indirect discrimination generally in employment on the grounds of religion or belief, disability, age, or sexual orientation. The **EC Treaty** was amended by adding two sentences to **Art 141 EC (now 157 TFEU)** which located within a Treaty base the principles of equal pay for work of equal value and positive discrimination previously contained in Directives only, which meant that they could not previously have given rise to direct effects against other individuals (no horizontal direct effects of Directives—*Marshall*). The *Mangold* and *Kükükdeveci* judgments, noted here, may, though, have circumvented that limitation. The **Lisbon Treaty** has attached the **Charter of Fundamental Rights** to the Treaties which has further provided for equality rights. Furthermore, **Art 10** of the **TFEU** provides that the Union in its policies shall aim to combat discriminations including sex and sexual orientation. A general summary article on gender equality law has been provided by Masselot.[9]

[9] Cited in the 'Taking Things Further' section at the end of the Chapter.

Positive discrimination

Measures of positive discrimination have, however, been given a mixed reception by the CoJ and rules of positive discrimination which try to promote the appointment of women to achieve more substantive rather than just formal equality have been subject to exacting criteria to ensure that men are not then discriminated against. See the case of *Marshall* **(C-409/95)**.

[10] Your conclusion may range from considering that the Union and, in particular, the CoJ have contributed significantly in promoting and enforcing equal treatment rights for women, to the view that it has only done what was to be expected or not enough so far.

Summary[10]

In summary, although **Art 119** provided the only specific mention of equal treatment in the original **EEC Treaty**, it formed the basis upon which the principle has been expanded into areas beyond equal pay, and has become a fundamental social principle of the Treaty **(now 157 TFEU)**. Whilst the amount of legislation is limited, it has been subject to very liberal interpretations by the CoJ far beyond a literal reading of the Articles in cases more often brought by individuals rather than the Commission in **Art 258 TFEU** actions; see the *Garland*, *Defrenne*, and *Marschall* cases.

+ LOOKING FOR EXTRA MARKS?

- Making reference to and discussing the potential of the EU Charter of Fundamental Rights for extending the general rights' provision in the EU would be a useful addition.

- You might also mention though that attempts by the Commission to promote a general Directive on equality rights, including covering sexual orientation discrimination, has thus far not been approved by the Council where it required unanimous support under **Art 19 TFEU**.

Q — QUESTION 2

Meg and Nicola work part-time for the telephone call centre of the 'Chaste Direct Bank'. They discover that even though they were working what they considered to be antisocial hours (from 6.00 pm until 12.00 midnight), they were receiving less per hour than their full-time colleagues working during daylight hours. There are 18 female and 2 male part-time evening workers. The daytime staff are evenly divided between male and female workers. Meg complains to her boss, Mr Branston, that this appears to be discrimination. He explains that it is far easier to get staff for evening work and, in particular, women find this a very suitable way of combining their commitment to a family and childcare sharing, and being able to earn money. He has very many applicants for the part-time evening work but in contrast far fewer for the daytime work. Soon after, Meg is dismissed on the grounds of displaying a poor attitude. She has found it difficult to obtain alternative employment as Mr Branston has failed to respond to enquiries for a reference for Meg.

Nicola became pregnant but suffered ill health as a result of the pregnancy. She was forced to take time off during the early part of the pregnancy but, after a successful birth she returned to work at the end of her 14 weeks' maternity leave. Her rights to the Sports and Social Club were suspended during her maternity leave. However, since the birth of her baby, the health problems which had first manifested themselves during pregnancy flared up again and, combined with the depression from which Nicola also suffers, has meant she has been absent for 25 days in 12 weeks. She was dismissed because she exceeded the number of days off which could be taken on the grounds of ill health.

The call centre has advertised for a new manager. The shortlist for applications consists of two equally qualified persons only. George is an internal candidate who already works for the company and Posy is an external applicant. 'Chaste Direct' stated its positive discrimination policy for filling job vacancies in the advertisement and as a result has appointed Posy as the new manager. George has protested that he has been discriminated against by the company and threatens to take the matter to court. In response the company issue him with a formal warning that he will be dismissed if he causes any more difficulty. Shortly afterwards another management position is advertised and George applies again but under the name Georgina. Appearing at the interview, George/Georgina states that he intends to undergo a sex-change operation. This time there was no equally or better qualified female applicant. George/Georgina, however, was dismissed.

Meg, Nicola, and George seek your advice as to their rights, if any, under EU law.

CAUTION

■ This is quite a complex and involved question with a number of points to be addressed.

■ Given that this is such a long question, any general treatment must be brief to give you time to deal with the many substantive issues arising.

DIAGRAM ANSWER PLAN

Identify the issues	■ Identify the facts which give rise to legal issues
Relevant law	■ Introduce **Art 157 TFEU**, the applicable Directives, and the various issues.
Apply the law	■ Equal pay (*Jenkins*, *Bilka-Kaufhaus*, and *Enderby* cases) ■ Pregnancy rights (*Lewen*, *Larsson*, and *Brown* cases) ■ Positive discrimination (*Marshall* and *Badeck* cases) ■ Dismissal of George (*P v S* case) ■ Procedural difficulties with direct effects in the national courts.
Conclude	■ Conclusion

SUGGESTED ANSWER

[1] As a general introduction to this problem on discrimination you could state the narrow Treaty base for EU law, but that a number of Directives have been issued.

Introduction[1]

The area of law applicable to the factual situation in this problem stems originally from a very narrow legislative base in the **EEC Treaty**. This is **Art 119 (now 157 TFEU)** which was the sole primary legislative provision for the EU to concern itself with sex discrimination. It is concerned predominantly with equal pay but also, following the **Treaty of Amsterdam**, with positive discrimination. There also exists a growing body of EU law on the subject following the enactment of a number of Directives, on matters of equality between men and women. Case law on these, as with the original Treaty provision, has extended the scope of protection further.[2]

[2] Point out that the Court interprets these rights liberally, to give the maximum protection to the rights provided.

The facts

The factual circumstances in this question give rise to a number of issues to be resolved. They are:

[3] You must identify the issues, which start with part-time pay, an old favourite but nevertheless still frequently appearing in exam questions. This may be an equal pay claim or possibly equal pay for work of equal value.

[4] There is a possible objective justification which needs to be discussed.

[5] Then include the dismissal of Meg and the failure to give a reference.

[6] Nicola's treatment during pregnancy and dismissal afterwards.

[7] Finally the issues affecting George. These are the failure to be appointed, which includes an aspect of positive discrimination, and the dismissal.

[8] With reference to the appropriate statutory provisions first, and case law where relevant, you should suggest the outcome of these issues.

(a) part-time pay[3]
(b) the possible objective justification[4]
(c) the dismissal of Meg
(d) the failure to give a reference[5]
(e) Nicola's treatment during pregnancy and dismissal afterwards[6]
(f) the failure to appoint George and his dismissal.[7]

The part-time staff, who are predominantly women, receive less pay per hour than the full-timers. Meg is claiming that she has been indirectly discriminated against compared to full-time workers and despite the fact they are paid the same as male part-time workers, of which there are only 2 out of 20.

The law applicable[8]

The principal enactments we are concerned with are **Art 157 TFEU** and the consolidating **Directive 2006/54**. It is well-established law that the prohibition of discrimination in pay under **Art 157 TFEU** applies not only to direct but also to indirect discrimination. The cases of *Jenkins* v *Kingsgate* **(96/80)** and *Bilka-Kaufhaus* v *Weber* **(170/84)** confirm that this situation will be regarded as indirect discrimination, when a disadvantage falls on a category which is predominantly female, unless it can be justified objectively. Indirect discrimination in this area is covered in the consolidating **Directive 2006/54** which takes its definition from the earlier general discrimination Directives as 'where an apparently neutral provision, criterion, or practice would put persons of one sex at a particular disadvantage compared with persons of the other sex, unless that provision, criterion, or practice is objectively justified by a legitimate aim, and the means of achieving that aim are appropriate and necessary'. The *Bilka-Kaufhaus* case provides three guidelines to determine whether a difference in pay is objectively justified. The measure employed must:

- correspond to a real need on the part of the undertaking
- be appropriate to achieve the objective
- be necessary for that objective.

It is, though, in the end, a question of fact to be decided by the national court but the CoJ has further held in the case of *Dansk* v *Danfoss* **(109/88)** that the burden is to be placed on the employer to prove that the difference is justified and that this should be transparent. The reasons put forward in the present case appear to be an objective justification because there is no shortage of applicants for part-time positions compared with full-time daytime positions. However, it is combined with references to marital and family status, which was expressly covered in **Art 2** of the **Equal Treatment Directive (76/207)**, namely that there shall be no discrimination whatsoever on grounds of sex either directly or indirectly by reference in particular to family or marital status, although that particular reference has been omitted from the consolidating **Directive 2006/54**. This would appear to be unlawful indirect discrimination but if there is a doubt, given the applicants for the positions, a reference under **Art 267 TFEU** to the CoJ may be necessary to decide the point.

An equal value claim?

There may also be an argument here that Meg has a claim for equal pay for work of equal value. **Article 157 TFEU** now includes the words 'equal pay for work of equal value', previously restricted to **Directive 75/117**. In the present case, Meg is comparing her wages with a male worker whose work is arguably of equal or lesser value because it is daytime work and she is working antisocial hours but receives lower wages. She could ask for a job evaluation scheme and should the company refuse to carry out a job evaluation scheme to test this, it can be imposed on them through court proceedings (*Commission v UK* (61/81)). Following *Murphy* v *Irish Telecom* (157/86) and *Enderby* v *Frenchay* (C-127/92), in which the CoJ held that **Art 119 EEC (now 157 TFEU)** could be used to make a comparison of work of equal value, this claim has a good chance of success. **Article 19 of Directive 2006/54** now removes the need to produce statistical evidence to support a claim of indirect discrimination in pay and that the burden of proof was on the employer to rebut this.

Meg's dismissal

Meg was then dismissed, which appears to be a reaction to her making a complaint, and this is specifically covered now in **Directive 2006/54, Art 24** which serves to protect complainants from unfair dismissal on the grounds that they have complained. The procedural difficulty that this is a private employer will be considered at the end of this answer.

Meg's reference refusal

Finally concerning Meg is the refusal to give a reference. This point is covered by the case of *Coote* v *Granada* (C-185/97) which held that a refusal to provide a reference would undermine **Art 6 of Directive 76/207** but which is contained now in **Directive 2006/54, Art 17**, under which Member States should take measures to achieve the aims of the Directive and must ensure the rights can be enforced by an individual before the national courts. The CoJ held that **Art 6 of Directive 76/207** also covers measures an employer might take as a reaction against legal proceedings of a former employee outside of dismissal.

Nicola's issues

Turning to Nicola, the suspension of rights during 14 weeks would appear to be a straightforward breach of **Art 11 of Directive 92/85** which serves to protect employment rights during pregnancy and maternity (see *Susanne Lewen* v *Lothar Denda* (C-333/97)). If there was any doubt about this, a reference to the CoJ would be necessary. However, the dismissal for absence outside of the 14-week protected period due to ill health arising from pregnancy would appear to be lawful according to the case law of the CoJ and not protected by either **Directive 76/207 or 92/85** and with no change under **Directive 2006/54**. See *Larsson* v *Dansk Handel and Service* (C-400/95), in which the CoJ confirmed that **Directive 76/207** does not prevent dismissals for absences due to illness attributable to pregnancy even where the illness arose during pregnancy and continued during and after maternity. **Directive 92/85** does not help as this also only protects against dismissal for the beginning of pregnancy to the end of maternity leave, as confirmed in *Brown* v *Rentokil* (C-394/96). Absences due to illnesses thereafter are treated in the same way as any other illness and may constitute grounds for dismissal according to provisions of national law. The case of *NW Health Board* v *McKenna* (C-191/03) confirms that this basis of comparison is acceptable. Hence, the dismissal appears to be lawful.

[9] For the purposes of answering the question, at least, you will have to assume that the stated intention of George is genuine.

George and gender discrimination[9]

George was not appointed and suspects the positive discrimination policy has actually discriminated against him. Positive discrimination is now located in **Art 157(4) TFEU** although the first cases arose under **Directive 76/207, Art 2(4)**, now recast in **Art 3 of Directive 2006/54**. In the case of *Hellmut Marschall* v *Land Nordrhein-Westfalen* (C-409/95), the CoJ held that clauses favouring women applicants would only be acceptable if they contained a 'saving clause' which provides that if a particular male candidate has grounds which tilt the balance in his favour, women are not to be given priority. Further, such clauses are acceptable provided the candidates are objectively assessed to determine whether there are any factors tilting the balance in favour of a male candidate but that such criteria employed do not themselves discriminate against women. This position is now supported by the *Badeck* case (C-158/97) which is based on **Art 141(4) EC (now 157 TFEU)**. The facts reveal no such clause in the present case, and unless there is such a clause or careful assessment by the bank, it is unlikely that the positive discrimination policy of the bank conforms with EU law.

George's dismissal

George was dismissed after stating that he was to undergo a sex-change operation. These facts fit within the case of *P* v *S and Cornwall County Council* (C-13/94) which involved a male-to-female transsexual who was dismissed from employment in an educational establishment after informing the employers he was going to undergo gender reassignment. The CoJ held that this was unlawful discrimination on the grounds of sex because it was 'based, essentially if not exclusively on the sex of the person concerned'. The dismissal would be contrary to **Art 24 of Directive 2006/54** which provides that Member States must introduce into their own legal systems such measures as are necessary to enable all persons who consider themselves wronged to pursue their claims by judicial process.

Claims in the national tribunals[10]

[10] Consider the right to pursue these claims before the national tribunals, because they are employed by a private employer, which may affect their rights to remedy in the national courts.

The final aspect concerns the difficulties which might arise in respect of pursuit of the claims in the national tribunals. Any claims made under **Art 157 TFEU** will be safe in all circumstances because this was held to be directly effective in *Defrenne (No 2)* **(43/75)**, both vertically against the state and horizontally against other individuals. If the Member State has accurately implemented the Directives, then applicants can invoke national law before the national court. However, if they have not been implemented or correctly implemented, the claimants will be unable to rely directly on the Directives because a private employer is involved and there are no horizontal direct effects of Directives; see the *Marshall* case **(152/84)**. The result in such a circumstance would depend on whether the national court could interpret any national law in compliance with EU law, thus following the *von Colson* **(14/83)** and *Marleasing* cases **(C-106/89)**. If this is not the case, a further possibility exists in that a claim may be made against the state, in accordance with the *Francovich* case **(C-6/90)**, for a failure to implement the Directive with the result that the claimant has suffered damage.

✚ LOOKING FOR EXTRA MARKS?

■ The final part of the answer above may be regarded as coming within this feature, unless you are advised on a particular course that a full discussion of the procedural aspects of the case must be given.

■ A brief statement of the problems and possible solutions will complete an answer in a question which essentially concerns sex discrimination.

Ⓠ QUESTION | 3

'Strange Fruit', a wholesale fruit merchant, advertise for a full-time permanent secretary and also for a temporary sales post for four months to provide cover for a member of staff on secondment to another workplace. All the existing secretarial positions in the company are part-time appointments.

The two main contenders for the permanent position are Tony and Astrid. Their qualifications are broadly equivalent but Astrid has slightly more experience, but not so much as to make her a clear favourite. In line with their policy of positive discrimination to appoint staff of the minority sex to

Ⓥ

posts predominantly staffed by the other sex, they decide to appoint Tony. As a part of that policy they have increased Tony's salary by 10 per cent pro rata over and above that paid to the existing part-time secretaries and provided him with a 20 per cent pension enhancement. The appointment is challenged by Astrid and the increased pay and pension payments have been questioned by Karen, an existing secretary. SF argue that their policy conforms with EU law and argue that the pension enhancement is linked to the state pension age and the fact that men generally work to an older age but die younger, so their policy helps to ensure that male employees get to enjoy the fruits of their labour in the shorter period of retirement likely to be available to them. The increased pay is to attract full-time workers, which, it is argued, is more cost-efficient for the employer.

In the interview for the temporary post, the applicant Clare was asked if there were any grounds which would prevent her from fulfilling all the duties of the contract during the busiest fruit sales period of spring and summer. She replied that there were no obstacles and was subsequently appointed, starting work on 1 May. Clare knew she was pregnant at the time of the interview and after just three weeks in work announced that she was due to give birth at the end of June and was taking maternity leave as from 1 June. When she left work one week later, she was dismissed and paid only for the time actually worked.

Advise the various parties of their rights under EU law.

CAUTION

- Note that it is intended by the question that you take account of case developments.
- Hence, you should concentrate on these developments.

DIAGRAM ANSWER PLAN

Identify the issues	■ Identify the facts which give rise to legal issues
Relevant law	■ Refer to **Art 157 TFEU**, especially **paragraph 4** and **Directive 2006/54** and the positive discrimination provisions.
Apply the law	■ Review case law of *Kalanke*, *Marschall*, and *Badeck* ■ Equal pay issue cases (*Jenkins*, *Bilka-Kaufhaus*, and *Enderby*) ■ Pregnant temporary worker dismissal cases (*Webb*, *Mahlberg*, and *Tele Danmark*)
Conclude	■ Summarise and conclude

[1] This question revisits positive discrimination and the dismissal of Clare who applied and was appointed to a temporary position when pregnant but was subsequently dismissed when the pregnancy was revealed.

[2] Provide a general introduction to the area of law and the problem before moving on to consider the factual issues arising.

[3] In particular, positive discrimination is a feature of this problem.

Introduction and issues arising[1]

This question is concerned with some of the more recent developments of equality law, which has become one of the fundamental policies of EU substantive law.[2] The issues which arise are the appointment of a worker on the basis of the application of a policy of positive discrimination, which then gives rise to Astrid's claim to equal access to employment under **Directive 2006/54**. It is also concerned with indirect discrimination between full-time and part-time workers and finally the dismissal of a pregnant woman from a temporary contract.

Positive discrimination[3]

A limited form of positive discrimination is provided in **Art 3 of Directive 2006/54** and **paragraph (4) of Art 157 TFEU**. **Article 3** of the Directive provides that the Directive shall be without prejudice to measures to promote equal opportunity for men and women, in particular by removing existing inequalities which affect women's opportunities. It would seem therefore to concern women only but not exclusively, as seen in case law. Hence, despite the actual words contained within the Directive, it was not limited to women. **Article 157(4) TFEU** provides:

With a view to ensuring full equality in practice between men and women in working life, the principle of equal treatment shall not prevent any Member State from maintaining or adopting measures providing for specific advantages in order to make it easier for the under-represented sex to pursue a vocational activity or to prevent or compensate for disadvantages in professional careers.

The Treaty Article is thus aimed at covering both men and women but is specifically addressed to the Member States. It would nevertheless have direct effects. The facts of the present case involve a private employer; therefore the Treaty Article would need to be applied if there were any doubts about the Directive. **Article 3 of Directive 2006/54** provides that Member States may maintain or adopt measures within the meaning of **Art 141(4) EC (now 157 TFEU)** with a view to ensuring full equality in practice between men and women, thus backing up the amended Article in the Treaty.

It has already been observed in the cases of *Kalanke* **(C-450/93)**, *Marschall* **(C-409/95)**, and *Badeck* **(C-158/97)** that where a policy of positive discrimination is employed it should not automatically favour one sex and that procedures must be included within any such policy to ensure that an objective assessment of the individual candidates is undertaken. This position was made even clearer in the case of *Abrahamsson* **(C-407/98)** whereby a female was appointed to a university chair in preference to a male applicant on the basis of a positive discrimination regulation and despite a clear vote in favour of a male applicant (5:3), his qualifications, and the overall higher ranking of the male. The university contended that the difference was not so great as to breach the objectivity requirement. However, the CoJ held that EC (EU) law, primary or secondary, does not support appointments based on automatic preference for the underrepresented sex irrespective of whether the qualifications are better or worse and where no objective assessment of each candidate has taken place. Whether that would be enough in Astrid's case to support her claim for unlawful discrimination in access to employment contrary to **Arts 1 and 4 of Directive 2006/54** is difficult to say with certainty in the absence of more detailed facts. A reference to the CoJ may be needed.

[4] The other issues must, of course, still be addressed, starting with the pay difference.

The pay difference[4]

What is clear from numerous cases and pronouncements of the CoJ is that the additional salary for Tony as a full-timer in comparison with the female part-timers could only be accepted as lawful if objectively justified (see the cases of *Jenkins* (96/80), *Bilka-Kaufhaus* (170/84), and *Enderby* (C-127/92)). Here, there does not appear to be an overwhelming objective reason to support this. The increase in pension is also to be regarded as pay following the *Barber case* (C-262/88) and must therefore also be at the same rate unless similarly objectively justified. It may also be argued that it is up to the pension fund actuaries to determine the pension payments and the amount needed to be paid into the pension fund and not for the employers themselves. Indeed, this will have already been taken into account in calculating payments, thus removing the need for the employer to do so, in which case it appears more like an unlawful discriminatory measure. Again, in the event of uncertainty here, a reference to the CoJ should be made.

[5] Dismissal during or as a result of pregnancy is an issue which has received close attention from the CoJ.

The dismissal of a pregnant worker[5]

The final issue here concerns the dismissal of the pregnant worker from a temporary post. However unjust it might be felt in certain quarters that the employer is suffering unduly in such a circumstance, a line of cases from the CoJ show clearly that the CoJ upholds fully the rights provided now by **Directive 2006/54, Art 15** and **Directive 92/85, Art 10** in protecting women workers from dismissal whilst pregnant including those on temporary contracts (see the cases of *Webb* (C-32/93), *Mahlberg* (C-207/98), and *Tele Danmark* (C-109/00)). In the last case, the pregnant worker had also not informed the employer of her pregnancy; however, the CoJ held quite clearly that 'Had the Community legislature wished to exclude fixed-term contracts, which represent a substantial proportion of the employment relationships, from the scope of those directives, it would have done so expressly.' The only distinguishing factor would be that in the present case, the employers specifically asked whether there would be any grounds on which the applicant could not fulfil the entire contract. Once again, only a reference to the CoJ on this point would determine whether it would make any difference to alter the previous view of the court. I would suggest it would not, particularly in the light of *Busch* (C-320/01) in which the pregnancy of a worker returning to duty was not revealed to the employer, although there is clearly scope for argument.

Summary

Overall then, the employer appears to be in breach of EU law provisions for the actions it has undertaken.

+ LOOKING FOR EXTRA MARKS?

- Some discussion on positive discrimination would be interesting, if there is time. After an initial flurry of cases, you might suggest that this seems to have stalled, with no new cases recently.
- If there is time, you might also mention the improvement in remedies and damages available for those suffering discrimination has helped in realising the overall aims of equality.

Q QUESTION | 4

To what extent has the EU moved from prohibiting discrimination on the grounds of sex to the provision of much more far-reaching equality protection? What is the evidence of the elevated status of a general principle of equality?

! CAUTION

- As with similar very open questions in this book, be careful that you do not write a long rambling answer on anything and everything without focusing on any topic in particular and without, in the end, answering the question.

◻ DIAGRAM ANSWER PLAN

> Outline the original Treaty provisions outlawing discrimination

▼

> Highlight the considerable extension of gender and other discrimination prohibition

▼

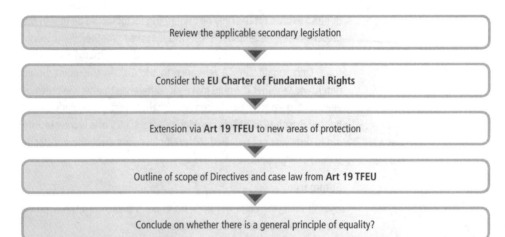

Review the applicable secondary legislation

Consider the **EU Charter of Fundamental Rights**

Extension via **Art 19 TFEU** to new areas of protection

Outline of scope of Directives and case law from **Art 19 TFEU**

Conclude on whether there is a general principle of equality?

SUGGESTED ANSWER

[1] This question seeks your knowledge of equality, which the EU has now incorporated, and how equality is developing into a general principle and being supported by the Court of Justice.

[2] You need to commence with an outline of the limited original provision for prohibiting discrimination (then just equal pay).

[3] Then, but only briefly, outline its extension over time to considerable provision for gender equality to the now much more extensive scope of equality protection.

Introduction[1]

The EU originally provided a Treaty base that only prohibited discrimination in relation to the pay of men and women[2] (**Art 119 EEC**). This was, however, expanded over the years by both increased Treaty provision and directives to outlaw discrimination between men and women and then into other areas of discrimination protection.

Expanded the Treaty provision[3]

Article 157 TFEU (ex 119 EEC and 141 EC) on equal pay for equal work originally provided the only specific mention of equal treatment of the sexes in the **EC Treaty**, but, following amendments to the Treaties, equality provisions are more extensive. In addition to the main Treaty Article, **Art 157 TFEU**, the **Treaty of Amsterdam** introduced as one of the goals now outlined in **Art 2 TEU**, 'equality between men and women', and **Art 3 TEU** states the aim 'to promote . . . equality, between men and women'.

Equality between men and women in the working environment was also included in the **1989 Community Social Charter**, which was brought into **Art 136 EC (now 151 TFEU)**. The amended **Art 137 EC (now 153 TFEU)** provides that the Union shall complement and support the activities of the Member States in the field of equality between men and women with regard to labour market opportunities and treatment at work.

Article 157 TFEU was amended and added to by the **Treaty of Amsterdam** which added two sentences to locate within a Treaty base the principles of equal pay for work of equal value and action to promote equality but which falls short of out-and-out positive discrimination.

There are now a number of examples of express prohibitions of discrimination within the Treaty, but there is not, as such, an express general principle of non-discrimination or equality. The specific prohibitions do, however, support the emergence of a general principle in the EU legal order that is additionally supported by the judgments of the CoJ and academic commentary. In addition to the ones noted elsewhere, the Treaty Articles that seek either to prohibit discrimination or promote equality are:

- **Article 8 TFEU**, general statement on equality between men and women
- new **Article 10 TFEU**, general statement on equality
- **Article 18 TFEU**, on nationality
- **Article 40(2) TFEU**, concerned with equality between producers and between consumers in the **Common Agricultural Policy (CAP)**
- **Articles 45, 49, and 56 TFEU**, providing for equal treatment of workers and the self-employed
- **Article 106 TFEU**, on public undertakings
- **Article 110 TFEU**, on taxation.

All of these Articles support the development of a general principle of equality by the establishment of a legal culture that does not tolerate the different treatment of like, or the same treatment of unequals across a range of subject matters.

[4]Highlight the importance of **Art 19 TFEU**.

Finally, as far as the Treaties are concerned, a new enabling power has been provided in **Art 19 TFEU (ex 13 EC)**, which provides:[4]

the Council, acting unanimously in accordance with a special legislative procedure and after obtaining the consent of the European Parliament, may take appropriate action to combat discrimination based on sex, racial or ethnic origin, religion or belief, disability, age or sexual orientation.

[5]Outline the expansion of rights protection by secondary EU legislation.

Secondary legislation[5]

The first secondary legislative interventions in this area were enacted following the publication of a social action programme in 1974 by the Commission. Three Directives concerned with equality between men and women were adopted:

- the **Equal Pay Directive 75/117**
- the **Equal Treatment Directive 76/207**
- the **Social Security Directive 79/7**.

A second social action programme in 1982 led to the enactment of **Directive 86/378** on equal treatment in occupational pensions and **Directive 86/613** on equal treatment of the self-employed and protection of self-employed women during pregnancy and motherhood (now replaced by **Directive 2010/41**).

The amendment of the **EC Treaty** by the SEA in 1986 resulted in the enactment of the **Pregnancy and Maternity Directive 92/85**. The **Maastricht Treaty** led to the **Parental Leave Directive 96/34**, repealed and replaced now by **Directive 2010/18**, the **Burden of Proof in Sex Discrimination Cases Directive 97/80**, and the **Part-time Workers Directive 97/81**. The more recent secondary legislation includes **Directive 2004/113** on equality in the access to and the supply of goods and services, and **Directive 2010/41** providing for equal treatment of the self-employed.

EU Charter of Fundamental Rights[6]

[6]The **EU Charter of Fundamental Rights**, which further supports a general principle, must also be included in your answer.

The **EU Charter of Fundamental Rights** further provides **Arts 20–23**, which prohibit discrimination on any grounds in **Art 21**, i.e. sex, race, colour, ethnic or social origin, genetic features, language, religion or belief, political or any other opinion, membership of a national minority, property, birth, disability, age, and sexual orientation. The CoJ is now making reference to it and it will no doubt feature much more in case law in the future.

Article 19 TFEU Directives[7]

[7]Consider whether there is a general principle of equality within the EU legal order and if there is evidence of this. The scope of the Directives issued under **Art 19 TFEU** are crucial in this expansion of equality rights.

Article 13 EC (now 19 TFEU) provided the Treaty with a new legal base for the enactment of legislation to tackle discrimination across a range of issues. The Article does not actually prohibit anything in its own right, but empowers the Council to take action to combat discrimination based on sex, racial or ethnic origin, religion or belief, disability, age, or sexual orientation. Two Directives were enacted in 2000 that, between them and the 2006 recast Equal Treatment Directive, encompass many of the matters identified in **Art 19 TFEU** where action was deemed necessary to combat discrimination.

The Racial Equality Directive (Directive 2000/43)

The first Directive adopted under **Art 13 EC (now 19 TFEU)** seeks to apply the principle of equal treatment to persons regardless of racial or ethnic origin in matters of employment, social protection, education, and access to public goods and services, including housing (**Art 3(1)**). An exception is provided whereby differential treatment can be justified where a certain characteristic is a genuine and determining occupational requirement (**Art 4(1)**).

The Framework Employment Directive (Directive 2000/78)

This Directive deals with all of the other forms of discrimination identified by **Art 19 TFEU (ex 13 EC)**, with the exception of the matters covered by the Racial Equality Directive and Directives on equality between men and women. It provides that there should be no discrimination, direct or indirect, on the grounds of religion or belief, disability, age, or sexual orientation. As with forms of indirect discrimination under previous Directives, indirect discrimination can be objectively justified provided that it is proportionate (**Art 4**). An exception exists whereby different treatment can be justified by a certain characteristic that is a genuine and determining occupational requirement (**Art 4(1)**). There is also a special exemption for access to employment in religious organisations (**Art 4(2)**), and there are further exceptions in respect of disability (**Art 5**) where measures to accommodate disabled persons would cause employers a disproportionate burden, along with numerous exceptions in respect of age (**Art 6**).

In 2004, **Directive 2004/113** was enacted to implement the principle of equality between men and women in the access to and supply of goods and services. It applies to the provision of all public and private sector supply of goods and service outside the sphere of private and family life transactions.

[8] Turn to the CoJ and its case law to support your view. The cases of *Mangold* and *Kükükdeveci* are most instructive here as to the development and value of a general principle.

Case law from the Article 19 TFEU Directives[8]

Of the many cases now arising, the only examples provided here are those which clearly support the development of a general principle of equality and not those merely considering particular provisions of the Directives. *Mangold v Helm* (**C-144/04**) concerns age discrimination that resulted from a scheme to ease the employment of older workers. It was held that a change of German law to assist older workers in finding work went beyond the objectively justified exceptions permitted in **Art 6(1) of Directive 2000/78**, even though its implementation period had not expired. Mangold became subject to the change, which allowed workers over the age of 52, previously 58, to be employed on fixed-term contracts without accruing compensation rights on termination, as opposed to permanent contracts, which would allow such rights. The justification for the ruling was that non-discrimination on the grounds of age was part of the general principle of non-discrimination in EU law and thus applicable in its own right, but with reference to the norms contained in the Directive for assistance.

The decision in the *Mangold* case was subsequently affirmed by the CoJ in *Kükükdeveci* (**C-555/07**), which involved a dispute about a notice period between an employee and a private employer because a German law precluded periods of employment completed before the employee reached the age of 25 from counting towards the notice period. **Directive 2000/78** should have been implemented in Germany at the material time, but it had not. The preliminary ruling question was essentially: on what provision of law could Kükükdeveci rely? The CoJ held that the general principle of EU law prohibiting discrimination on the grounds of law, as expressed in **Directive 2000/78**, applies to preclude national law from discriminating.

Hence the existence and value of a general principle of equal treatment has been acknowledged and confirmed by the CoJ in a number of cases: recently, e.g. in *Chatzi* (**C-149/10**), in which the Court held that the principle of equal treatment is one of the general principles of EU law and is now affirmed by **Art 20** of the **EU Charter of Fundamental Rights** (in that case, to support the right to parental leave on an equal basis). A good overview of developments in equality law has been provided by Prechel.[9]

[9] Cited in the 'Taking Things Further' section at the end of the chapter.

Summary

Equality law provision in the EU has developed, from limited beginnings, a number of genuine and comprehensive legal instruments for the combating of discrimination in a range of areas. Furthermore, a general principle of equality is emerging more and more visibly through provision of a number of equality rights in the Treaties, secondary legislation, and the judgments of the CoJ. The CoJ will no doubt have opportunities to expand on the general principle endorsed.

➕ LOOKING FOR EXTRA MARKS?

- It may be too soon for you to state definitively that there is now a general principle of equality, but there is nothing wrong in you stating that in your answer; but try to weigh up the evidence thus far and perhaps then state that the development appears to be pointing in that direction.

- You may be of the view that there is now a general principle, in which case say so and say why you are convinced.

TAKING THINGS FURTHER

- Burrows, N and Robinson, M, 'An Assessment of the Recast Equality Laws' (2007) 13 EL Rev 186.
  Focuses on the consolidating equality Directive which incorporated much of the prior Directives and case law.

- Costello, C and Davies, G, 'The Case Law of the Court of Justice in the Field of Sex Equality Since 2000' (2006) 43 CML Rev 1567.
  A general overview of case law developments in this area.

- Dewhurst, E, 'Intergenerational Balance, Mandatory Retirement and Age Discrimination in Europe: How Can the ECJ Better Support National Courts in Finding a Balance between the Generations?' (2013) 50 CML Rev 1333.
  A focused look at the age discrimination rules.

- Masselot, A, 'The State of Gender Equality Law in the European Union' (2007) 13 ELJ 152.
  An overview of gender equality developments.

- Möschel, M, 'Race Discrimination and Access to the European Court of Justice: Belov' (2013) 50 CML Rev 1433.
- Prechal, S. 'Equality of Treatment, Non-discrimination and Social Policy: Achievements in Three Themes' (2004) 41 CML Rev 533.
  A focused look at the race equality developments.

Online Resources

www.oup.com/uk/qanda/

Go online for extra essay and problem questions, a glossary of key terms, online versions of all the answer plans and audio commentary on how selected ones were put together, and a range of podcasts which include advice on exam and coursework technique and advice for other assessment methods.

10 Skills for Success in Coursework Assessments

Introduction

In **Chapter 1**, some of the different or special considerations of EU law were outlined. In some of the other chapters, I indicated those questions which might be suitable as coursework questions. In this chapter, I will provide some guidance in tackling EU coursework questions. It may be that coursework is a percentage of or in some cases the whole assessment for your EU law module. In my experience, having been an internal or external EU law examiner in about 20 UK and European Universities, word limits do vary but, depending on the percentage value carried and whether stand-alone or combined with an exam, may be between just 2,000 words up to 5,000 for undergraduate coursework. Some coursework questions will be in the form of an essay-style question and some will be in the form of a problem. The problem questions are likely to be composite questions but are unlikely in EU law to be fully mixed questions involving both procedural law and substantive law, although it is not ruled out; there are over 100 law schools out there and they can vary considerably in their coursework requirements. In EU law, I have observed that longer coursework questions tend to concentrate either on one involving a number of procedural actions, or on specific substantive subjects such as the free movement of goods or persons, competition law, or discrimination law. The questions at undergraduate level are more likely to be set questions, but longer word limits might alternatively involve you in choosing your own topic.

The bottom line though, whatever length, form of question, topic, or combination of topics covered, is that the examiners are looking for the same thing, and indeed broadly similar if not the same as they would expect for an exam answer. Addressing the topic posed or chosen in a clear, well-structured, coherent way, well-argued, supported by relevant statutory or judicial authority, with additional support from academic work, and your work should be accurate and comprehensible. As was stressed in **Chapter 1**, it is not just what you write, it is how you write it. A clear difference from exam answers, where examiners are aware of the pressure, especially of time, and thus far more tolerant of minor mistakes, is that with coursework, a clear explanation and more accuracy are expected. Basic errors of any sort—spelling, grammar, misreading the question, getting the facts wrong—stick out like very sore thumbs and are unlikely to be tolerated even by the most generous of markers. We'll come back to proofing and checking your work at the end of this chapter.

Getting started: Researching, planning, and preparing to write

Don't delay. I expect most of you may have left coursework essays until the last minute, trying to convince yourself and all around you'll work better under pressure! If my long experience bears any witness, for the vast majority of you, frankly that is not true and you end up with a rushed, second class piece of work.

Start as soon as you get the question or on the release date of the coursework by jotting down notes on what you think you need to do and the general areas and ideas straight away. No harm in discussing this with your fellow students as long as the final submitted work is your own. Once you have decided generally what you need, start your research. You don't have to start at the beginning, especially if the question is divided. Like an exam, start with a question/part you feel confident with (to get something under your belt!) and move on to other questions/parts as your confidence in handling the material grows. You can do the same thing for coursework, except you know what the question is in advance. So get your notes from the course/module together, make sure you are clear on the law, and get straight any uncertainties.

Then plan your answer. If the question set is a problem question, use the IRAC breakdown (FLAC/ILAC in some Universities) and to build up a coherent argument (Identify the issues, the Relevant law (Treaty, secondary, case law, national law), its Application, and Conclusions), apply these to the facts, and conclude by offering the required advice to the person you are advising or discussing generally.

Critical analysis and evaluation

In problems this means applying the law to the facts and reaching a conclusion in a reasoned way, as set out above, and hopefully as has been demonstrated in the earlier chapters of this book. Are there contradictory cases which suggest that the opposite conclusion may be drawn? Are there any particular facts, unique to this problem which will alter your conclusion?

For essays you are trying to put together a clear and coherent piece of prose which outlines the issues, discusses them in the light of developing law (statutory and/or case law), and which reaches a conclusion for or against the particular direction of the question. Avoid the classic mistake of discussing everything you know about a given topic. As you prepare your answer, keep asking yourself, 'Am I actually answering the question?' Essay answers should follow the more traditional formulation of introduction, main body (containing your arguments and analysis), and a conclusion.

Relevance and sticking to the word and time limits

As noted above, are you answering the question, or off on a flight of fancy of your own, or drifting into discussing the bit of the course you actually liked, not the question which was set?

Exceeding the word limit can be fatal! Only using half your allotted words, whilst not fatal, is usually a pretty accurate sign that you have not done enough work. Even with high word limits such as 5,000 words, the common complaint, when you really get going with researching the answer, is that it is not enough. Penalties vary between Universities but can extend to a zero mark. Most Universities operate the so called 'de minimis' rule or policy, which means minor infringements are ignored. 'Minor' is usually provided as 'an up to 10 per cent excess will be tolerated'; above that penalties will apply. I have seen above 30 per cent leading to total failure. Check with your lecturers. It is, in any case, an important legal skill and good discipline to stick to the word limit. Staying relevant and answering the question set is a good way of doing it. You should try to stay within the limit if possible; then you know you are ok.

Putting text and material that should be in the body of work into the footnotes will not work as way of getting round or exceeding the word limit. Examiners will at best ignore such work or penalise you for it. Also, when ignored, it might make your remaining answer incoherent, so even if you are not actually penalised you may miss vital marks that way. If it's vital to the answer, it goes in the text; if not, leave it out.

Stick to the time limit: unless you have evidential mitigating or extenuating circumstances for missing the deadline, it is just plain silly to miss it; get your priorities right and submit on time! If you don't, penalties can vary from a percentage or grade reduction to complete failure. In any case sticking to the deadline is good academic and professional discipline.

Referencing and citation of legal authorities

In coursework you will be expected to follow academic standards of citation, including providing a bibliography, footnotes, and proper citation of authorities. The recognised and usual citation system for academic law writing is the Oxford Standard for the Citation of Legal Authorities (OSCOLA), although the Harvard citation system can also be required. It is worth getting used to this system during your course, as you will probably be required to use it when undertaking coursework and very much so for dissertations or extended essays. There are OSCOLA citation helps and generators to be found at https://www.law.ox.ac.uk/research-subject-groups/publications/oscola & https://www.lawteacher.net/oscola-referencing/.

Footnotes are for references, signposting to articles and citations and not text; see the above section. Any material which is not your own must be acknowledged in the body of your work in the form of a footnote and you need to provide a separate bibliography listing the primary source of legislation (Treaties and secondary EU law), cases, and secondary sources, which includes, books, articles and web references. The latter must include 'Last Accessed' dates.

Writing up, proofreading, and checking before you submit

Does your work make sense, do your arguments stack up? No harm in asking friends or family to proofread it; they may well spot inaccuracies in expression that you do not. You are probably more concerned with the legal content. By all means spellcheck electronically, then do it yourself. Spellcheckers miss correctly spelled unintended words (false friends). Classic examples: from/form, vary/very, weather/whether.

Bibliography of books on law coursework writing

Finch and Fafinski, *Legal Skills*, 5th edn (Oxford: Oxford University Press, 2015, ISBN: 9780198718840).
Higgins, E and Tatham, L, *Successful Legal Writing*, 3rd edn (London: Sweet & Maxwell, 2015, ISBN: 9780414037045).

A coursework Question on Free Movement of Persons and Citizenship

This coursework question following is at first sight a very general one but there are elements which will require you to dig a bit deeper. These will be pointed out as I outline the key elements and then back that up with providing a commentary on the key legal issues, the leading cases, and secondary literature. This would be a suitable question for a submission of 2,000 to perhaps 3,500 words.

Q

'European citizenship'[1] was initially regarded as an essentially weak concept and a more of a symbolic statement of aspiration[2] than providing substantive rights for EU citizens.[3] Furthermore the Member States were determined that it would not have an impact on their determination of nationality[4] or provide further EU law rights for persons and workers, outside of those already provided for in the Treaties.[5]

Critically analyse and discuss these statements in the light of the development of citizenship rights in the EU and the case law of the Court of Justice.[6]

[1] Hopefully, clearly the starting point for you by defining this and locating its base wthin the EU legal order. A bit of prior history to the citizenship provisions would do no harm but don't get carried away with this as it will eat into your word count.

[2] This suggests that it was not really appreciated or considered to be much worth initially, so you will have to investigate that to see to what extent, if at all, that is a correct statement.

[3] This is a follow-up statement suggesting in fact that citizenship might have been designed and introduced to do that very thing, i.e., provide substantive rights—so this is where you should start to introduce some evidence, mainly in the form of case law, but also literature where you can find some.

[4] On this part you are going to have to dig a bit deeper as, on the face of it, the answer is not obvious. You need to research, then, what reservations the member states may have had and if and how they were expressed.

[5] This is a corollary to the last part in that the Member States might not have intended citizenship to create new rights. It is also backward-looking in that you need briefly to look at the range of existing rights and whether in fact new ones arose and that will be your key into the instruction, which is the final part of the question in the next annotation.

[6] The final sentence sets out the general approach you need to take, which is to research and discuss all of the above within the overall development of the concept and with case law to support your submission.

Commentary

The plan does not follow exactly the order of the marginal notes as these dealt with the parts of the coursework task in the order they appeared. You have to plan out a more logical way, then, of presenting the information, roughly along the lines that follow.

☐ DIAGRAM ANSWER PLAN

Start with a general statement of what EU citizenship means and its Treaty base

▼

Outline the basic scope of the rights

▼

> Note they were perhaps considered to be limited particularly as they were essentially based on three Directives on general movement

▼

> Note that the rights were curtailed by the view that they were to be rooted in national concepts, not giving rise to an extensive range of additional rights

▼

> Show just how extensive the rights have become via the case law of the CoJ

▼

> Summarise your submission in a conclusion

SUGGESTED ANSWER

Introduction

The **Treaty on European Union (TEU)**, signed at Maastricht, introduced a small section on European citizenship to the **EC Treaty; Arts 20 et seq TFEU. Article 20 TFEU** provides that 'Citizenship of the Union is hereby established. Every person holding the nationality of a Member State shall be a citizen of the Union. Citizenship of the Union shall complement and not replace national citizenship.' **Article 21 TFEU** provides that 'Every citizen of the Union shall have the right to move and reside freely within the territory of the Member States, subject to the limitations and conditions laid down in the treaty and by the measures adopted to give it effect.'[1]

[1]See the introductory article on citizenship by Cygan, A, 'Citizenship of the European Union' (2013) 62 ICLQ 492.

The first matter to be considered is a definition of EU 'citizenship', which is an addition and not a replacement for Member State nationality or citizenship. Thus, there can be no Union definition of 'European citizenship'. The actual determination of Member State nationality was decided to be a matter for each of the Member States, as was expressly stated in Declaration No 2 on Nationality attached to the **TEU** before its removal by the **Lisbon Treaty**. It provided that nationality shall be settled solely by reference to the national law of the Member State concerned. This position was upheld in **Case C-192/99 Manjit Kaur**, in which the CoJ held that it is for each Member State to lay down the conditions for the acquisition and loss of nationality.

However, **Case C-135/08 Rottmann v Bayern** considered whether the false/illegal acquisition of nationality nevertheless brought the person within the material scope of EU citizenship. Mr Rottmann, an Austrian, had failed to reveal pending criminal proceedings when he applied for and was granted German citizenship (which necessitated the loss of his Austrian citizenship). The revocation of the German citizenship would however lead to him being stateless. The CoJ, not following the opinion of the AG, held that EU law did apply to him. The Court considered it had not interfered with the right of the Member States to decide nationality themselves, but the consequence of withdrawing nationality by a state had the result that a once-enjoyed right, EU citizenship, was also lost. The Court held that it was up to the national court to decide whether the decision to withdraw citizenship was proportionate in view of both national law and the loss of EU citizenship, even if the German citizenship was acquired by a lack of disclosure. It should also take into account whether his original nationality could be recovered and the gravity of the wrong committed by Rottmann, especially in view of the effect on his family, which case then seems to have added an EU element or consideration to determining or removing national citizenship.

The scope of citizenship rights

The rights provided by the treaty under citizenship remove the economic activity requirement of the previous free movement of persons regime and were based on the prior legal regime of three **Directives (90/364, 90/365, and 93/96)** which provided only limited rights of free entry and residence. The **Maastricht Treaty** added a number of so-called political citizenship rights in **Arts 22–24 TFEU**, including the right to vote and stand as a candidate at municipal and EP elections in their host country, but these are quite limited in scope and application.

The true scope of citizenship was not immediately obvious and this has only become clearer as a result of CoJ judgments. In place of an economic activity, proof of self-sufficiency is instead required **(Art 7(1)(b) of Directive 2004/38)**. The CoJ held in **Case C-184/99 *Grzelczyk*** that it may be possible to make a claim on the social funds of a Member State, provided that the burden on the state is not unreasonable.

From the case law, the following stand out.

In **Case C-85/96 *María Martínez Sala* v *Freistaat Bayern***, Sala, a Spanish national who had worked in Germany for many years, lost her job but had remained in Germany and had received social assistance from 1989. Her residence permit had expired, but the German authorities supplied her with certificates stating that she had applied for an extension to her permit. The authorities refused her child allowance because she did not have a valid residence permit, which she claimed was contrary to **Art 12 EC (now Art 18 TFEU)** because German nationals were not subject to the same condition. The CoJ held in any event that she was lawfully resident in Germany. Sala thus came within the personal scope of treaty citizenship and **Art 8(2) EC (now Art 21 TFEU)** acted to attach other rights, including the right to be protected against discrimination under **Art 12 EC (now Art 18 TFEU)**; this, in turn, applied to a right within the material scope of the treaty, such as the child allowance claimed in the case on an equal basis with nationals.

In **Case C-184/99** *Grzelczyk*, the CoJ emphasized that the new citizenship provisions and new competences in education, albeit limited, allowed it to hold that **Arts 12 and 17 EC (now Arts 18 and 21 TFEU)** preclude discrimination as regards the grant of a non-contributory social benefit to Union citizens where they are lawfully resident, even though not economically active.

In **Case C-413/99** *Baumbast*, Mr Baumbast was self-employed in the UK, where he resided with his Colombian wife and two children, who were being educated in the UK. He was subsequently employed by a German company and worked outside the EU. His family remained in the UK. Their residence permits were not renewed, however, and Mrs Baumbast and the children faced deportation. The case was referred to the CoJ, which emphasized the right of children of EU nationals under **Regulation 1612/68** to continue their education even if the worker, from whom their rights derived, was no longer working in the EU. The CoJ further held that the text of the treaty does not permit the conclusion that citizens of the Union who have lawfully established themselves in another Member State as an employed person are deprived, where that activity comes to an end, of the rights that are conferred on them by virtue of that citizenship. In the most important statement of the judgment, the CoJ held that his or her right to stay under **Art 18(1) EC (now Art 21 TFEU)** is conferred directly on every citizen of the Union by a clear and precise provision of the EC Treaty. Purely as a national of a Member State, and consequently a citizen of the Union, Mr Baumbast therefore had the right to rely on **Art 18(1) EC (now Art 21 TFEU)**. It held:

> The answer to the first part of the third question must therefore be that a citizen of the European Union who no longer enjoys a right of residence as a migrant worker in the host member state can, as a citizen of the Union, enjoy there a right of residence by direct application of Article 18 (1) EC [now Art 21 TFEU].[2]

[2] Three journal articles which look, through case law, at the transformation of the rights from very uncertain to rights of substance are: Kochenov, D and Plender, R, 'EU Citizenship: From an Incipient Form to an Incipient Substance?'; Hinarejos, A, 'Citizenship of the EU: Clarifying "Genuine Enjoyment of the Substance" of Citizenship Rights' (2012) CLJ 279; and Kochenov, D, 'The Right to Have What Rights? EU Citizenship in Need of Clarification' (2013) 19 ELJ 502.

In summary, the citizenship law, as developed through the CoJ cases, would appear to be as follows. **Article 21(1) TFEU** has been declared to be directly effective and it can be activated in favour of EU citizens in a variety of ways, such as: by exhausted free movement rights, that is, those once enjoyed by a member state national and which gained him or her lawful entrance and residence in the host state when exercised, but who no longer is or can be relied upon because of changed circumstances (as in the **Baumbast** case); and by the movement to another Member State to receive services (as in **D'Hoop**), which movement then serves as the economic activity to trigger the general rights of citizenship.[3]

There has been significant extension or rights in the Member States facilitated by or based on an EU citizenship status and which have made inroads into Member State social security.[4]

Welfare rights as an example

If an EU citizen is lawfully resident in a host state, this will trigger EU citizenship and the rights that conveys. The most important of these are not the political rights contained in **Art 22 TFEU**, but the general right to be treated without discrimination compared to nationals. A number of the decisions appear to go further than perhaps originally extending the welfare benefits rights of EU citizens who were not supposed to be a burden on the host Member State. These developments appear to show that the Union is more concerned with the welfare rights of EU citizens and the sanctity of their family than it is with any national concerns about the possible drain on national resources by the welfare claims of other Member State EU citizens. Where appropriate, welfare rights can nevertheless be claimed by EU citizens. In **Case C-256/04 Ioannidis,** a Greek national spent three years in Belgium obtaining a graduate diploma followed by a training course in France. On his return to Belgium to look for work, he claimed a tide-over allowance. This was refused on the grounds that he had not completed secondary education in Belgium nor pursued education of the same level in another Member State; nor was he the dependent of a migrant worker residing in Belgium. The CoJ held that Ioannidis fell within the scope of **Art 39 EC (now Art 45 TFEU)** whilst seeking work and that, according to the citizenship provisions of the treaty, under certain conditions, financial assistance cannot be denied Union citizens. The fact that Ioannidis had completed a diploma in Belgium had already provided such a link.[5]

In **Cases C-22–3/08 Vatsouras and Koupatantze v ARGE Nürnberg**, the CoJ was asked to consider the rights to social welfare under **Arts 18 and 21 TFEU** and the ability of member states under **Art 24 of Directive 2004/38** to deny social welfare to EU migrant jobseekers and their families. The CoJ held, in view of the treaty Articles and previous case law, that, provided that the EU citizens can establish a genuine link with the host state, such as previous employment, then a jobseeker's allowance, which is designed to facilitate access to the labour market, should be available. It was not to be regarded as a safety net social assistance, which could still be excluded under EU law, but a clear link must nevertheless be established.

[3] There are numerous other cases to choose from but journal articles such as Hinarejos, A 'Citizenship of the EU: Clarifying "Genuine Enjoyment of the Substance" of Citizenship Rights' (2012) CLJ 279 provide good overviews of them.

[4] See e.g. Shaw, J, The Transformation of Citizenship in the European Union, Cambridge University Press, Cambridge, 2007.

[5] Goudappel, F, The Effects of EU Citizenship. Economic, Social and Political Rights in a Time of Constitutional Change, Asser Press, The Hague, 2010.

Case C-333/13 *Dano* v *Jobseeker Leipzig* appears to backtrack slightly from the generous interpretation of the CoJ in previous cases and addresses the widespread Member State concern about welfare or benefit to tourism. The case involved a lawfully resident (but not with permanent status) Romanian woman who lived in Germany but was non-economically active. Whilst in receipt of some social benefits, she applied for a further non-contributory cash benefit but was denied that by the authorities. This was then challenged relying on **Article 18 TFEU** and **Article 24 of Directive 2004/38**, both prohibiting discrimination and both previously seen in similar cases (*Grzelcyck*, *Sala*, and *Baumbast*) of the non-economically active. In contrast to those earlier cases, in which the lawful residence status was the determinative trigger for equal treatment, the CoJ stressed that meeting the conditions of **Directive 2004/38** was the criterion required to trigger equal treatment, in particular under **Article 7(1)** that they are not an unreasonable burden on the social assistance system of the host state. It is that requirement, according to the CoJ, that allows Member States to discriminate against those citizens who do not have permanent residence and who claim social benefits. The CoJ did, though, state that each case much be considered by the national court after conducting an assessment of the individual circumstances and merits. Whilst not reversing the earlier case law, it does allow the Member States to focus on the 'unreasonable burden' element to deny social benefit claims. This has been followed up in **Case C-67/14** *Alimanovic* involving the claim for social security benefit (SSB) of an EU citizen in Germany who had worked temporarily for 11 months, which was originally granted but then withdrawn. In a reference to the CoJ, it held that according to **Art 7 (3) (c) of Directive 2004/38**, EU citizens who had worked retain their status for six months and have a right to SSB during that period under **Art 24 (1)**. Thereafter, they may retain status as a work seeker but not the right to SSB as per **Art 24 (2)**, so retain residence rights but not benefit rights.

Citizenship thus means provided that there is movement in some way, even back to the home state or lawful residence in the host state, EU citizens will be entitled to be treated without discrimination compared to nationals.[6]

Conclusion

The EU law provision for the free movement of persons has changed considerably from its inception and recently most extensively through the introduction of a section on European citizenship and the consideration of a number of cases. Thus far, we can tentatively say that if one is an EU citizen lawfully resident in another Member State, one

[6] See the articles by Cousins, M, 'Citizenship, Residence and Social Security' (2007) 32 EL Rev 386 and Foster, N, 'Family and Welfare Rights in Europe: The Impact of Recent European Court of Justice Decisions in the Area of the Free Movement of Persons' (2003) 25 Journal of Social Welfare & Family Law 29.

does not have to be economically active to be entitled to equal treatment. This includes, for example, equal treatment in non-contributory welfare benefits on the same basis as nationals.

Rather than being an empty aspiration, the EU provision on citizenship has expanded extensively the right of EU nationals to equal treatment in a host state. However, the limit of the range of rights to which EU law now applies is less clear. Whether it should apply to rule out all discrimination against host EU citizens in comparison with nationals in all areas of law is the question left by the present development of the law, but it remains clear that the legal regime regulating the citizenship has come a long way from the near-empty and little-used original provision for it.

Online Resources

www.oup.com/uk/qanda/

Go online for extra essay and problem questions, a glossary of key terms, online versions of all the answer plans and audio commentary on how selected ones were put together, and a range of podcasts which include advice on exam and coursework technique and advice for other assessment methods.

Index

T